WILDMAN OF RHYTHM

UNIVERSITY PRESS OF FLORIDA
Florida A&M University, Tallahassee
Florida Atlantic University, Boca Raton
Florida Gulf Coast University, Ft. Myers
Florida International University, Miami
Florida State University, Tallahassee
New College of Florida, Sarasota
University of Central Florida, Orlando
University of Florida, Gainesville
University of North Florida, Jacksonville
University of South Florida, Tampa
University of West Florida, Pensacola

UNIVERSITY PRESS OF FLORIDA

Gainesville · Tallahassee · Tampa · Boca Raton · Pensacola · Orlando · Miami · Jacksonville · Ft. Myers · Sarasota

WILDMAN OF RHYTHM

The Life & Music of

BENNY MORÉ

JOHN RADANOVICH

First cloth printing, 2009
First paperback printing, 2015

Library of Congress Cataloging-in-Publication Data
Radanovich, John.
Wildman of rhythm: the life and music of Benny Moré / John
Radanovich.
p. cm.
Includes bibliographical references and index.
ISBN 978-0-8130-3393-8 (cloth: alk. paper)
ISBN 978-0-8130-6186-3 (pbk.)
1. Moré, Beny, 1919–1963. 2. Singers—Cuba—Biography. I. Title.
ML420.M596R34 2009
782.421640929–dc22
[B]   2009011119

The University Press of Florida is the scholarly publishing agency
for the State University System of Florida, comprising Florida
A&M University, Florida Atlantic University, Florida Gulf
Coast University, Florida International University, Florida State
University, New College of Florida, University of Central Florida,
University of Florida, University of North Florida, University of
South Florida, and University of West Florida.

University Press of Florida
15 Northwest 15th Street
Gainesville, FL 32611-2079
http://www.upf.com

This book is for Uncle Pete
and my sons, Peter and David

CONTENTS

PREFACE

I vividly remember the night when my obsession began. It was 1993, and I lived on Royal Street in the French Quarter of New Orleans. I had moved there from New York to immerse myself completely in New Orleans jazz and to live a bit more than I had been doing in New York. The move was a great success, as far as I was concerned. I spent much of my days in coffeehouses, and evenings at Café Brasil or the Napoleon House. Every wilting Sunday afternoon I danced through the streets in second line parades in the Tremé neighborhood. I picked up the habit of always keeping a white handkerchief in my back pocket, ready for any parade I might encounter.

One humid evening, I took the streetcar uptown to a dinner party given by a new friend at her superb Italianate mansion on Camp Street. Night jasmine perfumed the air. I opened the iron gate, went up the stairs, and Kate met me at the door. A drink quickly appeared in my hand. While I was introduced to other guests, my host put on a pleasant compilation of old Cuban songs, a range of music from a span of fifty years. As always happened in that house, conversation was quick and engrossing; I could look forward to discussion of local politics, literature, and music far into the night.

But when I heard a particular song begin, I cocked my ear toward the stereo speakers. A piano played an open rhythm before brass instruments spoke a loose melody, a kind of jazz vamp. A man sang in Spanish, encouraging someone called Castellano to dance. Then the singer told someone called Generoso how well he played, and a trombonist took a solo that was like absolutely nothing I had ever heard.

A fervent lover of jazz who was raised from the cradle on his father's bebop and soul and gospel records, I had no point of reference for such joyful yet aggressive playing, nor for the singer's improvisational approach and interplay with the male chorus voices. I asked to see the CD cover, and there it was: "Qué bueno baila usted" (How good you dance). The recording was slightly older than I was, by a musician dead since just before I was born in

1963. While I listened, I reflected that the singer's first and last name made for a puzzling combination.

"What do you mean, you don't know who that is?" my friend asked me, surprised since she already knew I loved Latin jazz. "Come on now, John," she said, looking over her glasses. "Really, you don't know?"

"His voice is a little familiar, but I'm not exactly sure what kind of music it is," I told her. "How can that be Cuban?"

"That," she told me, "is Benny Moré." She sounded as if what I had to learn in this world far outweighed what I understood so far. The others at the little party all knew who this Benny Moré was and seemed in agreement with her assessment of me.

New Orleans may sound like a strange place to first discover the Cuban Sinatra, but the Crescent City has long historical connections to Cuba. Kate's own grandfather had left Cuba in the 1920s. As I was to learn over the next dozen or so years, Havana and New Orleans have a great deal more in common culturally than just being port towns made rich by sugar and slaves, with residents who are unable to say no to a good party. Colonial sister cities in many ways, these were the Spanish and French capitals of the Caribbean. The exchange of culture between the two cities practically wore a path across the surface of the Gulf of Mexico. French opera and chamber music went to Havana, and the habanera rhythm—of great importance to early jazz—went north to New Orleans. Sugar planters escaping Haiti brought music to Cuba and Louisiana both. Some Cuban immigrants went to New Orleans long before they started to go to Miami.

The house on Camp Street was also where I had my first Cuban cigar, fresh from the island. My friend, who had some family connections still left in Cuba, had just returned from a visit there. From journalist friends, I had heard how Cuba was becoming a destination for Americans willing to risk the embargo's penalties, and for men looking for Cuban women. Aside from that, Kate was right: I knew very little and had lots to learn.

I began to investigate Cuban music more earnestly. I had written about New York salsa but started to focus a bit more on its Cuban roots. When I heard Benny sing the intense "Babarabatiri" with Pérez Prado, I sensed that I would need to understand the African influence I heard, too. "Cuban music" is so vast and daunting—so many centuries and styles—that the more I found, the more there was to find. And I subjected anyone involved in Latino music to the same interrogation: tell me anything you know about Benny Moré.

I wrote a profile for *Offbeat* magazine of singer Celia Cruz. Her response was essentially that of everyone else who knew or knew of Benny. "Oh, Benny! Naturally," she told me, "he was the greatest." Her answer to one particular question was what I would encounter wherever I went: she had no idea how he got his first name.

Then I interviewed trumpeter Arturo Sandoval. I was aware that he was too young to have worked with Benny, but I sneaked my usual questions into our telephone conversation anyway.

"You should talk to Paquito," he told me from his living room in Miami. I could hear him puffing on a cigar, and traffic outside the window.

"Paquito D'Rivera you mean?"

Arturo played chords lightly on his piano. "John, just call Paquito. He knows a lot," he told me. His tone was suspiciously reminiscent of my friend Kate's when I confessed that I didn't know Benny Moré. Back then I still assumed that out there somewhere in the world I would find an expert on Benny.

Of all the musicians I pestered, I subjected no one to quite as much questioning as the saxophonist and clarinetist Paquito D'Rivera. Like his former bandmate Sandoval, Paquito was very young when Benny was at his height in Cuba, but Paquito's father had owned a music store in Havana, and everyone passed through the shop in the late 1950s. A musical prodigy who first went by himself to New York to play professionally at the age of nine, Paquito knows stories about any Cuban musician you might mention. Although he didn't know about Benny's name either, he had a guess that I have since heard—that Benny didn't care which way they spelled it as long as he got paid. Paquito did have his own answer for another question I had begun to ask: why Benny drank so much.

"Because he was an alcoholic! Ha ha ha ha!" Paquito's trademark hoarse cackle came loud and piercing through the telephone receiver. When he stopped laughing at his own joke and my expense, he told me that maybe I should try to talk to Generoso. "He's still alive, you know," he added.

"Generoso . . ."

"Jo-ohn. El Tojo!" he told me in that tone I was beginning to recognize. Every time Paquito said my name, it was the equivalent of how Cubans say

"¡Mira!" when they want you to pay extra attention to something. Sometimes he put "John" and *mira* together. Now he hummed the piano introduction to "Qué bueno baila usted." I didn't want to seem as ignorant as I was, but I tried a little bit of the song: "'Generoso, qué bueno toca usted'?"

"Of course that is him. *Mira*, John. You should go meet him," he told me with plenty of insistence in his voice. "He's getting older, but he's still very *listo*."

Once I had found Paquito, the next stage began in my learning about Cuban musicians in the United States, and their lives back in Cuba as well. Paquito was rarely home at his house in New Jersey, but he often spoke with me from hotel rooms all over the world, in his heavy touring schedules for both classical and jazz concerts. Although his time was very much in demand, Paquito told me lots of things about life and music in Havana; many of the interesting little details in this book come from him.

I was still living in New Orleans when the first Buena Vista Social Club record became an instant phenomenon in 1997. Although the arranging of those songs wasn't what I had been hearing in Cuban big bands of the 1940s and 1950s, I became, along with millions of others, a fan of those old musicians, especially after the Wim Wenders movie showed their personalities and hinted at the decay of Cuba. I wondered if any of them had worked with Benny Moré, of course. I wouldn't learn for some years that one had known him well, the singer Ibrahim Ferrer. I was as curious as anyone else: what would it be like to go to Cuba? Unlike other people who wondered, I began to seriously consider how I should go about it.

By 1999 I was back in New York, and covering New York Latin music and jazz for the *Record* newspaper. Information about Latino artists like Celia Cruz and Tito Puente was easier to come by, but I had trouble learning about anything that had occurred before 1960. That was another lesson learned.

Eventually I came across a biography of Benny Moré in the main New York Public Library on Fifth Avenue. Published in Cuba in 1985, the book was written by a man named Amin Naser. I rushed out to the lawn in Bryant Park behind the library and devoured the fragile book. It was a bit short on some of the things I wanted to know, but it contained lots of photographs. I felt as if I had found a never-before-seen handbook on the ancient Mayans. The fascinating snapshots from Benny's short life showed him happy at every moment. Multiple photos of the funeral and Benny in his coffin hinted at his idol status. There was a discography to guide me, and mention of clubs and musicians I would come to know well. A story of Benny once attacking an unscrupulous promoter in Venezuela deepened his portrait in my mind.

Alas, even the question of Benny's nickname was not addressed in that book to my satisfaction, except to say that he had gone to Mexico as Bartolo and come home as Benny. By the time I found the Naser book in New York, I had long known that Benny's name was nearly always written "Beny" on his early recordings in Mexico and for some recordings after that. Yet by the time he returned to Cuba in 1950, he was usually referred to as "Benny" in media stories. I checked; photographs in the Naser book showed his gravestone with the latter spelling.

I learned there was a more recent Cuban biography written by Raúl Martínez, but I found that it was more like a pamphlet than a book. This smaller book yielded very little to my search except a few photographs. This is all I had to go on until I began to hunt for those of Benny's contemporaries who knew him best. Benny remained mysterious even as the physical picture of him constructed itself in my mind.

The more I knew about Benny, the more chasing his ghost became for me something like searching for a long-lost father. From the very beginning, Benny reminded me of my great-uncle Pete. Like Benny, Pete was a magnetic personality, warm and humorous. Like Benny, he was a complicated character with many unusual traits. A Golden Gloves boxer who once fought Rocky Graziano, Pete was a published poet with an agricultural background that, like Benny's, never quite went away. He teased just like a Benny, too.

After his capture in North Africa, Pete spent more than two years in German prisoner-of-war camps, including the model for the movie *Stalag 17*. Pete's repeated escapes meant brutal beatings, and when he returned home he began to drink heavily. A *Stars and Stripes* newspaper photograph of him at his liberation shows Pete as handsome as ever, as if nothing had happened in all those months of starvation and brutality. It was vintage Uncle Pete and very Benny: as he walked down a German street toward the photographer he had a cigarette in one hand and a bottle of whiskey in the other. Nine giggling women fought to hold on to his arm. The photograph was the way we all try to remember him, in the same way that Cubans now remember Benny.

I was quite stunned when I learned that Benny had died of cirrhosis at age forty-four. Pete wasn't much older when he drank himself to death.

Although I kept up my search for Cuban musicians of a certain age, I wasn't completely aware how far I had come down the path of writing my own book about Benny. When I learned by accident how to find Generoso Jiménez, I began to wonder if a book on Benny might be possible after so many years of frustration about not being able to find anything on his life when I needed to. I kept waiting for another writer to appear with a book in English or French or Spanish. Not a single hint of one appeared, yet RCA continued to rerelease his recordings and musicians kept praising him to me.

One day toward the end of 1999, I happened across a rerelease of a long-forgotten record from 1965, *El Trombón Majadero*. Before the end of the first note, I knew immediately who the trombonist was. Within a few months, I was sitting in Generoso's living room sipping dark rum and eating fresh chicharrones.

With little more than an address in my hand and a phone number that didn't seem to work from outside Cuba, I went to Havana for the first time in 2000. Havana is overwhelming, to say the least, especially for a visitor with only basic Spanish and with no clear idea of exactly what he was doing in Cuba.

I took a cab from my *casa particular* over to the Cerro neighborhood where Generoso Jiménez lived in a 1830s townhouse with one daughter. Another daughter lived next door. Benny had been godfather at the christening of both girls, in fulfillment of a promise he made Generoso before they were born.

Generoso was eighty-two years old then. He greeted me stiffly, while both his daughters kept their eyes on me and minded what he said. At some point they realized that I wasn't there to steal any of his music, nor could I read music. I explained that I was a writer and hoped that he had gotten the letter I had sent earlier, saying I would be in Havana and hoped to meet him.

I began to learn how politics influenced what Cubans could say, even an old musician talking about the distant past. One of my first questions was how jazz had influenced Generoso's playing and arranging. He answered in a somewhat oblique way that jazz had never influenced him, only Cuban music. As the interview of several hours progressed, Generoso warmed somewhat. Although he couldn't solve the mystery of Benny's name, he mentioned names of other friends and colleagues now legendary to twentieth-century Cuban popular music: Obdulio Morales, Chico O'Farrill, Machito,

Bebo Valdés. My head swam as he talked about his years at the legendary Tropicana nightclub, but I was puzzled about the recent time when a musician of his stature was completely forgotten in Cuba. The musician Jimmy Durschlag, who rereleased *El Trombón Majadero*, had been responsible for getting Generoso new dentures, without which he couldn't practice.

Practice? I asked.

His daughters told me that he was going to make a new record, though to my eyes he seemed a bit frail, and trombone demands some physical strength. Little did I know that the record, Grammy nominated, would feature many Cuban musicians who lived in the States, including Paquito D'Rivera. Yet another lesson: that many Cubans have an extraordinary capacity to function into and beyond their eighties.

At the end of the interview Generoso posed for my camera, holding his trombone up for me. I was completely shocked when he put it to his lips and began to play riffs and complex melodies. This was the Generoso of all the songs I had in my head, a Generoso I had assumed belonged only to the history books. I had found *that* Generoso—not just a man of amazing stories, but one who still had it! I took out the bottles of Generoso's favorite rum I had been advised to bring with me. The four of us drank glasses of rum neat, as Cubans nearly always do.

In 2007 I returned to do as much proper research as I could into Benny's life. I interviewed his cousin Enrique Benítez, as charming a man as I have ever met, in Havana. Like Generoso, Enrique was forgotten in his country, even though he had taught Benny to sing and had written some of his hit songs. I finally went to La Cumbre, the barrio on the outskirts of Havana where Benny had lived in a modest house, raising his farm animals out back. There I met his daughter Hilda and spent a pleasant afternoon talking about her memories of him. Although both said things that surprised me, things few people had known about Benny, neither could say whether he had taken his stage name after Benny Goodman, as I now believe. Although Hilda did tell me of Benny's love for American big-band jazz and especially Benny Goodman, she wasn't sure if he had named himself Beny or Benny in Mexico.

I traveled out to Santa Isabel de las Lajas, Benny's birthplace in the sugarcane fields near Cienfuegos. I uncovered many things about Benny's early childhood, saw where he had absorbed much of his Afro-Cuban heritage, and spent an afternoon in the town's museum. I heard the two Santería legends surrounding the Casino de los Congos where Benny had learned drumming and dances. No one I met on that trip could answer the simple question of the spelling of Benny's name.

As I finished writing this book, I was surprised and a little disappointed to realize that Benny's private, interior thoughts and beliefs remained largely hidden to me. The few times he let down his guard to a friend, or a brother, or a journalist afforded very rare glimpses. One such moment is an unreleased, informal recording his doctor made at Benny's house in La Cumbre, in Benny's final days. Benny sang along with a new electric guitar, an instrument he never used on a record.

I believe that Benny knew this would be his last recorded message, and so he took off the entertainer's happy mask. The songs can be described only as the sounds of an intensely sad human being dying a terrible death. When I heard that recording in 2007, I felt a sense of Benny's soul for the first time. Inescapably, I thought of my uncle Peter at his similar end, too.

This book, I hope, gives some sense of what the life and times of Benny Moré were like, both the public and the more precious private personality. Although he deserved a much longer life and career, Benny's gifts to the larger library of world music are as rich and lasting as any musician from the Americas has ever left behind for us to discover.

ACKNOWLEDGMENTS

First, I must thank Roly Moré, to whom I owe an enormous debt for all his cheerful help with my many questions about his grandfather and family. Benny's daughters Bárbara, Lázara, and Hilda provided stories about their father. Tuti Jiménez and his sisters Regla and Regina helped with information about their father, Generoso. Thanks to Enrique "El Conde Negro" Benítez for our long and pleasant afternoon in Havana. Thank you, Bebo Valdés, Graciela Pérez, and Chocolate Armenteros.

In the music industry I need to thank Detlef Engelhard of Termidor Musikverlag and Timba Records, Jimmy Durschlag of Bembe Records, Diana Nazareth, Nat Chediak, Ian Morrison at Passion Music, and John Parker-Rees. Thanks to Norman Isaacs of Norman's Sound and Vision in New York who first steered me to Eddie Palmieri and then backward in time to Benny. Frank Grillo Jr. told me about his father's friendship with Benny. I especially owe Paquito D'Rivera for the years he patiently answered all my questions and more. Joseph Levy of the Vinyl Tourist helped with information on Pérez Prado. Tatyana Praino helped with questions about Cuban music history, and about her father, Rudy Calzado. Thank you Tom Tierney, archivist at Sony BMG. Thanks to Ileana Rodríguez, and many others inside Cuba whom I can't thank in print but wish I could.

Many writers contributed invaluable advice and information about Cuban music, including Ned Sublette, Isabelle Leymarie, Robert Farris Thompson, and Sam Charters—who lent me the English version of his book on Bebo Valdés. Raúl Fernández contributed many hours of correspondence and Cuban music expertise. Professor David García and Richard Davies provided information about contemporaries of Benny. Michael Dregni gave needed advice on the writing. Judy Cantor helped with information on Panart Records.

I cannot thank Rosa Lowinger and John Storm Roberts enough for advance reading of the manuscript, and a great deal of other help and advice. Vicki Gold Levi gave expert advice on photography and design, and other assistance and encouragement. Ramiro Fernández supplied advice and the use of the photograph from his collection. Others who helped include Ann Bardach and Frank Argote-Freyre, with information on Fulgencio Batista.

Marcos Salazar in Mexico provided lots of previously unknown information about Benny's time in that country. In Colombia, Sergio Santana also helped with Benny's early years. Mexican historian Nicolás Argamasilla provided enormous help with Benny's years in Mexico and Cuba, most of it also previously unknown.

Thank you to collector and music expert Jaime Jaramillo. Keith A. Llorens lent me his photograph of Nat King Cole. Carlos Flores and Walter German Magaña Sandoval helped with research.

Rosa and Mario helped me innumerable times over the years.

Richard Simon and Tanya McKinnon belong in their own special category of thanks. Paul Bresnick supplied editorial advice and the book's title. Thanks to Ian Mount for helping read my proposal early on. Linda Cullen helped at a critical moment. Thanks to Ann Marlowe for copyediting. My old friend Dave Miss helped me yet again, this time with expert work on restoring photographs and illustrations.

Thanks to Drs. Mallay Occhiogrosso and Howard J. Worman for information on alcoholism and cirrhosis.

Special thanks to Veronica González and Myra Nemeth at the Díaz Ayala Cuban and Latin American Popular Music Collection archives at Florida International University. Cristóbal Díaz Ayala himself fielded many questions and gave invaluable advice.

Perhaps most important in my fixation on Benny and his world, my wife Berrie sacrificed years' worth of nights and weekends to the writing of this book.

This book was written with the help of a grant from the State of Florida Arts Council, Florida Division of Cultural Affairs, and the encouragement of the University Press of Florida.

WILDMAN OF RHYTHM

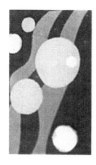

Prologue

He was the greatest singer Cuba has ever produced. Among Cubans and Cuban exiles alike, his name evokes overwhelming nostalgia for the power of his expressive boleros, his tributes to beloved *guajiro* (country) towns, and for the irresistible excitement of his faster pieces. He was a lightning rod at the center of one of the richest historical eras of the entire twentieth century, the golden age of Cuban music, itself a very special moment in eighty or more years of Cuban popular music history. Born Bartolomé Maximiliano Gutiérrez Moré Armenteros, he is known to millions of Cuban music fans as Benny.

Moré lived at a time that can seem as fantastical and exotic as a fictional kingdom in Voltaire's *Candide*. And just as impossible to find again once you leave it. From the vantage point of the tourists, everything in the 1950s in Cuba looked like a gorgeous stage setting: the atmospheric cabarets, the dance reviews beneath the palms, the rum and cigars, the men in linen suits beside women in evening gowns, the big American cars, the Mafiosi, the grand orchestras.

Moré is representative of Cuban big-band music and an entire era in the same way that Frank Sinatra epitomizes indelible memories of postwar America. Moré's early and terrible death recalls the tragic loss of other musicians so evocative of their times and countries: Edith Piaf for the French, Carlos Gardel for Argentines, Otis Redding and Jimi Hendrix for Americans.

Personally and artistically Moré represents the height of Afro-Cuban mu-

1

sic and culture. Even his own racial combination perfectly embodies the two great cultures that created something so uniquely Cuban: his father was a white Spaniard, and his mother's parents had been slaves.

Despite being unable to read music, he composed some of Cuban music's most memorable and lasting standards. His success owed something to the wild times he lived in, but the excesses of the era contributed to his early death just as they floated him to his triumphs. Cubans are very fond of their icons, and his passing at forty-four gave them another to adore. The god of thunder Chango gets his own shrine and statue; Benny Moré left music on 78s and 45s that is given a reverence usually reserved for figures like the revolutionary José Martí.

In the 1950s, really good sin may have been hard to come by in the United States, but thanks to efforts of the American Mafia and a cooperative Cuban government, this wasn't the case in Havana. The Mafia presence in Cuba hit its full stride during the brutal, felonious reign of Fulgencio Batista, when he opened his country to Meyer Lansky, the mob accountant and brain behind the casinos. Other underworld figures who took advantage of Cuba included Santo Trafficante Jr., another gambling wizard, and Lucky Luciano. Lansky set about creating the glitz by inviting Hollywood celebrities and high-roller gamblers. For publicity buzz Lansky flew Ginger Rogers down when he opened the Riviera Hotel in 1957, but the famous had been coming long before that.

The celebrities who visited Havana cabarets appeared just as often in the papers back home, in lurid stories about their antics in Cuba. Like other Americans attracted to Cuba, they went there and then went completely wild. Maureen O'Hara was found dead drunk in a theater. Robert Mitchum, already famous for a marijuana arrest and hard-drinking ways, smoked a joint at a crowded party in Havana and felt compelled to take off everything but his wristwatch. Ava Gardner, in a publicized adulterous affair and later marriage to Frank Sinatra, visited with Frank often, as he had many favors to return to his early underworld sponsors. The stunning and capricious Ava tried to leap from the balcony of the Hotel Nacional on her honeymoon night with Frank Sinatra. There was nothing calm and relaxing about visiting Havana in the 1950s.

When Americans who liked their entertainment naughty and dark learned of the debauchery of the movie stars and the wide-open excitement of the casinos and live sex shows, they began to arrive in droves. They took the ferries from Florida and flights from cold Midwestern airports to stay at infamous luxury hotels like the Nacional, the Riviera, and the Capri. They partied past sunrise every night of the week at clubs like the Sans Souci, the Tropicana, and the Montmartre.

Although the average Cuban saw little of the monetary wealth lavished on the island, Batista and the Mafia had created a unique moment when Cuban orchestras could flourish because of these dollars. There was such a hunger for music that it was easy to play two or three gigs every night of the week. The musicians were bursting with ideas; they left their last shows and hurried to little dives and cafés, to continue in the jam sessions called *descargas* to hone the flood of musical ideas until they were completely exhausted and the roosters had long since crowed.

Through their fog of rum-and-Cokes, the majority of tourists may not have noticed the rich music beyond the nightclub extravaganzas, but visiting musicians and composers had been learning in Cuba since before George Gershwin, as far back as Louis Moreau Gottschalk. American jazz stars and Cuban exiles would later combine Cuban music with bebop to create Latin jazz, and New York salsa.

Moré and his contemporaries were born in Cuba's colonial past, and knew the other Cuba, isolated by internal and external forces. His recordings belong to a long history of cultural trade between his country and the United States. Had it not been for the closing of the "mango curtain," Benny Moré would have found a far larger worldwide audience, even despite his untimely death. When the door to Cuba closed, Moré's music and importance continued outside Cuba, mostly in the United States itself, thanks to Puerto Rican musicians and those Cubans who left for the New York City area.

Moré's group and a handful of others spread Afro-Cuban big band music in general, *son* in particular, to New York, Central America, South America, and even back to Africa. *Son*, which means "sound" in Spanish, is the perfect hybrid of Spanish melody and African rhythm, and is the basis for all music now referred to as salsa. Without Moré and his peers, American jazz would be weakened, there would be no New York salsa, and the music of the Americas in general would be greatly diminished. To hear his infectious music for the first time is to be completely thrilled. It is hardly formal tea-dance music for partners who bow to one another before gently holding hands. It is blasting, wild, complex dance stuff, "all about the thing between man and woman," as Generoso Jiménez has said.

Moré couldn't read a note of music, yet he wrote more than a dozen Cuban standards, including "Qué bueno baila usted" and "Mi amor fugaz," and is known for performing many songs of longing for Cuban towns, like "Manzanillo" and "Santa Isabel de las Lajas." His orchestrations, the caliber of his musicians, and the excitement of the musical cultural scene in those days make the hottest contemporary New York salsa band you can name pale in comparison. Much of Moré's sound was due to his best arranger, Generoso Jiménez, also a superb bandleader and a genius trombone player. His dizzying solos were the first on that instrument in Latin music, and all Latin and Latin jazz trombonists are influenced by his style. As Moré did with other arrangers, the two formed a powerful team: Moré hummed or sang his compositions while his arranger sat at a piano and wrote out the notation. In this way, the pair worked for many hours on the Afro-Cuban rhythmic intricacies of their songs.

Moré was born into a deeply African subculture whose ways took years to absorb, and from which he learned everything he would need in life. Moré's legacy is taking African dance polyrhythms and transferring them to a big-band format without losing the original vitality and uniqueness of the drum sessions where he learned his rhythms. He never forgot his African patrimony or his simple country roots. He often referred to his Banda Gigante as *mi tribu* or "my tribe," and at the height of his fame he chose to live away from the noise of Havana on a little farm, surrounded by common farm animals. He parked his big Cadillacs out front, leaving behind the clubs, and the demands of the women and record companies and radio show schedules. It was there that he sat among the animals, smoked, drank dark rum, and composed songs on his guitar.

Moré had a singular personality, witty and eccentric. Always a character, he loved practical jokes and teasing: he named his hogs, chickens, and peacocks after famous musician friends, or called a favorite pig Chuleta, which means "pork chop." Like a Django Reinhardt or a Louis Armstrong, no matter how great his success, he never lost his original "countryness" and unusual ways.

Onstage, he mesmerized audiences who came to dance but stood by the thousands to watch his antics while he sang, clowned, and led the band with twitchy gestures. Gangly and tall, he preferred white suits with suspenders, an extra long jacket of nearly zoot-suit length, a big Cuban cowboy hat, and his Congo cane. He drove the band forward with a strange electric energy, and they played hard, wiping the sweat from their necks when they had a second.

Moré's incandescent talents and timeless song credits place him at the top of a bewilderingly large list of talented musicians who influenced popular music around the globe. Cuba has given us some of our greatest rhythms and forms: habanera, mambo, rumba, danzón, cha-cha, the *son* and all its offshoots, bolero, descarga, tango. With these forms came specialized instruments, now also widely found in other styles around the world: maracas, bongos, conga drum, tres guitar, timbales, guiro, shekere, bata, marimbula, and the simplest but most important, two ordinary wooden sticks—claves. Moré was an expert in most of these Cuban forms, and unequaled in at least two: *son* and boleros. Just as important, he was expert on the instruments themselves.

The African element in Cuban music is indispensable to its entire identity, just as it was to Moré's personality. As a child who inherited a strong Lucumí culture, very early on Moré was taught the Afro-Cuban encyclopedia of vibrant African and Santería religious rituals, with their emphasis on holy drums and sacred rhythms to honor each god. Benny Moré was the quintessential rural Cuban man who literally put down his cane machete, hung a battered guitar from his shoulder, and left home to join the music being created in that marvelous chaos of Havana.

ONE

La Guinea, 1919–1935

The poorest neighborhood in the isolated country town of Santa Isabel de las Lajas is called La Guinea, in reference to the African origins of the black Cubans who lived there and worked the fields outside of town. On Heredia Street, close to the train station, is a small, single-room structure where no one lives yet everyone visits regularly. Black Cubans from the neighborhood have crossed the porch and filled the hall with dancing and singing for at least a century. The Spanish referred to such buildings as cabildos, but the descendants of the slaves brought to labor in the sugar fields called their place of worship El Casino de los Congos.

By chance, the colors of the building reflect the Cuban flag. White paint peels from the wood siding, the tile roof burns red in the hot sun, and the trim and the columns supporting the front porch are painted blue. There has never been a permanent door at the front entrance, only a piece of fence propped at the doorway to keep out goats and dogs. In the shade inside is a large altar with blue conga drums along the wall, ready for the next makuta. On either side of the steps grow two large basil plants used in ceremonies by believers. Beside one of the plants is a large granite rock that members of the Casino believe has been magically growing ever since being placed there by a freed slave. The other legend of the Casino is that whenever a member dies, the drums inside begin to play themselves, and then stop just as mysteriously.

The children of Africa who landed on the dazzling green shores of the

Caribbean floated there, pushed by the same trade winds that each year bring tropical rains and violent cyclonic storms. The slaves from Gambia, Senegal, Nigeria, and Guinea brought more than riches to their owners; they brought customs and arts that filled up the New World with unique culture as fast as the Europeans took out the gold and silver, sugar and timber. Because Cuba was the second-to-last nation to free its slaves, in 1886, African culture remained remarkably intact there. For the unfortunate slaves this may not have been happy history, but for the future of the music of the world, someday this would be very good news.

Just as for any poor, fatherless child in the Cuban provinces, the hurdles facing Bartolo were enormous. Like the other boys he grew up with, he was eager to know his African heritage, which meant that he had to undertake a considerable amount of study down at the Casino de los Congos. Among the lessons was the significance of the makuta, a social dance of Congolese origin. Drums for this dance would be transformed into an early form of the conga drums. In these Palo ceremonies, dancers also use a special stick to strike the ground in a rhythmic accompaniment to a song.

The African elements from a variety of countries infused Cuba with a mixed culture so unique that there are only two other places in the world where similar cross-pollinations occurred: Brazil and Louisiana. Although Brazil's Africanness mixed with Portuguese traditions, Louisiana's musical history and Cuba's habanera had a great affinity and contact between them. It is not much of an exaggeration to say that without Cuba, American jazz couldn't exist in the form we know it, and without the influence of jazz, modern Cuban music would be very different.

As elsewhere in the Caribbean, wars of race and independence caused a great deal of turmoil and bloodshed. Just before Bartolo was born, a race war took place throughout Cuba in 1912, and thousands of blacks were massacred by frightened whites, especially in Oriente Province in the east. Executioners from white militias displayed severed heads and bodies as a gruesome warning in public places and along rail lines.

Because there were so many slaves in Cuba, and because slaves were still imported very late into Cuba (legally and illegally), tribal cultures lasted well into the twentieth century. In many ways African cultural elements of religion and music were passed on undiluted to the next generations. As usually happens in history, a mixing of people at cultural crossroads creates a new

tradition, a new art form, and a new language. Explaining the real source of
Cuban music, musical genius Generoso Jiménez would say with a shrug, "El
Español ama a las negras"—the Spaniard loves black women. Some mixed-
race children like Bartolome perfectly embodied the complementary traditions they represented.

All of Bartolo's grandparents had been slaves—except for one. His father's
father had never been a slave because he was white, a Spaniard. The man
had owned slaves in the area, and ate off dishes with the Spanish royal seal.
Bartolo's white blood was something he didn't know about himself until he
was an adult. One thing he did know was that he was related to Colonel
Simeón Armenteros, a figure in the war of independence from Spain with
Maceo. Black and mulatto boys like Bartolo who played beneath Armenteros's
statue in the Lajas park looked to him as a black Lajero who meant something very important in the larger history of Cuba. Little did Bartolo or his
friends know that someday he would become the most famous black man in
Cuba, and Armenteros would be forgotten.

* * *

Bartolome's childhood took place in the perennial summertime of the Caribbean, in a country located entirely below the Tropic of Cancer. Aside from
the short-lived cold fronts that made it across the Florida Strait in winter,
the cycle of the year was marked only by harvest seasons, Carnival before
Lent, and then the rainy months. Summer came ferociously hot, humid, and
mosquito-ridden. In Lajas the scent of the ocean drifted inland on the sea
breeze. Almost the only chance for a break from the harsh summer sun came
with the numerous tropical storms and hurricanes. Sickness, infant mortality,
intestinal worms, dengue, hepatitis—these were still facts of life for country
children of Bartolo's generation. And yet Cuba with all its natural and cultural wealth was not a sleepy banana republic, and had been vital to Spanish
and North American interests long before his birth—for centuries, in fact.

As an adult he never complained about hardships in his childhood, but
being a black boy in rural Cuba was far from easy. Although the sugar industry brought some prosperity to the countryside in the 1920s, by 1928 the
market had completely crashed from oversupply, and the world economy
sank into depression not long after. For the Third World, the economic issues
were far more intense than in the United States and Europe.

Although as a child he knew his stepfather Silvestre Gutiérrez as his only father, Bartolo's real father was a wealthy young European named Augustiano Moré, a field manager who took a liking to Bartolo's mother, Virginia Secundina Moré, when she was a girl. When Virginia's mother learned that her daughter was pregnant, she drove her from the house. Not long after that, Silvestre became Virginia's common-law husband. Silvestre helped raise the family, but he disappeared from the historical record at some point. In all, the diminutive Virginia would give birth to an astounding eighteen children. Virginia tried to control her oldest by various methods, but none worked. He was headstrong but good-natured, and it was not easy to resist his tricks for getting what he wanted. He earned his whippings, but he was very good at getting out of some of them, too.

Even if he was an illegitimate boy in a fast-growing family that lived in the poorest neighborhood in Lajas, as a young boy he lived in a world rich in culture and entertainment. His childhood was essentially the same as his mother's, for Virginia also grew up in a place that valued performance and music but could offer little more than that in life. Far out in the countryside, there were no permanent movie theaters yet, and professional musicians rarely traveled outside the cities. But Bartolo was born right at the beginning of commercial radio. Its powerful influence on his early life and career never waned, even when television made him a superstar in his own and nearby countries.

Virginia had sung at parties as a teenager and as an adult, and had even studied violin for a time, so she encouraged her children to sing and play music as soon as they could hold an instrument. For musically inclined Cubans, which means the majority, the influence begins in the crib. So many sounds reach a Cuban baby's ears that it might as well have been an orchestra Bartolo was hearing: accompanying a girl's voice singing lullabies came the roosters, the tropical birds, dogs barking, donkeys braying, horses that whinnied as men rode them past the porch, women cooking and laughing in the hot kitchen, loud children next door, the heavy downpours on the roof. And of course the drums, percussion, and guitars of the *guateques* that took place several times a week. One thing has never changed from 1919: Cuba was and still is the most musical country on earth. Street vendors have their own special songs—the peanut vendor, the man who fixes pots, the one who sharpens knives. Although few people in town had phonographs, many had radios, and so a Cuban child also heard danzón, comedies, American jazz, the Spanish light opera called zarzuela, and best of all the exciting *son* music. In a time before cars, it was still a pleasantly noisy childhood, and noise in the street is a universal element of the energy of Latin American life.

The Casino de los Congos served as church and social center for Bartolo and his siblings and all their friends and relatives. The religion Bartolo inherited was largely Santería, in his case a very heavily Africanized version of Catholicism. The Casino was established by Bartolo's great-grandfather Ta Ramón Gundo Moré, a freed slave on Virginia's side. Family members believe that they are descended via Ta Ramón from a kidnapped African king. A powerful African influence also emanated from the nearby village of Palmira, one of the most African-rich cultural hotspots in Cuba; its light fell strongly on Santa Isabel de las Lajas, and especially on La Guinea, located on the side of town closest to Palmira. On the feast day of St. Anthony, believers sacrificed a goat. They carried stews, okra, and corn in gourd cups to the Casino. For days before and after, the entire neighborhood participated in the dancing and singing. Benny's inheritance from Heredia Street would turn out to be immensely rich, both as it formed him and, someday, monetarily as well.

Bartolo got his early musical education not only at the Casino but in small groups he sang with in the village. And when there was no group, he would sing alone. Virginia later laughed that keeping him in the house, even when he was very young, was impossible whenever he heard the tuning of a guitar or the rattle of bongos.

One often-told story starts after midnight while Virginia, who worked as a laundress, was finishing her ironing. When she checked on the boys, she saw that Bartolo was no longer in bed with Teo. Teo told her that his brother had gone to the *son*. "You don't hear it, Mama? That's where he went," he told her. Benny had heard a party a few houses down, climbed into his shorts, and sneaked out. He was, she remembered, about four or five at the time.

Virginia set off angrily to search for him in the guava grove. Because the moon was full, she superstitiously put a scarf over her head. She didn't look forward to using the switch on his little leg, but she took it down from the shelf and put it in her apron. When she found him, he was at the neighbors', standing barefoot on a table in the middle of the room, making up song verses to the people who were crowded in to hear him.

She was about to order him off the table, but he saw her come in and started to sing her arrival into his act, improvising "So the lady has come ... I'm going to get a whipping ... she's going to be very mad ... I don't know when I will sing again ..." It was impossible not to be affected by such cheek, and she smiled behind her hand.

The owners of the house begged her to let him stay a while longer: he was their star attraction. She was tired, and the wife promised that she would keep an eye on him, so Virginia shrugged and let him stay. When she returned an hour later he was still improvising.

This story is often repeated in what little information there is on his early life. While it may sound a bit apocryphal, it is very plausible. Even toddlers in any Cuban family already know many dances, have begun to sing, and can follow the all-important rhythm with claves or clapping hands.

Virginia claimed that Bartolo made guitars from thrown-away boxes by age six, and Teodoro remembered their using sticks as claves, along with a bongo that Bartolo made from two condensed milk cans. He said that Bartolo was already organizing and leading his brothers and sisters, urging, "Don't start until I say."

With sugar prices at an all-time low, it was a period of severe economic hardship for Cuba, and with a growing family, Virginia needed help from her oldest. At the end of fourth grade, in 1930, Bartolo left school to go to work. Although he had enjoyed his schooldays at José de la Luz y Caballero and was good at math and reading, he was very excited to leave behind the hot classroom and feel like a grown man who was needed by his family. Presumably he soon wished himself back in the classroom, because he got up even earlier and worked all day in the blazing sun. There was still the washing and ironing to help with, but now he worked all of the daylight hours carrying food to the field workers. He and later Teo also carried canteens of water out to the workers in nearby Caracas. In the evenings he began singing with an informal group that included Manolo Mena, Loreto Madraza, and Eliseo Fernández, usually over at the little park across from the train station.

By 1932 Virginia was forced to move for work as a washerwoman to faraway Vertientes in Camagüey Province, where she had relatives. Although this must have been a hardship for the children and Virginia herself, the town would play a very important role in Benny's life. At first the boys stayed with Virginia's father in Lajas and kept working in the yucca fields, but at least they didn't have to help with the wash in the evenings. Few people speak about Bartolo's stepfather, Silvestre, but it is likely that he came and went. It is also likely that his comings and goings were due to searching for hard-to-find employment, as millions did in all the countries affected by the Depression; for a black man in Cuba, the only work was seasonal cane and other agricultural labor. Eventually they did all live permanently in Vertientes, Virginia and Silvestre and all the children.

Characteristically for his restless childhood, Bartolo decided one morning that it was high time for him to leave Lajas and join his mother. He shook his brother early.

"What?" said Teo, slapping at Bartolo's hand. Teo was still dreaming and not happy about being awakened.

"Let's get out of here, Compay," Bartolo said, and told him to get dressed, that they were going somewhere good.

Teo, used to his brother's cheerful orders, obediently began to dress. This took some time, since he kept putting his pants on backward. It seemed like whenever Bartolo had brilliant ideas, they somehow always interrupted Teo's sleep.

As they left, Teo remarked that the moon was still up. He assumed they were going fishing down at the river, but then he realized they were taking a different way out of town. He pulled up short. He had woken sufficiently to notice that they had left the bamboo cane poles at home.

"Bartolo, where are we going?"

"To where the old lady is at," the thirteen-year-old Bartolo told him confidently.

"What are you talking about?"

Bartolo only grinned and pointed to his head and said, "See this coco?" which always meant "I know what I'm doing."

Neither Bartolo nor eleven-year-old Teo had any understanding of Cuban geography. Vertientes is located to the south of the city of Camagüey, in the province of the same name, 250 kilometers away—one-fifth the length of the entire island—as the crow flies. But in Cuba the crow seldom flies along a path that even remotely resembles a straight line. Roads never seem to take the direct route from town to town or region to region, but are often old colonial roads developed by the Spanish with the influence of local rivers, marshes, and mountains. Although Bartolo and Teo had many first cousins scattered around Lajas, they had met only those within close range. Alfredo "Chocolate" Armenteros, who would become Bartolo's first orchestra leader, lived at the same time in Ranchuelo, a town somewhat bigger than Lajas and less than thirty kilometers away to the east, but Alfredo and Bartolo would not meet for another twenty years. Alfredo was only a small boy when Bartolo left Lajas. Decades later in his apartment in New York's Spanish Harlem, Alfredo agreed that "yes, it was close by, maybe a short ride on a horse, but where would you get a horse?" For poor black boys in the country, visiting relatives in neighboring towns was as unlikely as escaping the legacies of sugar plantation slavery.

To get to Vertientes, the boys would have had to leave either from Cienfuegos or, more likely, Santa Clara. If they went via the latter, they would miss the view from the road along the Caribbean, and the colonial masterpiece city of Trinidad, as well as Sancti Spíritus, but they must have passed through Ciego de Ávila and then drifted southward to Vertientes from Camagüey. It is unlikely that they had enough money from their jobs to pay for even the cheapest rail ticket, so they would have traveled to Vertientes by a combination of sneaking on trains and begging or paying a small amount for rides along the way. How long it took them is unknown. Until someone told them to go east, they didn't even know in what direction they were headed. Virginia was quite shocked when they made it.

Although the boys would go back and forth for work and family reasons, Bartolo never lived in Santa Isabel de las Lajas permanently again. He had left behind the woods and flat plains of Lajas for humid Vertientes, near the Gulf of Ana María, with its mangrove coast and hundreds of cays offshore. It wasn't far from where the Cuban saltwater crocodile once prowled the marshes and passes between the islands.

TWO

Rumba, *Son*, and the Orchestras

Son was disliked by the authorities from the moment it first appeared in Santiago de Cuba, in the easternmost provinces. Rock and roll carried its hint of sexuality and raciness, but for early *son* it wasn't implied, it was clearly displayed. *Son* dancing uses a hip thrust and twisting that leaves little doubt what it stands for. *Son* and other badges of Africanness were frowned on by many powerful Cuban officials, but it was the Caribbean, after all, and while the whites may have controlled the laws, in the end they had little real influence over popular culture.

If the Africanized culture of New Orleans and São Paulo seeped into society from the bottom up, culture in Cuba went both ways: from the ballroom and the opera house downward, and from the cane fields and the porches of mountain *bohíos* upward to popular and then to symphonic music. Spanish lyric songs were carried by the first settlers, drums and polyrhythms came with the Africans, and French Creoles fleeing Haiti brought the ballroom contredanse. Similar to what happened in Louisiana and Brazil, these elements cooked in the hot climate to give birth, in the case of Cuba, to la danza, el danzón, the cha-cha, and many less formal styles.

Historically the music of Cuba casts a giant shadow that covers all of Latin America, especially Mexico and the Caribbean. The edge of the shadow falls onto Louisiana, where Cuban rhythm colored early jazz and provided what Jelly Roll Morton called the Latin tinge. Later this influence reached much farther, 2,400 kilometers north to Manhattan and the Bronx, where so many

Puerto Rican immigrants had settled. When Puerto Ricans arrived on the U.S. mainland, they added their own traditions to Cuban forms, and the style of music everyone played from the 1940s on would become what is now called salsa. Where Cuban musicians met big-band jazz, their tradition fascinated bebop musicians like Dizzy Gillespie, and the result of this next intermarriage was Latin jazz.

In 1928, the year Bartolo turned nine, President General Gerardo Machado officially outlawed the playing of the most important instruments in *son* music, bongo and conga drums, across the entire island. A former cattle thief and hero of the war of independence from Spain, the repressive Machado hoped to elevate Cuban popular music by surgically removing its threatening African elements. Thus he also outlawed comparsa, the exciting Carnival music that originated in Santiago de Cuba. The ban specifically targeted conga and bongo drums, and any religious drums of African origin, which in the past had been used to make war.

The next year the white mayor of Santiago followed suit to ban congas and bongos, and he outlawed the conga line—the wild and chaotic Carnival dance. The mayor of Santiago was Dr. Desiderio Arnaz, and he had been trying to suppress the conga lines from the city's Carnival season since 1925. A Machado supporter right to the last minute, he would later help haul bags of gold coins to a waiting airplane when Machado fled the country. Dr. Arnaz was the father of Desi Jr., who happened to find fame in American television partly by mimicking Afro-Cuban music. Ironically, the charismatic Desi, though not a particularly talented singer, would help introduce the conga line dance to the United States: his signature song was the afro-cha "Babalú ayé," which in the Dahomeyan language is the name for the Yoruba god of sickness. Desi brought only his good looks to the song, since he was imitating the version that Miguelito Valdés had made famous in Cuba.

Machado's culture-control laws forbade the playing in public of African instruments, although they allowed timbales, which look something like the drums used in European music. African instruments represented the ever-present menace of African culture and, as religious, liturgical tools, were often played by secret followers of the Palo or Santería religion like Bartolo and the other Congo members. Any drum played with the hand was now a target of federal and local law.

Oddly enough, General Machado didn't exactly hate *son* and even had his own favorite group, Septeto Habanero, the most popular band of the 1920s. For them alone he was willing to suspend his ban on bongos. With the advent of 78 rpm records and radio, this group did as much for the future of *son* as Machado's banning of drums in public. The Septeto formed the basis for *son* orchestration to which the blind bandleader Arsenio Rodríguez would later add congas for the first time. During Machado's dictatorship, upper-class Cubans stuck to their danzón and jazz in the country clubs and society concerts, but everyone else went crazy for *son*. Eventually, white Cuba came around too, but not until racism had worsened through the 1930s. In that atmosphere, even international stars Josephine Baker and Joe Louis were refused hotel rooms in Havana.

In the end, and in spite of the ban, *son* flourished throughout Machado's dictatorship and then exploded when he left power. The music bans functioned something like blue laws: periodically enforced but not really affecting what people did in the privacy of their own homes. In fact, by forcing drumming and Palo beliefs underground for all those years, Machado strengthened the African element of *son* by concentrating it among stubborn followers who were even more keen on its survival. The moment they could, the believers brought their bongos and conga drums right back out into public parks, plazas, courtyards, and front yards in the black neighborhoods of every city and town across the island. By the time Arsenio Rodríguez added conga drums as an afterthought to his band in 1942 and created the orchestration and format that led the way for Benny Moré, *son* was the biggest sensation to hit Cuba since the danzón. It was at this time that *son* was mistakenly named rhumba and began influencing composers like George Gershwin.

In the 1930s in the neighboring Dominican Republic, the equally repressive dictator General Rafael Trujillo took a lesson from his friend General Machado. More successfully applying the Machado method, he sought to mold merengue by likewise downplaying its African rhythmic elements and history. Like *son* and jazz, the music had organically emerged as a cross-pollination of Hispanic melody and rhythms of former slaves, but merengue dancing with its rolling, below-the-belt hip thrust was considered a lascivious outrage by the white Dominican upper class. For the same reasons, an early form of merengue had been fully banned in Puerto Rico as far back as 1849. Naturally, the Dominican dictator's favorite band was renamed the

Orquesta Presidente Trujillo. General Trujillo succeeded in whitewashing merengue, and repressed all other forms of indigenous Dominican music so successfully that his approved brand of merengue became the national music of that island.

When Machado attempted to mold popular culture and take away *son* from young boys like Bartolo, it was as if Calvin Coolidge had forbidden Louis Armstrong to play anything but waltzes instead of his "funky butt" blues, or if Dwight Eisenhower had called Elvis in 1954 and warned him he could only play pure hillbilly music from then on.

Son and drum language were Bartolo's birthright, and culture laws from Havana meant little out in the country. He still took his drum and dance lessons at the Casino de los Congos the nights when he could, or watched when younger boys were taught their lessons. He had long been able to take part in the groups that played in the informal but intense music parties at the country festivals called guateques, and he was already an improviser, a *rumbero* who knew all the rhythms of the rumba brava: the guaguancó, the yambú, and the columbia. He used milk cans to build a bongo set and practiced the rhythms constantly with his brother Teo and their friends. Three Kings Day and the feast of San Antonio were still a time when the Casino celebrated openly for days, and Bartolo and the other novices couldn't unlearn all the *firmas* they knew—the pictograph drawings in chalk used for Palo ceremonies. Dictators come and go in Cuba, but Africa in the Americas, at least in Cuba, wasn't about to disappear.

THREE

Sugar, Guitars, Vertientes, 1935–1940

Until Virginia had to move to Vertientes, Bartolo still had his chores at home, and little brothers and sisters to look after, and the animals to take care of. Whenever his stepfather went on a bender, he would have to do even more. Already he helped pick mangos in June, sweated away in the garden, burned the weeds the goats wouldn't eat, cut tough plantains for tostones, milked the cow twice a day, fed the chickens and ducks and pigeons, helped butcher the chickens, hunted in the grass for hen and duck eggs, and, if there were extra, washed them every morning for sale at the market. Although he sometimes hated doing the milking and found dealing with eggs boring, he never disliked any job that was out in the sun. Even if he had just come in from helping his stepfather all day in the cassava fields or in the lime groves, if his mother put a bucket in his hand when he came to the well for a cup of water, he happily took the bucket and picked guavas so she could make jam. And as the oldest boy, Bartolo would never stop supporting his family, even after he had made a succession of his own families.

On very rare occasions in Lajas, they went to the beach. Black guajiros had less leisure than the poor white guajiros, but on some feast days or times when the agricultural work permitted, Bartolo got to go along to the secluded Rancho Luna beach near Cienfuegos. Among his most cherished memories were wading in the shallows for conch shells and coaxing the mean but delicious crabs into a net by tugging a fish carcass tied to a string through the water. Like his time learning the dance steps and drums at the Casino, running along the beach while Virginia warned him to be careful of the waves was something he never forgot. Nor did he forget the first time he tasted lobster, roasted on the beach by his uncle on a smoky driftwood fire with only lime and drops of seawater for seasoning.

Although he was one more restless country boy who would be attracted toward the perfumes of Havana, at age nine Bartolo still thought he would never leave Santa Isabel and was sure it was the best place to live on the entire island, if not the whole world.

But by 1935 when he and Teo went to Vertientes, sugar prices had come back. The two boys now learned the meaning of really hard work—they began to cut cane. They worked for the Maduro Company in the town of Jaronú up along the north coast in Camagüey Province. When the mill was built in 1920 by the American Sugar Company, it was the largest in the world. Bartolo and Teo lived and worked near gorgeous beaches offshore on Cayo Romano and Cayo Cruz. They surely never spent a day off there, but Bartolo did meet the musician Alejandro Castellanos and the tres player Victor Landa while in Jaronú.

The stay for the two Moré boys lasted only seven months before Bartolo again became restless; their mother had gone back to Lajas, and when he heard the news in a letter, he told Teo to pack his things. When Teo asked why, Bartolo told him the same thing he had months earlier:

"Because I want to go to Lajas to see the old lady."

"The old lady?"

So that was that. Teo wasn't about to stay in that awful mill town by himself. Unsurprisingly he had been more thrifty with his earnings than Bartolo, for whom acquiring and saving money would never be a priority. Teo still looked up to his brother, and so he let him have half of the money. Bartolo promptly bought a guitar in Morón on the way, although he still wasn't much of a guitar player yet. They may have had enough money for train fare, and could have bought the guitar near the station while waiting for a connecting train, but chances are that they hitched a ride on the highway to Morón and Bartolo came across a guitar he decided he couldn't live without. It was a lovely instrument, the two boys agreed. It would be several years before Bartolo learned to play guitar properly.

The boys had been in Lajas only a few days when Bartolo announced to everyone that he was leaving for Havana. He had talked incessantly to Teo about his plans the entire way back to Lajas, especially once he had that guitar. But because he had almost no money, his mother wasn't all that concerned that it would happen.

After dinner he went over and kissed Virginia. "I'm not going to see you for some time, Mama," he told her, making sure he caught her attention.

She rolled her eyes while he told everyone about his plans to go to Havana. All she would say was "Wave to the president for me when you go by the Capitol."

Virginia was in fact quite surprised that he would "run away and leave her," as she put it, but by then she must have understood his stubborn nature, a boy who forever had a purpose. He was the type of child that adults describe as never afraid to get what he needs in life. Bartolo had no more idea what he would do when he got to Havana than the times he had traveled many kilometers to rejoin Virginia, aside from the initial burning urge to go there. In this case he must have imagined he would become a musician as soon as he arrived, though merely seeing Havana would have been enough of a reason.

That night he hopped the 11 o'clock train and rode the fifteen kilometers to the town of Santo Domingo. He was an expert at stealing away beneath a train, but with his beloved guitar along, and barely hanging on the undercarriage with the ties passing beneath his hip, he was relieved to get off when the train stopped at a crossing.

At Santo Domingo he hitched a ride on a truck hauling cabbage from Las Villas Province to the market in Havana. He told the driver that his mother was sick in the hospital in Havana—a story he knew no Cuban could resist—but the man was afraid of the police, since Bartolo looked like a minor and a vagrant.

"Get under the tarp, make a little spot in the cabbage pile," the man told him. He shook his finger for emphasis. "And don't move. You hear me?"

Bartolo nodded earnestly. He hopped up onto the truck bed and burrowed under the tarp while the man tied the corner back down. The man slapped the side panels, looked both ways down the dark highway, and off they went.

The trip took all night, and Bartolo napped as well as he could among the hard and powerful-smelling cabbages. The man would take him only to

Catalina de Güines, sixty kilometers from the outskirts of Havana. Bartolo made his way to the nearest local Congo, where he asked the caretaker for help. True to the Casino's role as a benevolent society for black Cubans, the caretaker fed him and gave him enough money to get to the city.

When he entered the dream world that was Havana, he was stunned. Magnificent women sauntered past, hips swaying, shoulders just barely moving. Appreciative male onlookers called out *piropos* that were lost in the noise of enormous honking cars flashing by, street arguments, music. Enticing food smells floated everywhere. Bartolo was so fascinated by his first sight of a Chinese laundry that he stood on the sidewalk to stare and listen to the workers. He had come to the greatest city the Spanish had ever built outside the Iberian Peninsula, the place where so many guajiro boys had found success. Not many of them were black, but those who did make it were entertainers.

He stayed with Virginia's brother, his uncle Tomás, in a one-room apartment at 111 Calle Paula and worked for him selling bruised fruits and vegetables and medicinal herbs from a pushcart. He lasted only six months before he got homesick. He may have had a guitar now, but it wouldn't magically play itself, and he remembered only a few chords. Just about anything new can become a chore after six months. This was when Bartolo's own self-timer seemed to go off, to tell him that it was time to move on and see more of the world. The next thing he knew, he was a cane cutter again.

Once more Bartolo and Teo ventured out together, cutting cane at the Las Marías mill, far away near Ciego de Ávila in the province of that name. Sometime in that same year they went back to Vertientes to work at the Guano Alto mill, shifting along with the other cutters to the next region's harvest. A few years later Vincent Astor would issue stock certificates in the Vertientes Camagüey Sugar Company to raise capital for investment in the mills. Astor, son of John Jacob Astor IV who had made so much money in real estate in Manhattan, was only one of the superrich to invest in sugar in Cuba. American investors would also have sweetheart deals with puppet regimes that made fortunes in nickel, coal, coffee, and other goods.

Someone who would play a major role in Bartolo's future lived in Vertientes—Enrique Benítez, who would later be known throughout Cuba by his nickname El Conde Negro, the Black Count. Benítez was a second cousin to Bartolo, whose great-grandmother was Majulia Benítez. Born in Lajas in

1916, Enrique had moved with his family to Vertientes by the time Bartolo was born in 1919. His mother was Virginia's aunt, and this family connection is what had drawn Virginia to Vertientes to work, with Bartolo and Teo to follow in 1935.

This first visit to Vertientes was when young Bartolo, who was eager to sing, first encountered the very musically inclined Enrique. As with so many Cubans, musicians and otherwise, Enrique would eventually be known only by his nickname, the tongue-in-cheek El Conde Negro. The name was a boast of his success with women, and the irresistible Benítez with his dark skin, handsome face, and sly look would engage his cousin in a lifelong contest over their conquests. Bartolo, always less aggressive with women, did not feel a need to actively participate in the contest. It was a good thing he didn't try, because Benítez would eventually father fourteen children with twelve different women. The cousins had a great deal in common, aside from family ties: both were raised in the same Africanized atmosphere, both had a small-town background, and both were naturally talented musicians who would always draw on their deep cultural sense of rhythm and harmony. And although Bartolo wouldn't learn this about himself until later, both boys had white Spanish blood.

Benítez had been taught to play some guitar and tres by a white player named Ñiquito from Cienfuegos. Enrique had formed his own trio, Los Vertientinos, with whom Bartolo sang on occasion in 1935. By 1937 Enrique too had been to Havana, singing and playing with the Cuarteto Continental. In their spare time in 1939 the cousins formed a group to sing at get-togethers and dances, and guateque parties. Bartolo, not yet a lead singer, sang backup behind Enrique. Their first group together, Conjunto Avance, included Horacio Landa and others, but consisted largely of a trio that comprised Enrique, Cheo Casanovas, and Bartolo. It may have been Enrique's show, but Bartolo was smart to join.

During the very long day making money to send back home, the Moré boys swung machetes to fuel the mill with sugarcane. Bartolo might have spent his life in the hard world of sugar harvests, ruining his hands and back with the work of the Caribbean slaves—the reason he was born in Cuba and not Africa in the first place. Although Cuba had a wider variety of crops to harvest, in Jamaica during the brutal years of slavery hundreds of thousands of slaves were deliberately worked to death in the cane fields. The mortality rate of men, women, and children in Jamaican sugar harvests was so high that the Western African slave ports struggled to ship enough new slaves to take their place. Only two generations away from enslavement in Cuba, Bartolo and his friends and relatives encountered conditions in the sugar business that were essentially little changed from the 1880s.

But the same lucky accident befell both Moré brothers at the same time, and probably kept them from being cane cutters for the rest of their teenage years or longer. Both of them, in superb condition by then, found that their energy was flagging, that they could hardly get out of bed. Teo had trouble sharpening his machete. Bartolo would have teased him if he didn't have the same problem, and he soon had the same terrible headache and nausea. They had both been afflicted by one of the cane cutters' many hazards: mosquito-borne malaria. When a company car took them, boiling with waves of fever and shivering with chills, to the hospital, the doctor Horacio Rodríguez Moya warned them that they must do different work, once they got better. He saw to it that the company wouldn't put them back in the cutting crews that were first in the wet fields, which the mosquitoes seemed to own just as firmly as the American investors.

When they had finished their time in bed, Bartolo became a cart driver. This unfortunately was just as hard in its own way as cutting cane. It was more backbreaking, and he spent much of his time in close proximity to the roaring furnaces, which felt like walking on purpose into the winds of hell. Bartolo already knew that he would never work in the sugar industry for a moment more than he was forced to, but at least the cane cutter's knife was no longer a part of his life, making his hand stiff and sore from gripping it so long. His youthful energy kept his body going during the day, but all he could think of, and all he and Enrique talked about at night, was Havana.

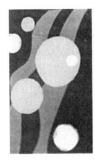

FOUR

Havana Apprenticeship, 1940–1943

For a country boy, to think of going to Havana is a great daydream.
But being there for real? Nothing could ever surpass that feeling.
It's true that it was very hard. There were plenty of nights when I
had a lot more hunger than I had sleep, but I was in Havana.

When Bartolo left for Havana this time, he was armed with a clearer purpose and much more earned experience of what it meant to spend your entire life far out in Camagüey or Las Villas Province as a sugar worker. This experience supplied him with all the more determination to avoid going back. Enrique and he agreed on that, and they agreed that they made a great team. Cheo too had tired of life in the provinces and was easily persuaded to go along.

Havana life in 1940 felt the shortages and rationing endured in America and Europe, though nowhere near the same degree of hardship. Still in its final decades of American domination, Cuba had officially sided with the Allies, yet luckily didn't have to send troops off to fight. Unfortunately, tourism plummeted from the moment fighting began, which meant less money for entertainers, so in some ways Bartolo had arrived in one of the most difficult periods. Not until after the war ended would clubs like the Sans Souci reopen and the former soldiers and sailors arrive to spend freely in the casinos and the cathouses. Bartolo, or Benny, wouldn't live in Havana then, and returned only when tourism had completely eclipsed all prewar figures.

Benny told *Bohemia* magazine that it took him a lot longer to get somewhere than he would have preferred, three years of living hand to mouth. The trio found that the city was crawling with musicians from the provinces who competed for the few available spots, so all they could do was join the other strolling musicians who worked the cafés and little bars in Habana Vieja and down along the waterfront.

Bartolo again stayed with his uncle on Calle Paula, and worked for him pushing a cart and selling fruit and vegetables in the central market. He may have been pushing a cart again, but at least it wasn't loaded with hundreds of pounds of fresh, wet cane. And with singing to sell his products, he had already entered into the wonderful, centuries-old tradition of the *pregones*, little songs or musical phrases used by street vendors to advertise their goods and services, often turned into popular song. Knife sharpeners, shoe repairmen, a blind man selling pots, the ice cream lady, the tamale man—all street vendors in Cuba have a little song to go along with their goods. Just as Italian opera composers used regional folk songs for inspiration, many *pregones* were street advertisements heard by a composer, then updated for current popular forms. "El botellero," "El mondonguero," "Frutas del Caney," and "Mango mangue" are the best-known *pregones*. Some, like the early American blues songs on 78s, were risqué and full of double entendres, such as "Atesame el bastidor" (Let me straighten your bedframe). The *son-pregón* "El manisero" or "The Peanut Vendor" is one of the most famous songs ever exported from Cuba. Originally written by Moisés Simons for the singer Rita Montaner, it may have been influenced by the New Orleanian composer Louis Moreau Gottschalk, who was influenced in turn by Cuban folk song. In Cuba every strolling street musician will always know the key to play it in, and its charming lyrics.

"El manisero" debuted in Paris in 1928 and then on Broadway in 1931 when the Don Azpiazu orchestra's "rhumba" version became immediately successful. It was a very important moment in American popular music. Although a Latin tinge had first seeped into jazz via the Cuban and Mexican musicians who brought it to New Orleans before the turn of the century, by the 1930s it had taken up residence in Tin Pan Alley for good. The Azpiazu version of "The Peanut Vendor" sold a million copies and more forcefully introduced the habanera rhythm, mistakenly called rhumba then, to American music. Judy Garland sang "The Peanut Vendor" in *A Star Is Born* in 1954. And the version Louis Armstrong had recorded on December 23, 1930, for

Okeh Records with Lionel Hampton on drums, is one of the more charming examples of the use of Cuban music in American jazz.

Even though *pregones* are an urban invention, most likely Bartolo had been singing "El manisero" for some time already on the dusty streets of Lajas and Vertientes before he ever came to Havana.

After the nights of roaming with the group, his worst problem now— apart from the bees and flies that pursued the fruit on his cart—was staying awake long enough to get to a siesta in the afternoon. The lady who came by to sell coffee in a thimble-sized cup knew Bartolo very well. He often cranked his arm dramatically while finishing one cup of sweet coffee, meaning "Keep them coming!" Both he and Enrique pushed carts, but mostly Enrique worked as a stevedore during the many years he held a day job in Havana.

They had become night people, and took their place with the clubbing types, the insomniacs, and the prostitutes. Along with their hours they also shared a verb, *fletear*, which can mean either to play as strolling trouba- dour musicians or to "street walk" as prostitutes do. For years Bartolo never owned more than one pair of pants; when those wore out, he had to find another pair. He channeled a country boy's loneliness through his voice, and the drinks the musicians often got as payment temporarily took the edge off the hard reality.

In Havana in 2007 Enrique recalled those days:

We had our trio in Havana, Trío Benítez-Moré—Bartolo, me, and Cheo. He played maracas and clave. I was the lead, Benny accompanied. Obviously Benny became a better singer than me, but then he wasn't really a singer yet, so he sang backup. We played in bars and restaurants. Havana in those days had many, many bars. We would go from street to street, and bar to bar. We might begin at the Bodeguita, the Sala Rosana, or the Costa Blanca. Then we would make a left after the Floridita, out toward Habana del Este. There was a bar near the tunnel called Caballero. If it was slow, we went down to the launch for La Regla. Over there was the bar Mar y Tierra, the Mexico, the Barrilito. All this for four, five, maybe six pesos, but it was still better than in La Guinea.

The cousins and Cheo strolled beneath the pale light from the gas lamps along the tourist-filled streets, beside the open restaurants and sidewalk ca- fés along boulevards like Prado. At a table along the street a woman, with legs crossed and a little shoe hanging off the end of her foot, sipped a daiquiri while her movie-star-handsome date clapped for the trio and gave them a peso from his stylish suit pocket. Bartolo shot Enrique a look that meant "Check out the lady," but Enrique didn't need to be told when there was a pretty girl nearby: his radar was always working. Besides, Enrique liked to play it cool around women, while Bartolo just liked to play around.

"And that's why I get a little more love and you get a little less," Enrique would tell his younger cousin.

"Maybe so, but the love I get is of a higher quality than the love you get. Cheo, tell him the truth about those ugly girls. The real truth, heifers!" he said, running from Enrique's thrown shoe.

The writer Eduardo Robreño remembered seeing Bartolo singing with a group called the Trío Raga in a café restaurant called Las Culebrinas that was open day and night. That group, led by Alfonso Raga, had a black tres player from Camagüey named Aristides, with Chino Aurelio on guitar. It was very early in the morning. Robreño said he heard Bartolo first singing, "Cantan las mirlas por las mañanas su dulce canto al rayar del día." Robreño claimed that Bartolo's skills were so advanced that he could sing the Spanish versions of "La Siciliana" from *Cavalleria Rusticana* or Arlecchino's aria from *Pagliacci*. Bartolo sang a Gardel song that goes "Solo en la ruta de mi destino, sin el amparo de tu mirar, soy como un ave que en el camino rompió las cuerdas de su cantar." It was during a period of gasoline rationing, and so it was a time of strolling troubadours and walking everywhere in the city for your entertainment. When Robreño tried to give Bartolo a little something for singing, he wouldn't take anything but a drink of rum.

Bartolo's abilities were trained and molded under Enrique's guidance from the time the two first met. In an interview much later Bartolo said, "Let me tell you right now that a great part of who I am I owe to my compadre El Conde Negro." They would love each other like brothers until the end. The Conde Negro apprenticeship that began in 1935 took six or seven years before Bartolo began to surpass Enrique's singing abilities and was able to sing successfully with other musicians.

They lived at a time of very exciting music in the most exciting city in the Americas. Arsenio Rodríguez was around, and many other musicians who would soon become major figures in Cuban and American music still remained in Havana. In 1940 American big band jazz was calling to the players in Havana, but no one had left yet for Manhattan and the Bronx. The great Enrique Jorrín was creating cha-cha-cha with the López brothers in the late 1940s, but he wouldn't write "La engañadora" until 1951. All the famous forms except for mambo were present. It wasn't only men: an excellent big band of all women players, Anacaona, kept busy, as did other all-female groups. Sometimes Bartolo went to the club Panchín in Marianao to hear a singer he admired, Panchito Riset. Bartolo's first composition was a bolero, "Dime que sí." Though he never recorded it, the Benítez-Moré trio sang it in the streets.

This was also the time of the great Cuban radio shows. Station CMQ at Monte and Prado ran a gong-style talent show called *Corte Suprema del Arte*. Another station had a similar show called *Todo el Mundo Canta*. The CMQ show was known for harsh treatment of those who dared to perform live, and at his first appearance on the show, poor Bartolo was booed off the stage. Anyone who has seen the talent night at the Apollo Theater in Harlem knows how it works: when the audience dislikes the performer, it is a painfully humiliating experience to be forced off the stage. As legend has it, a very determined Bartolo went back for a second attempt, and that time he won first prize.

Bartolo finally left behind busking and playing for pennies on the street and began to work with a succession of groups, first in a duo with a singer named Anselmo. Next he sang for the Cuarteto Cordero, and then the Conjunto Cauto, which was directed by Mozo Borgella—a man who would provide the connection to the next stage in his life. By now he was living in the Belén barrio and was singing with the Sexteto Figaro, and with Lázaro Cordero on a radio show for CMZ.

Bartolo was a very ambitious guajiro boy among thousands and thousands who came to Havana for work, and who loved everything as he did: the people with "huevos" (slang for money), the giant cars they called "máquinas" (machines), the noise, the music everywhere, the saucy looks from the bold women who swayed as they walked in a way that mesmerized any man who watched. In Havana everything was eroticized, and everything was musical at the same time. From an African sensibility, Bartolo appreciated the sexualized atmosphere of Havana, where even the language itself was charged with sexuality. When he first arrived, he would laugh to his friends about how you can't say "papaya" in public unless you mean to use a vulgarity (if poetic) for a woman's privates. He also loved how saying "fruta bomba" instead made you feel even more self-conscious and a little more dirty because you were avoiding saying "papaya."

In 1944 Bartolo was thrilled to have a visit from his brother Teo, who got to see him sing at the 7:30 show on Mil Diez (Radio 1010). By then the crowd cheered him, and he was never booed again.

Bartolo was persistent and impatient. He still had hungry nights, but they only sharpened his focus. A secret known to many hunters for getting a bird dog to work harder is to deny him a meal before a hunt; the dog is more aggressive and runs and hunts all the harder. It was a long three years until Bartolo got regular meals, but he sang in public. There is immediate satisfaction in that, too, once you are good enough. And by the early 1940s, he was.

When Bartolo met Miguel Matamoros in 1944, he still owned nothing more than a guitar and one suit, and a single pair of shoes that had become well known to the shoe repairman on the street. Even if he rarely had enough money to keep more than one extra E string around for his guitar, by then Bartolo had learned all the guitar chords he needed and, just as important, had mastered rhythm guitar. He and Enrique had also worked on composing songs, but soon playing guitar would only be something he did when writing songs and singing in private. He was about to join one of the biggest groups in Havana.

FIVE

Conjunto Matamoros, 1944–1945

At the time when Santiago de Cuba native Miguel Matamoros first heard Bartolo sing in 1944, the Conjunto Matamoros was one of the most famous bands in Havana and across Cuba. Its recordings and tours had helped spread Cuban music throughout the world, and Matamoros records sold as well in the United States and Europe as in western Africa. Along with Siro Rodríguez and Rafael Cueto, Miguel had formed the original Trío Matamoros in 1925. For the trio and the larger group, Matamoros played guitar and sang lead, Rodríguez sang backup and played maracas and claves, and Cueto played rhythm guitar and sang chorus. They toured the United States and many European countries and later assembled the larger band in 1942 to play the mob-owned Hotel Nacional. Miguel's family name was a very old one, earned back when the Spanish were busy pushing the North Africans off the Iberian Peninsula and forcibly converting Jews and Muslims who stayed behind: Matamoros means "Moor killer." For Bartolo, this name would come to mean something much more positive—career maker.

Miguel Matamoros's biggest hit was "Son de La Loma," and another of Miguel's compositions, "Lágrimas negras," would be revisited by Bebo Valdés and flamenco singer Diego el Cigala for a Grammy award in 2005. The patient and calm Miguel was born in 1894 and had paid his dues. He had worked as a miner, farmer, telephone repairman, carpenter, and house painter, and wasn't able to work full time as a musician until he was in his thirties. Discovered in Santiago by RCA's Cuba director, Miguel was still working as a private chauffeur when he made his first recordings in Camden, New

Jersey, at the Victor studios in 1928. The music his group played was romantic, atmospheric *son* and boleros, beginning to sound a little old-fashioned to Bartolo's more modern ears by the time he came along. But Bartolo, like all singers in Cuba, loved the Matamoros three-part vocals and knew all of their music intimately. Some of Matamoros's biggest hits included "La mujer de Antonio," "Lágrimas negras," "El paralítico," "Veneración," "Las maracas de Cuba," and "Frutas del Caney." Rafael Cueto added to the trio's sound with a *tumbao* beat made by hitting the guitar body with the meat of his hand while playing rhythm. Ned Sublette says that their soft style was perfectly suited to the new format of radio, and this helped their early success.

The larger Conjunto Matamoros functioned as a sextet or octet, adding to the trio the pianist Ramón Dorca, trumpeters José Macías and José Quintero, bassist Cristóbal Mendivé, and bongo player Augustín Gutiérrez. In 1943 the conjunto was working for stations CMQ and on Mil Diez's *Onda Colectiva Hoy*.

Besides Bartolo, another musician who would go on to fame after working with Matamoros was violinist-turned-conga-player Mongo Santamaría. In those days Santamaría was still in Havana, working as a mailman by day and moonlighting on recordings and gigs with Matamoros and other groups around town. Santamaría went on to play with Pérez Prado and, most notably, jazz vibraphonist Cal Tjader. Santamaría helped popularize Latin jazz, and he wrote the Latin jazz classic "Afro Blue." In 1963 he recorded a masterful Afro-Cubanized version of Herbie Hancock's "Watermelon Man" that far outsold the original jazz version from Hancock's first record. Santamaría would also bump into Bartolo again in 1948, when the two of them were working in Mexico City.

Just back in town from a heavy touring schedule, an exhausted Miguel Matamoros had contracted laryngitis. He called Mozo Borgella and asked if he could borrow one of his singers to help with lead parts for a few shows, so that afternoon Borgella took Bartolo over to Mil Diez. It was Miguel's first introduction to the lanky kid, but Siro had already met Bartolo at a party where Bartolo was singing. When Siro and Bartolo were introduced that night, they liked each other right away. Siro also remembered seeing him sing at the Templete bar on Avenida del Puerto, and continued to be impressed with his skills. So when Miguel brought him around a few days later before the show at Mil Diez to try out with the conjunto, Siro recognized him.

Reportedly, Bartolo had also been singing with blind tres genius and modern *son* pioneer Arsenio Rodríguez. When he left for the Matamoros gig at a club in the Hotel Nacional, Miguelito Cuní replaced him in that band.

It was quickly apparent that Bartolo had the capability to be more than an occasional fill-in for Miguel. All three of the original band members were immediately impressed with Bartolo's skill and sense of rhythm with a full group; although Siro couldn't take all the credit for having discovered Bartolo, he could claim to have heard him first. Everyone in the conjunto liked him as well, and Miguel was secretly a little relieved to have found someone to take the pressure off his singing so much of the lead. They had to buy Bartolo new clothes to sing in public with the band, but otherwise he was ready to go. One of the first engagements when they used Bartolo was for station 1010. Having heard and performed Matamoros's hits many times, Bartolo knew Miguel's parts before he showed up to practice the first time with just the trio.

Because of the war, shellac for pressing 78s was rationed and in short supply, but radio stations and jukeboxes picked up the slack to offer cheap entertainment to a population that had very little money but an insatiable taste for the latest sound and the latest dance. And since the record companies couldn't afford the risk of pressing expensive records without testing the music first, radio had grown quickly as a place to identify what the listeners really wanted, and to let the chaff settle out. This upsurge in radio also helped create big stars who became household names without selling millions of records. Television, looming on the horizon, would take those bands to a higher level of success, and even quicker.

Bartolo recorded in the studio with the conjunto that year, and although he may not have received public recognition, for the very first time he heard his own voice on a 78. The first release he made with Matamoros was "Buenos hermanos" (Good brothers), and his voice is clearly superior to Miguel's; he was already using a swinging technique that swayed with and over the melody like American jazz singers he heard on the radio.

Because Matamoros was in the RCA Victor stable, Bartolo had finally come under the all-seeing eye of the American-owned conglomerate that dominated recording in Latin America. Bartolo's business sense may not have been developed enough to know what it could mean to be RCA Victor property, but he was so excited that he couldn't sleep. All he cared about was that he was singing for Miguel Matamoros, and he had a 78 with his own voice to send to Virginia and the rest of the kids. To have recorded his voice so that he could hear it was the most thrilling and satisfying thing that had ever happened to him, and he could be pardoned if he spent a good while in his room staring at that record and drinking toasts to it. In 1962 he told a reporter for *Revolución*:

> My name wasn't on it but it had my voice, and I knew that it was my voice. It made me so excited and happy at that moment. Nothing has ever felt that fantastic.

Bartolo had practiced and played regularly with Matamoros long enough to be considered a band member when Miguel got an offer to take the full conjunto for a long gig in Mexico City. The trio had been to Mexico before, but only to the port of Mérida on the Gulf side of the Yucatán. They had been hearing lots of talk about the booming film industry, and they knew of many musicians who had found work there, so everyone was eager to go. Bartolo had a relationship at this time with a woman who called herself Inés Moré Armenteros, but it is not known if he had any children with her before he left for Mexico.

With Bartolo being a band regular now, Miguel often directed the group and let Bartolo take over his old parts, even on songs like "Son de La Loma." So going to Mexico meant they would have to take Bartolo along. In those days he finally had a little bit of money in his pocket, but he didn't even have time to get a telegram off to Virginia in Lajas. He rushed around Havana to get his passport, and barely made it to Rancho Boyeros, now known as José Martí International Airport. It was an enormous thrill to be in an airplane for the first time, though he would never learn to like flying.

Before he went to Mexico with Matamoros, Bartolo had been living in an awful flophouse, so he was very excited at the thought of staying in hotels while on tour. One of the guys in the band told him that Mexican women were as hot as Mexican food, and Bartolo replied that he wasn't that interested in hot peppers, but he would see what Mexican women were all about.

They left for Mexico City on June 21, 1945. Hitler had been dead since April, and the Germans had surrendered to Soviet and American forces. In another few weeks the Americans would drop atomic bombs on Japan, and the Cold War would begin almost immediately after that. When the

American GIs went home, they would be eager to celebrate and forget all they had seen, and soon many of them would escape the winters to spend time in Havana again. While he watched white lines of birds drifting over the hot green surface of Cuba from the airplane window, Bartolo had no idea that he wouldn't see home again for five years.

Down in Lajas, the neighbor Machito Ponce brought a message to Virginia that Bartolo had gone away to Mexico with Matamoros. She felt sick to her stomach when she found out. Perhaps she sensed that he had gone away for a long time, but she must have been excited to know that he was now a touring member of the great Conjunto Matamoros.

# SIX

In the Land of the Aztecs, 1945–1948

The level of influence Cuba has had on Mexican popular music is nearly as important as the Spanish guitar's or the accordion's. The two countries do share a history of intensive meddling from the United States that radically altered their fortunes and, in Mexico's case, geography. Even without the enormous territories that were annexed into the western United States, Mexico is seven times larger than Cuba, but the Caribbean island has influenced the music of Mexico more than any other country, second only to Spain.

Although the Cuban bolero arrived in Veracruz at the end of the nineteenth century, Cuban inspiration first entered Mexico much earlier. In the late 1700s a dance called chuchumbé came ashore when two ships from Havana sailed into port at Veracruz. This dance form still exists in the Yucatán. One of the many music styles in the Yucatán is the *son jarocho*, of mixed African and Spanish origin; the original "La Bamba" that Ritchie Valens heard played on harps was a *son jarocho*. To this day, Cuban danzón is still popular in the dance halls of Veracruz, Mérida, and Tampico where, as Robert Thompson Farris puts it, "time stopped in 1939." *Son* music from Cuba put a heavy stamp on Mexican orchestras, but it would be mambo that exploded not from Cuba but from Mexico, where it spread around the world in a flash from Dámaso Pérez Prado's recordings. The overarching term the Mexicans use now for Afro-Cuban music is *música tropical*, to differentiate it from the *norteño* cowboy accordion music styles, and the mariachis.

Mexico may seem an unusual place for a Cuban musician to make his name, but Cuban musicians had been there for many years. The clubs were packed night after night, and the end of the war meant that more money and energy could be put into entertainment. Mexico City and Tijuana were becoming very busy again.

Bartolo didn't know what lay in store for him in Mexico, but he knew it could shape his future. He would meet everyone and would play with most of them.

Under contract with Mexican radio and television pioneer and RCA talent scout Emilio Azcarraga Vidaurreta, Matamoros played first in July at the cabaret El Patio, which often booked Cuban acts. Like Mexican films of the time, the bill was a bit of a variety show. It opened with two acts of dancers, one featuring Venezuelan singer Eduardo Lanz and ballerina Gloria Luz of the Ballet Panamericano, the other the Cuban rumba dancer Esther Lafayette, doing La Danza de los Puñales (the Dagger Dance). El Patio was among the most popular nightspots in town, and it served food. Straight-up margaritas arrived at the table alongside pork enchiladas and chicken mole. Tobacco smoke hung heavy in the air, and the music went on all night. It was the kind of place you could go with a date, have a big meal at nine p.m., start dancing at eleven, and not leave until the sun was up. As elsewhere, Cuban music was returning to the popularity it had seen around the world in the 1920s and 1930s.

Esther Lafayette, who was listening backstage after her act, remembered a roar erupting from the Mexican audience. They were going wild for Bartolo's singing because "they had never heard a voice like his before." A rumba dancer better known as Reina Karula (Queen Karula), Lafayette watched from the wings while Bartolo, dressed in red pants and straw hat, sang Obdulio Morales's "La culebra." She said that Miguel was quite pleased with the reception of his young singer in his first international performance, and every night they had the same reaction from the crowded house. Lafayette also claimed later to have been the one who bestowed Bartolo's new name on him.

Bartolo must have been encouraged and emboldened by all the attention he received at every show, and at the various venues where they appeared. The precise moment when he decided to stay and take his chances in Mexico may be unknown, but it couldn't have taken very long. Within just a few weeks, he was another new Cuban resident of Mexico City—and this was the lesser of the dramatic changes that he embraced.

Matamoros had a contract to play at the popular cabaret Río Rosa along with Son Veracruz. Just like back in Havana, they were booked in several locations on a given date. They also played the Club Montparnasse and did live radio from the studios at XEW, the station that RCA helped build, as well as from XEQ. Radio XEW is where Bartolo met a young woman named Juana Bocanegra, and also Emilio Azcarraga, who among his other activities was the head of XEW. Marcos Salazar, a Mexican researcher and expert on Bartolo's time in Mexico, believes that it was Azcarraga along with fellow Río Rosa owner Vicente Miranda who would come up with the new stage name for Bartolo, not Esther Lafayette. The issue continues to puzzle musicologists, and several opinions exist with compelling arguments for each one, but definitive proof is still elusive.

Eulalio "Lalo" Ruiz de Mantilla led the other group playing at Río Rosa, Son Veracruz. Ruiz de Mantilla was born in Daiquiri, and grew up in Santiago de Cuba, like Miguel. Chico Piquero and Modesto Durán played in the band along with two authentic Mexican Veracruzanos, Manuel Peregrino and Raúl de la Rosa. Lalo also played Río Rosa with the Orquesta Antillana led by Arturo Núñez, which is when Bartolo first met Núñez. Bartolo was beginning to know the core group of Cubans in Mexico, and his teasing and country personality made people like him immediately. The Distrito Federal—DF to Mexicans—was a very exciting place, even after Havana. The food was excellent, the tequila addictive, even the rum was pretty good, and they had decent tobacco—a Cuban could be happy here. The weather in the capital may not have suited Bartolo's clothes, but he found a great sense of humor in the Mexican character. He could trade jokes and leg-pulling with the Mexican guys as if they were shooting soccer passes back and forth. In some ways Mexicans, with their family firmly at the center of their culture, and never complaining about hard work, reminded Bartolo very much of life in Lajas. Only in Mexico could a group of men at manual labor make the work look something like a party. He found happiness in Mexico in many and surprising ways.

In all, Bartolo would record ten singles that were released while Matamoros was in Mexico, and more on another trip when the group returned. Besides "Buenos hermanos," Bartolo took over lead from Miguel on seven singles:

"La cazuelita," "Se va a morir," "Ofrenda criolla," "Seré dichoso," "¿Qué será eso?" "Penicilina," and "Me la llevo." It is clear that Bartolo was holding back on the recordings, proving his acceptance and understanding of ensemble playing. Others with Matamoros included "Mexicanita veracruzana" and "Las ruinas de mi bohío."

Bartolo first met Clemente "Chico" Piquero at the General Motors hour on station XEW when Chico was playing bongos with the gigantic sixty-piece orchestra directed by José Sabre Marroquín. Jorge Negrete, who later played with Trío los Panchos, also played with the big group. Along with all the other musicians, Chico hung around to watch the renowned Conjunto Matamoros do the radio show that was on next. Because he was a little removed from the center of Cuban music now, he was surprised to see that Matamoros had another lead vocalist, a young-looking kid who he believed incorrectly at the time had come from Santiago de Cuba. Anyone who stayed to hear Miguel sing was quickly satisfied by the change in lineup. Chico was sure he had heard this kid strolling with a guitar through bars and nightspots back in Havana; he remembered the voice and the face. While members of both bands relaxed at the radio station's snack bar, Chico introduced himself and told Bartolo that he had seen him sing on the street in Havana.

"Well, how did I sound now, Negro?" Bartolo asked him.

"Terrible, Papi," Chico said with a straight face. "It all started out so good, percussion, piano, Matamoros. Everything was great. And then you started singing. Awful. Like cats making love," he told Bartolo, who bent over laughing and hooted when Chico added, "We aren't not talking about nice love, either."

"You know something, Negrito? My throat is really dry from all this abuse, and from my own countryman, too. I think you better start buying the drinks and not stop until I cheer up!" It was the first of thousands of drinks and jokes they would share over the years. From that moment on, they would be drinking buddies and close friends for life. Chico would also be the major impetus for Bartolo's next career move.

Having taken the job as Miguel's singer, Bartolo was already showing good sense (combined with some very good luck) about moving his own career forward, and his skills and drive had shown Miguel what he could do. In Mexico his decisions would be controlled more by a developing business sense and less by luck. There at age twenty-six he would make a sharp turn that surprised people who knew him back home, with the exception of old friends he had grown up with like Enrique Benítez. Bartolo's shrewd decision-making in this case had two interdependent elements, and without the first his success in Mexico could never have come about.

Now that the war in Europe and the Far East was nearly over, and the Mexican film industry was doing so well, Bartolo couldn't have arrived at a better location, or at a better time, for his singing career.

Bartolo and some members of the band were staying at a hotel called the Forno, and whenever he had a moment he wandered the capital's amazing streets, smelling the hot chocolate and churros, the grilled corn, the tortillerías. He loved the mariachis on the corners, and the stocky Indians purposefully walking their children across the boulevards. Being one of the precious few black faces in the entire country made him an exotic, and to Bartolo the city couldn't have been more exotic and strangely beautiful. He never felt anything other than warm welcomes everywhere he went. He was in the place Cubans often romantically refer to as the Land of the Aztecs, and everything glowed in a rare mountain light. At their first chance, Bartolo and some of the guys went to climb the superb pyramids and walk through the famous Valley of the Moon ruins north of the city. It was the first summer he had ever spent in a temperate climate, and although he would never come to love chilly weather, it was a welcome break from the storms and mosquitoes that were facts of life where he had grown up.

Bartolo had been in Mexico for two weeks when he met Juana Margarita Bocanegra Durán on the second of August when Matamoros played the live show at XEW radio. Bocanegra, whom everyone called Juanita, was a nursing student and worked for Dr. Ortiz Tirado, who was also a singer on the side. Juanita worked at XEW part-time. Though naïve and innocent, she was very flattered and excited by the idea that this obviously talented boy had taken a liking to her. She was plain and didn't have a lot of experience with boys, but Bartolo was so nice. She just knew that her mother would like him. She also knew that her father would dislike him no matter what, for he had all her father's least favorite characteristics: black, a musician, a flatterer, not a penny to his name. Juanita may have been plain, but she was a nice, fun girl from a good family.

Because he wanted to talk seriously and didn't have enough money for drinks, Bartolo took her for ice cream for their first date. He played a dance song on the jukebox. She turned out to be a good dancer, so he immediately nicknamed her Negrita, which made her laugh since she wasn't black. "Close enough," he said, since she came from Veracruz. Just calling him Bartolo made her giggle, because in Mexican Spanish it's the common name for a donkey, equivalent to "jackass." She would laugh so hard that she could only point to him when she wanted to ask him something.

Bartolo's inclination to stay must have gone hand in hand with meeting a nice Mexican girl, and likely Chico Piquero had advised him that to remain as a foreign musician in Mexico was becoming more difficult. A tourist visa was one thing, but to actually work in Mexico with its historically powerful unions and musicians' protection would have been impossible on a temporary visa. Bartolo had looked around and seen all the work to be had in Mexico, and he knew that he would make better progress than back in the slow and competitive market of Havana. Even though he was singing for one of the greatest bands, he was already a bit impatient with having to sing Miguel's parts Miguel's way. What he really wanted was to sing a more driving *son* with his own interpretation and improvisation, and in front of larger orchestras. In Havana, he knew, he could wait forever to sing for another authentically pure *son* group like the one led by Arsenio Rodríguez. Miguelito Cuní had already taken the spot Bartolo had held briefly with Rodríguez before leaving to go with Matamoros. Bartolo deeply respected all that Miguel had achieved and was grateful for the chance Miguel had taken on him, but Miguel's idea of *son* was too polite, not the aggressive music Bartolo yearned for. Nor did Miguel love American jazz quite as much as Bartolo and his friends did. Bartolo never said it in public, but for him Matamoros's style of music was a little retrograde.

When he told Miguel and the other guys that he planned to stay, they were shocked. Rafael Cueto believed that Bartolo left the group simply because he had learned all there was to learn; he had warned Bartolo over a drink in a quiet cantina that if he stayed with the group, he would never be able to change the songs or come out of the shadow of Miguel and Miguel's rigid ideas of how their songs should be sung. So Rafael also believed he had encouraged Bartolo's leaving, though he certainly didn't want to say that to Miguel. After he told Bartolo that his was a narrow role to play, Bartolo had said, "*Bueno, chico,* then maybe I'll stick around to see what I can do here." Rafael also warned him to take care to get his working papers or he wouldn't be able to stay.

Siro Rodríguez said that when Bartolo told them he was going to stay because Mexico was a good place to be, Cueto warned him to change his name so that Mexicans wouldn't laugh every time they heard him announced.

On their next date, at the Impala restaurant, Bartolo proposed to Juanita. He told her that he wanted to get married to her legally, but when he said he was poor, he wasn't kidding. He showed her all he had to his name: a little less than 50 pesos among the lint and guitar picks in his pocket. It was enough for the meal and not much more. She said yes anyway.

She was right about her mother liking Bartolo—and about her father not liking him. Her father threw his hands in the air when he heard Bartolo's name.

"¡¿Un negrito que se llama bartolo?! ¡Perfecto!" (A black boy named Jackass?! How perfect!)

Her mother tried her best to help, though it was a hard sell. When Juanita said the "amigo" she would like to bring home was "a Cuban musician," her mother thought this sounded perfectly romantic, and she looked forward to meeting him. Bartolo knew women and knew that they instinctively liked him, so getting Juanita's mother on his side wouldn't be that hard. He also knew Cuban men and fathers of daughters. Assuming Mexican fathers were the same, he was prepared.

Juanita's father was suspicious from the moment he met Bartolo, who by then was calling himself Benny (or Beny), but Juanita had already decided that she wanted to marry him no matter what. And so they did, on August 25 in a courthouse civil ceremony at noon, the day after Bartolo's twenty-sixth birthday. Later that afternoon they had the traditional ceremony at the church of San José, the Bocanegra family's parish. Mexican singer Miguel Aceves Mejías gave away the bride. Juanita's family paid for the party, and gave the priest and altar boys money, since it was obvious that no one else could. Siro and Rafael served as witnesses. Because Mariano Rivera Conde joined Miguel Matamoros in acting as Benny's groomsmen, this means that either Benny had already been signed by Rivera Conde to RCA Victor or he would be soon enough. Esther Lafayette came to the wedding and party as well. Not only had Benny's name changed but so had his possibilities in Mexico, being married to a Mexican citizen.

It was a wedding reception in Mexico with lots of hard-living Cubans and music industry people in attendance, so it was an old-fashioned everyone-gets-smashed party at her place at 124 calle Balderas. The Matamoros trio played, and Benny sang, which must have impressed Juanita's father, whom Benny did his best to please alternately with staying out of his way. He wanted to joke with Juanita's father that at least he wasn't a "bartolo" anymore, but thought better of it. Past tipsy like everyone else, Benny gave a speech between songs to thank her family and the guests for coming, and proclaimed that Juanita was far prettier than any old Cienfuegos town girl. He got so drunk that he ended up sleeping it off on the rug in the living room, and presumably didn't consummate the marriage that night. When it was time for the guests to leave, Benny told Juanita that he wanted to lie on the floor for just a minute. He lifted his face as if to say something, and then rested his chin on the tile and began to snore. Juanita put a pillow under his head and covered him with the matrimonial blanket her mother had given them as a wedding present.

In their eight years of marriage, he was always kind and attentive to her, and she was the only woman he would ever legally wed. Later he dedicated one of his own compositions, the bolero "Dolor y perdón" (Pain and forgiveness) to her.

With so many successful friends, Benny and Juanita received plenty of household gifts and money for the wedding, but it wasn't long before they needed to look for a cheaper apartment, since Benny was out of work for some time.

The next day they started their honeymoon by boarding a train that traveled across the mountains, on to Guadalajara and Mazatlán, and then through the vast Sonoran Desert, whose stark beauty stupefied Benny. He kept Juanita laughing the whole long, dusty trip.

When it was time to go back to school, Juanita settled into a berth in the sleeper car alone, because Benny stayed in the busy border town of Tijuana to work. Without a musician's union membership, he was better able to find work away from the watchful gaze of the powerful union based in the capital. He lived alone from August until November, playing with Manolo Berrío, Cristóbal Mendivé, Ramón Dorca, and probably others, in the clubs and bars that were beginning to fill with U.S. servicemen celebrating the end of the war.

When he came back to the capital, Benny found it tough going for a while. He was often over at Chico's place at 87 calle López, eating, getting drunk early, playing music, smoking too much, and frequently falling asleep there too. Chico's friendship went beyond mere drinking buddies, and Benny never forgot him for it. Chico was playing then for the Orquesta Sabre Marroquín.

The historical record of how Bartolo became Benny is anything but clear. Even the spelling of his new name is still disputed six decades later. On the original Mexican 78 recordings Benny's name is listed as "Beny," but Esther Lafayette said she pulled a slip of paper bearing the name "Benny" from a hat at the restaurant Lido in 1945. Stories from musicians who worked for him in the Banda Gigante days, as well as Moré family tradition, hold that Benny chose this name, with this spelling, after the big-band leader and clarinetist Benny Goodman. Benny was a lifelong fan of American big bands and had a collection of Glenn Miller and Benny Goodman records. In Cuba his name usually had this spelling, though not on some of his more famous later LPs.

However, some historians are adamant that when Benny changed his name it was "Beny" all along and that the spelling with two *n*'s is a later mistake made permanent. Before Benny began to record, he was listed on handbills and advertisements for the Río Rosa cabaret as "Benny." On other advertisements for the Río Rosa shows he is listed as only "B Moré," and at the Montparnasse and Club La Habana he is billed as "Benny Moore." Mexican historian Marcos Salazar has collected the advertisements and made a timeline to show that on December 15 Benny was listed along with Lalo Montané as "B Moré," but that on December 18 he is listed along with Montané as one of the singers for José Ramírez's Conjunto Tropical Veracruz and his name is "Benny Moré." And by 1947 he was listed in the show *La Voz de Oro de Cuba* as "Benny," yet the Mexican 78s he recorded still list him as "Beny." Salazar believes that Vicente Miranda and Emilio Azcarraga of XEW were the ones to suggest that Bartolo become Beny, with one *n*, for commercial reasons, and that somehow the name became "straightened" to Benny.

Not helping to clarify the question, on a page of sheet music for the 1949 song "El timbero de Belén," Humberto Cané has arranging credit and Benny the composer is identified as "Benny Moré," but he has signed one version of the score as "B Moré." And on August 19, 1949, he is listed on an advertisement for Club La Playa with Núñez, Chucho Rodríguez, and Lalo Montané as "Benny."

Other tantalizing questions include these posed by musicologist Sergio Santana: If Benny's name was changed while Esther Lafayette was present, who else was there? Members of Matamoros, other dancers, Juanita herself? What were the other names in the bag that he might have chosen?

Ultimately "Benny" was accepted as the correct spelling in Cuba, and became standard after his return there. This spelling appears on his death certificate and tombstone. Much of the confusion over such basic information can be blamed on the American embargo as well as on government control of all information in Cuba after 1961. RCA archives do little to clarify this issue, either.

Benny went often to calle Miave, where Cuban and Mexican musicians and sports figures hung out. Among the musicians were Florecita and Modesto and the singer Candita Quintana. From the baseball world came the pitchers Basilio "El Brujo" Rosell and stocky Manuel "Cocaína" García, who got his nickname from his seeming ability to numb the batters.

Many of the guys spent time in a cathouse named Bandidas, and although the Mexican singer Marco Antonio Muñiz said they went there to sing music only, it is likely that they made use of the charms of the girls there when they could afford it. Prostitution is still legal in Mexico, and in the 1940s it was certainly a man's prerogative to visit a house of prostitution from time to time. Muñiz also said that all the musicians in town in those days played music there as well. Muñiz, who would become a very successful ballad singer, was working at radio station XEW when Benny arrived in the capital. At one time he acted as chauffeur for Benny, and it can be taken for granted that Rivera Conde had placed Muñiz on the "Tipsy Benny Detail" to make sure that Benny got to and from gigs safely and on time.

One night Benny told Chico that he was dying to work but kept getting turned away without a union card.

"Look, I had to sell my return ticket to Cuba, and this is all I have left," he told Chico miserably. Now he couldn't run home with his tail between his legs even if he wanted to.

Chico helped Benny find them a cheaper place and did his best to keep Benny's spirits up. However blue Benny got, he was still optimistic. It was just like the time when he moved to Havana, believing in his voice and himself and praying for a little luck.

Chico provided vital help to Benny at a pivotal moment in his career. On one of his days off, Chico met with the general secretary of the music union, and his intercession finally won working papers for Benny. As soon as Benny got the forms taken care of, the two of them went to see Pancho Aguirre, manager of the Río Rosa, who booked and then recorded Benny with his own money. From then on, things went well for Benny, and although several years would pass before he formed a professional relationship with the other most famous Cuban musician who ever went to Mexico, he didn't lack for work. Beginning in December he started playing regularly at the Río Rosa, his first gig with his new working papers.

From his shows at the Río Rosa, Benny befriended Lalo Montané, a singer with Son Veracruz. Sometime in December of 1945 they formed a success-ful duo that they called Dueto Fantasma (Ghost Duo) or sometimes Dueto Antillano. Montané said that they were fast friends the moment they met. He said that both wanted to do a live act, but Benny had the idea to re-cord, and they did so with the Arturo Núñez orchestra. Live, they performed some of Benny's hits from Matamoros, with Benny sharing the parts. He told Montané, "If I can't do it, you can. If you can't do something, I'll do it." It was a sign of Benny's unproprietary nature, and how he and Miguel Matamoros had traded off on their solos. Montané certainly already knew these Matamoros recordings before he met Benny; they were played often on all the Mexican radio stations.

With the exception of Ignacio Villa—a piano genius known as Bola de Nieve, who began living in Mexico permanently in the 1930s and who would play a large role in a notorious episode in Benny's later career, in Caracas—most of the Cuban musicians Benny would work with in Mexico City had begun to arrive in the 1940s. There was always a demand for Cuban music in Mexico. Besides the work in the many clubs, there was the lucrative spillover work recording music for the film industry.

At the time that Benny arrived with Matamoros, there were dozens of Cuban musicians doing very well in the Distrito Federal. Some, like Silvestre Méndez, Mariano Mercerón, Arturo Núñez, Pérez Prado, Aurelio Tamayo, and Enrique Tapann, relocated to Mexico permanently. Other well-known Cubans—Humberto Cané, Kiko Mendive, Eulalio Ruiz de Mantilla—stayed for many years but eventually left for other places. Benny would fall into a third category, musicians who stayed for a shorter period, like Justi Barreto, Chico Piquero, Modesto Durán, and Mongo Santamaría. Many others came and went between Havana and Mexico. Arturo O'Farrill was born in Mexico while his famous father Chico lived there for a time before moving permanently to the United States. Benny's longtime friend Olga Guillot would move to Mexico permanently after the Cuban Revolution. All the Cuban musicians who performed and recorded in Mexico left their mark on that country's musical history.

During those vibrant postwar years in Mexico City, other busy music spots included Club France, Panamericano, and Maxim's, which were "reserved for the upper class." Gonzalo Martré remembered a show at Club France sometime in the late 1940s when he saw Pérez Prado, Ary Barroso, Luis Arcaráz, Juan García Esquivel, Ismael Díaz, and Arturo Núñez, with Benny Moré, Lalo Montané, Bernardo Montesinos, and Kiko Mendive all singing. It was an alignment of the planets that could never happen again.

Mexico, with hundreds of radio stations and a huge appetite for music, was a place where singers could become famous. One of the more important Cuban entertainers there was Silvestre Méndez, who moved to Mexico City in 1946. Born in Havana in the Jesús María barrio sometimes called Amalia, Méndez appeared as a rumba dancer or percussionist in many films in Mexico, traveled the world, and saw his compositions recorded by Machito among others. In Havana he had worked on RHC Cadena Azul with the conga player Chano Pozo, who went on to fame with Dizzy Gillespie and was later murdered outside a club in Harlem over a bag of marijuana.

Méndez played in the Arturo Núñez orchestra at the Oaxaqueño and at the dance halls Swing Club and Núñez's Antillano. Méndez played in the orchestra directed by Chucho Rodríguez, star of radio XEW. Méndez and Benny knew one another from playing at various times in both bands. Méndez formed his own band called Silvestre Méndez y Su Tribu, a name that Benny would borrow seven years later for his own tribe.

Méndez was also under contract to RCA Victor, signed by their A&R (artists and repertoire) man who either discovered or signed everyone of consequence in Mexico City, Mariano Rivera Conde. Rivera Conde had Benny record more than one of Méndez's compositions, the first being "Merengue pa' ti" with the Conjunto Humberto Cané, and eventually the slinky "Yiri yiri bom" with Rafael de Paz. Méndez said that he gave his song to Benny to record, and that "in Benny's hands that guaracha-mambo was tremendous palo."

Méndez wrote "Yiri yiri bom" on the spot during a visit to the studio where the film *Delirio Tropical* was being shot. The dancer in the film, Amalia Aguilar, was a friend of Silvestre's and had invited him to the set. All the music had been recorded, but when asked if he had anything handy that would fit a scene that the band Trío Nodarse could record, he came up with "Yiri yiri bom" within minutes. Among the many Cuban dancers who lived in Mexico, Méndez said the best rumba dancers were Amalia Aguilar, María Antonieta Pons, and Ninón Sevilla. Méndez later lived for two years in New York City, where he became friends with Sammy Davis Jr.

Benny's first recording in Mexico may have been done with recent arrival Mariano Mercerón, on a song called "La televisión" in 1946. In 1947 he recorded "Manzanillo" with Mercerón, and for Columbia Records he recorded the medley "Pensamiento–Soy Lucumí–El fiel enamorado" along with a single, "La sitiera," with Arturo Núñez's group. (*Lucumí* is the old Nigerian word long used in Cuba to refer to Yoruba people or culture. In Cuban music, declaring yourself Lucumí or Yoruba means that you are a Santería follower.) On any recordings Benny did for Columbia at this time, his name had to be hidden under a pseudonym, because he was signed with exclusive rights to RCA Victor. Duets he sang with Lalo Montané as "Lalo y Homero" include "El can can," "Mira que eres linda," "Siguiéndote," "Tengo para ti," and other songs released on LP.

Benny recorded six songs with another orchestra leader, Humberto Cané, including the *son* made a hit by Cascarita back in Cuba, "Puntillita." Humberto, son of the founder of the Sonora Matancera, Valentín Cané, had joined his father's band, first playing tres and recording vocals on the guaracha "Gozando bailando." In 1946 Cané went to Mexico, where he learned to play bass and switched to that instrument.

From time to time RCA summoned Benny to the studio with orchestra leader Arturo Núñez, and they recorded throughout his time in Mexico. A pianist, Núñez had gone to Mexico in the early 1940s and put together his dance orchestra to play at El Patio, where he spent three years. He assembled flutist Domingo "Mango" Vernier Robich, Arsenio Núñez Molina on bass, Nacho Soriano on trumpet, Alejandro Torres on sax and clarinet, Aurelio Tamayo on tarolas, and Che Toledano playing conga and flute, with Kiko Mendivé doing vocals. As a sign of the difficult times during the war, band members earned the wage, miserable even in inexpensive Mexico, of eight pesos per day. Knowing that he couldn't keep a band together forever on such poor pay, Núñez asked Vicente Miranda, who owned El Patio in addition to being part owner of Río Rosa, for a raise. When Pancho Aguirre, the manager of Río Rosa, heard about it, he offered Arturo ten pesos per musician, with a raise for the bandleader as well. It may not have been a large salary, but it was steady work and it was a 25 percent increase, so Núñez moved over to the Río Rosa, which became one of the clubs known for booking Cuban bands.

Chucho Rodríguez was another good bandleader with whom Benny would work, but this pianist was Mexican-born and had arrived in Mexico City in 1942. They first met in 1945 in Havana while Benny was still with Matamoros. In Mexico they became friends while they worked at XEW.

RCA Victor offered Benny a contract for a three-month trial, which Rivera Conde then extended to a year. Aside from "La televisión," Rivera Conde first brought Benny into the studio for a session with the orchestra Mariano Mercerón y Sus Muchachos Pimienta (Mercerón and His Spicy Boys) for "Me voy pa'l pueblo"—attributed to Mercedes Valdés but actually written by Marcelino Guerra—and "Desdichado."

Mariano Rivera Conde, A&R man and eventually vice president for RCA Victor Mexicana, was the Ahmet Ertegun of RCA's Latin American business. When he had attended the wedding of Benny and Juanita, Conde was himself recently married, to Consuelo Velázquez in October 1944. His wife, who was as famous as any Latin American musician at the time, was a concert pianist. She became a darling of Hollywood for writing "Besame mucho," and also "Amar y vivir" and "Cachito." "Besame mucho" has been covered by countless artists—Sinatra, Sammy Davis, Xavier Cugat, the Beatles—but Consuelo's reputation was made when Nat King Cole's version appeared in 1944. After her husband's death in 1977, she became a member of the Mexican parliament from 1979 to 1982. She and Mariano had met while they were working in programming at XEQ. Their attractive looks and power-couple aura must have been a little dazzling for Benny when he was invited to their opulent house for parties. Benny had become a much bigger fish in a smaller pond, but it would be three years before he crossed paths with someone who would become the biggest fish in the Mexican pond and one of the biggest in the entire sea of Cuban-born musicians, Dámaso Pérez Prado.

At the same time that Benny was busy in Mexico, Mongo Santamaría also passed through town and decided to stay for a time to work in film with the other Cuban players. In 1947 he invited Havana bongo player Armando Peraza to come to work with him in the *son* group Clave de Oro. By the next year they were both living in New York City when Peraza took part, along with Mario Bauzá, Charlie Parker, and Flip Phillips, in recording one of Latin jazz's greatest songs, Bauzá's "Tanga," arranged by Chico O'Farrill. Peraza went on to a very busy career that included a long period with rock guitarist Carlos Santana. Santamaría would soon tour with Pérez Prado.

Among the better recordings Benny did in Mexico, "Me voy pa'l pueblo" was the A side for "Parece que va a llover." As in much of the Mexican material, the vocals are particularly strong, if the arrangements themselves sound dated.

Songs of note recorded in Mexico include "Rumberos de ayer" and "Sopa de pichón." A Machito composition, "Sopa de pichón" was a New York Puerto Rican joke about eating pigeons, but it contains an irresistible melody and rhythm. Benny also recorded the Ernesto Duarte song "¿Dónde estabas tú?" with Rafael de Paz; it would become a fantastic cover later by Tito Puente. Although not released until 1952, one of Benny's greatest hits and one his best career performances came on "Mata siguaraya," also with Rafael de Paz.

In the 1940s Mexico had the best recording industry in Latin America. The modern studios and soundstages there recorded endless amounts of music that helped fuel the hunger in Mexico for Spanish-language feature films. Many Mexican singers like Agustín Lara were turned into huge stars by radio and record companies. Hollywood had already tried and failed to make Spanish-language films for the Mexican and Latin American markets. Instead, Mexican filmmakers concentrated on what they thought would sell, and they threw anything they could at the wall to see what would stick.

Benny had landed smack in the center of the golden era of Mexican cinema, which lasted from the mid-1930s into the 1950s. Typical films were sometimes a strange mix of musical stage theater, slapstick, and high melodrama interrupted by music. Kitsch was king: bullfighters, cowboys, noir detectives, hookers, knife fights, fistfights, cantina fights—they had everything that might appeal to the largest possible audience. Most films had weak plot lines but good music, and many were hugely popular, affordable entertainment for a poor country.

The industry grew into a web of mostly national film companies and studios. The director Luis Buñuel was among the filmmakers in Mexico City, where he went into exile. Ricardo Montalbán—one of the biggest foreign stars of Mexican cinema—bared his chest in *Sombra Verde* in 1954. Another famous name in Mexican cinema was Dolores del Río, who also crossed over to Hollywood. The lobby cards and movie hall posters were masterpieces of lurid artwork to match the lurid stories: stabbed hearts, bad girls in fishnets and devil horns, virgins hiding behind cactus spines with cowboys fast approaching, pistoleros, the priest crossing himself at what he sees, laughing mariachis, a popeyed detective at the moment the bullet enters his chest. Titles included *Donkey Plays the Flute, House of Perdition, Fallen Woman,* and *Magnificent Beast.*

Although Pérez Prado later said that Benny didn't have the stomach for film industry schedules, Benny got a fair amount of paying film work at this time, in at least eleven films. He first had a chance to sing on a soundtrack in 1946 for *Carita de Cielo* (Heaven's darling), starring the Cuban rumba dancer Ninón Sevilla, who got him the job. With Juan Bruno Tarraza's conjunto he sang "Ya son las doce" for *Ventarrón* (Gale) in 1949. That group had Humberto Cané on bass, as well as Alejandro Cardona, Lucas Hernández, "Caramelo" and Manolo Berrío on trumpets. Also in the group were songwriter-percussionists who would provide several of Benny's future songs, Justi Barreto and Silvestre Méndez. Juan Bruno Tarraza's group was the same that accompanied Toña la Negra and visiting Cuban singers Elena Burke and Celia Cruz in 1948.

Benny provided a vocal but no appearance for "Cabio sile" by Silvestre Méndez in the film *El Rey del Barrio* (*The King of the Neighborhood*), providing backing for rumba dancer Yolanda "Tongolele" Montes. Other appearances included *En Cada Puerto un Amor* (A girl in every port) (1949), *Novia a la Medida* (Bride to order) (1949), *Cuando el Alba Llegue* (At the crack of dawn) (1949), and *El Derecho de Nacer* (Birthright). Sometimes he made appearances as a singer, but often it was soundtrack work.

A new Cuban face had appeared on the scene, that of Dámaso Pérez Prado. No Cuban musician had greater success in music and the film industry than Pérez Prado did in Mexico, and few Cuban musicians have approached his worldwide sales.

SEVEN

Locas por el Mambo, 1948–1950

The music that played at ear-splitting volume in the whore-houses of Mexico in Jack Kerouac's *On the Road* may have been enhanced for the characters of Sal and Neal by the joints they smoked and the mescal they chugged, but that wild, jungle-crazy mambo music was the real thing. From its danzón origins, mambo became one of the most prominent world music forms in a decade that saw some formidable new sounds: rock and roll, be-bop jazz, cha-cha. Although never as popular in Cuba as elsewhere, mambo is one of the most universally recognizable Cuban styles in the world, largely due to Pérez Prado.

The doomed Austrian Maximilian I, crowned as emperor of Mexico, re-quested a habanera before his execution. For American and European listen-ers, hearing a habanera is a far more pleasant experience: the one in Bizet's opera *Carmen* is the most recognizable example in the style of danzón. Just as recognizable for American and European listeners is the sound of mambo. One definition of mambo is "danzón that was irradiated with *son* that was irradiated with a little jazz plus Toscanini plus *anything.*"

Benny came to Pérez Prado when the bandleader was just rolling down the runway, at the moment before his wheels came off the ground. As Pérez Prado was soaring, Benny's own career was taking its turn to queue up on the runway, but Benny had to leave Mexico for this to happen. Benny was associated with Pérez Prado for only about two years, but his mature voice was heard from then onward on Pérez Prado vocal hits throughout Latin

America. One proof of mambo's success could be seen in its official denunciation by the Catholic Church. In Peru, the cardinal of Lima refused absolution to anyone who dared dance the mambo; given the enormous sales of Pérez Prado records, this would have sent most of his flock to hell. One Colombian bishop called the music "devilish inventions brought from hell to upset an already morally rotten society."

Cristóbal Díaz Ayala has called the relationship of the two most famous Cuban musicians of modern times a "marriage of convenience" and believes that Pérez Prado didn't really want another figure bigger than himself in his band. If this is true, Benny's leaving just as his voice was becoming known worked out well for the two of them. Pérez Prado also would capitalize on Benny's recorded voice for as long as he could, even doing so in a questionable manner after Benny had gone back to Cuba. Although he did work with other singers, Pérez Prado would seek commercial success after Benny by concentrating on instrumentals.

Dámaso Pérez Prado was born in 1916 in Matanzas, the "crucible of rumba," famous for its guaguancó dancers and rich in Afro-Cuban culture. Just a few years older than Benny, Pérez Prado saw much quicker business success when he took his musical chances in Havana, but he also had that success taken away from him by powerful hands. He may never have slept on park benches with a growling stomach as Benny had, but he went from steady paychecks and turning down work to being forced to leave Cuba—or not work at all.

Trained in classical music, music theory, charanga, and danzón as a child, Pérez Prado came to Havana in the early 1940s, playing first with the Pennsylvania orchestra in Marianao. With his piano and orchestration skills, he was able to keep plenty busy. Like everyone else, he put in his time at the port playing for the sailors and night people. Pérez Prado was doing gigs at the tough waterfront bar Kursaal with Arturo Mesa's group, and arranging for Ernesto Roca at Peer Music, when Cascarita heard about him. By then Pérez Prado was already one of the better-known arrangers in town.

Singer Orlando "Cascarita" Guerra was looking for arrangers to expand his repertoire. He asked Pérez Prado to be musical director and pianist for the Casino de la Playa, one of the best orchestras ever to play Havana. After Miguelito Valdés left for New York, Cascarita, who was a genius of the guaracha, became the most popular big-band singer in Cuba. He had sung pieces orchestrated by some of the very best arrangers in Cuban popular music history: René Hernández for the Julio Cueva orchestra, Bebo Valdés, and now Pérez Prado. The Casino de la Playa pioneered a Cuban version of a jazz orchestra, which helped lead the way for Benny and similar bands later.

The two genius writer-arrangers René Hernández and Bebo Valdés, like Pérez Prado, were writing with mambo rhythms in mind, and they contributed many of the orchestra's hits. Very quickly Pérez Prado was taking his place among the most powerful musicians in Cuba. The competition for arrangers with rights that brought extra income was, in the difficult war years, intense and complicated.

The dispute over who created mambo comes down largely to who created the rhythm, but Orestes López, brother of bassist Israel "Cachao" López, seems to have written a mambo rhythm while in Antonio Arcaño's orchestra in 1938. He described the song "Mambo" as "un danzón de nuevo ritmo." The group, Las Maravillas de Arcaño, were the best practitioners of a modernized dance form called charanga, which uses flute, bass, violin, and percussion. Arcaño's band was essentially a danzón group, and after changing instrumentation a bit, he led a revival of the danzón in the late 1940s.

The blind *son* bandleader and tres player Arsenio Rodríguez also claimed to have been using a mambo—which he called the "diablo" portion of repeating trumpet lines—since the 1930s. Many historians believe that some of his boasting came from the constant competition Rodríguez felt with Arcaño's band, but Rodríguez did use his diablo early on. As for writing mambo for larger bands with some jazz touches, Bebo Valdés seems to have been one of the first. He told Max Salazar in 1954 that in the 1940s he was under contract to the Cubaney orchestra and so couldn't be named as arranger for others. Instead, Pérez Prado got the earliest arranging credits for mambo compositions, since his could be printed and sold as sheet music. René Hernández also wrote early mambo arrangements for the Casino de la Playa orchestra until he left for New York to become Machito's arranger.

A bit unfairly, then, Pérez Prado would be referred to as the King of Mambo—a term that was partially a marketing ploy and partially true. He certainly was its greatest salesman, spreading mambo across the globe, but was not its originator. The New Yorker Tito Puente, who learned plenty from the Pérez Prado method of bandleading, would also come to be called a mambo king, and half-Cuban Tito Rodríguez was another great practitioner. All were immensely talented and recorded the mambo rhythm and approach at the place where Cuban music and jazz intersected, with the rhythms of both Orestes López and Arsenio Rodríguez not far away. Later when Benny recorded with Pérez Prado, the dispute was in full bloom, and a vocal Benny recorded on *Locas por el Mambo* would make fun of the argument.

Obsessed with American jazz, in particular Stan Kenton's more dissonant and experimental pieces, Pérez Prado began to write arrangements in Kenton's challenging style. In 1946 he recorded four sides for RCA Victor, two with vocals by Cascarita and two instrumentals, one of which was called "Trompetiana." Neither record sold. By 1948 the only recording company willing to gamble on this sound was Panart, where Ramón Sabat did two recordings with Pérez Prado. Panart was one of the few alternatives to the 800-pound gorilla of RCA Victor and, unlike Pérez Prado's future label, was owned and operated by a Cuban in Havana. Sabat later recorded some of the most influential music to come out of Cuba in his *descarga* jam sessions with Bebo Valdés, Chico O'Farrill, and Cachao, just before Cuba was closed off in 1960. But when Sabat made the recordings with Pérez Prado, again the Cubans didn't fall in love with them.

Worst of all, Pérez Prado's music displeased one high-placed man in particular. Like the conservative preachers in the United States who condemned early rock and roll and the R&B music it imitated as "degenerate," New York music executive Fernando Castro (a Mexican, no relation to Fidel) made it his mission to "purify" Cuban music. Although the sheet music of Pérez Prado—and of everyone else in Latin America—was published by Peer International–Southern Music Company, Fernando Castro of Peer/Southern's Latin Division took exception to Pérez Prado's tastes. Castro believed that Pérez Prado with his jazz leanings was single-handedly destroying Cuban music, and so he traveled to Havana to forbid anyone in the entire industry from using the "extravagant" Pérez Prado mambo arrangements that were causing Cuban music to "lose its original values."

Castro exerted considerable pressure on industry leaders to keep Pérez Prado from working, as well as from doing arrangements for others and selling sheet music in Havana, which accounted for a good part of his earnings. Pérez Prado found himself out in the cold. Forced to tour, he performed in Buenos Aires, Puerto Rico, Mexico, Panama, and Venezuela. The best work and best atmosphere, he decided, were in Mexico City, and he emigrated there in 1948. Except for a couple of decades in the United States, he lived in Mexico the rest of his life.

Forcing out Pérez Prado would prove a big error on the part of Castro, as

RCA Victor would soon far eclipse all previous figures by selling Pérez Prado. Although the Cuban public taste for records and live music already made record companies good sums without much need for foreign sales, RCA Victor was about to make multimillion international sales on single records.

With the Ramón Grau San Martín administration in its last, worst year, it was a good time to get out of Cuba anyway, and everything about Mexico seemed easier—except for getting working papers. In Havana, Grau had closed down Radio Mil Diez. Carlos Prío Socarrás was elected president in July 1948. In October, Grau's former minister of education José Alemán stole 19 million American dollars from the Cuban treasury and fled to the United States. Pérez Prado had left with only his talent and a stack of arrangements in a few suitcases. Benny felt lucky to be where he was, and had no plans to leave Mexico anytime soon.

Pérez Prado's early road in Mexico was quite a bit smoother than Benny's. As she had done for Benny, the Cuban actress Ninón Sevilla helped Pérez Prado to get work in the film industry. His first film work came on *Coqueta* (Tease) with Sevilla in 1949. Within a year Pérez Prado would record or appear on eighteen soundtracks. When sound engineer Juan Pedro Rivera asked Pérez Prado why Benny didn't take as much advantage of film work as he had, and why Benny hadn't appeared in the Pérez Prado film *Al Son del Mambo*, Prado told him that "Benny was not made for that kind of environment," adding that "Benny only functioned at night after his usual dose of rum." Other sources claim that Benny couldn't take part in filming *Al Son del Mambo* because of contract issues. Whatever the reason, another singer, Yeyo Cané, was used. The short Pérez Prado was known by the nickname Cara de Foca, seal face. His pompadour hair and white tuxedo suits would come later.

Cuban music history was once again aided by the unofficial but well-connected emissary Chico Piquero. Piquero talked to the musicians' union president, who said that as long as half of Pérez Prado's orchestra was made up of Mexican citizens, he could work with a full group. Because Pérez Prado was going to pay the musicians himself, he was forced to follow these rules. Once this was accomplished, he was granted a one-month license to play in the country. With his band organized and rehearsed after their trial shows at the Brasil club, Pérez Prado had his big debut show of *Al Son del Mambo*, later the title of a movie that helped spread his fame.

This group used four saxes to play rhythm in the lower register, five trumpets (the same as Kenton and Woody Herman), and a single trombone. Pérez Prado wanted commercial success, so he developed an attention-getting style of bandleading, including jumping around onstage. He eventually dropped singers for instrumentals and added American-style trap drums to his groups; these changes and heavy promotion by RCA meant huge hits.

That original group for the live *Al Son del Mambo* show included Benny Moré on vocals, Modesto Durán on conga, Aurelio Tamayo on timbales, trumpeters known only as Florecita and Perique, Chico Piquero on bongos, and Pérez Prado himself on piano. The rest of the group were all Mexicans. From the very beginning, Chico says, it was a dizzying, crazy time.

When Chico introduced Benny to Pérez Prado, who was looking for the best singer he could find, Benny had worked with many full orchestras, sang duets, wrote compositions, and knew something about how *son* instrumentation worked. Best of all, he could sing anything. He was able to support himself and Juanita, and could concentrate on advancing his career by looking around and choosing wisely. All he needed was to sing on big hits. From Pérez Prado he learned one final lesson: how to lead a groundbreaking orchestra while being a showman at the same time. It was the beginning of some of the most exciting music ever performed in the twentieth century, and Benny and Pérez Prado were two branches of the same tree.

Benny and Chico traveled to Panama with Pérez Prado for Carnival in 1949. They heard Benny's voice on records everywhere they went, in a country that would always have a great fondness for his singing. When they returned to Mexico, they did shows at the Folies Bergère theater and the Waikiki. They worked the clubs on the same nights as Juan Bruno Tarraza and the rumba dancer Tongolele, in whose honor Benny, in his "Mangolele," wrote the line "La Tongolele me gusta más." The slinky, diminutive Tongolele (Yolanda Montes) was born to a Spanish/Swedish father and a French/English mother in Spokane, Washington. She moved to Mexico City just after the war and never left, becoming one of the more famous American expatriates in Mexico. Her face and the shock of white hair through her wild brunette mane are best known to Americans from her role in the Boris Karloff film *Isle of the Snake People.*

That year Pérez Prado also signed with RCA Victor for international release. His first recording session for them, in Mexico City on December 12, 1949, resulted in "Qué rico el mambo" (also known as "Mambo Jambo") and

"Mambo No. 5" being released on either side of a 78. Benny's vocal on "Qué rico el mambo" is one of his best-loved songs, and "Mambo No. 5" was a smash hit. It took in millions in sales, and continues to sell to this day. With Pérez Prado, Benny sang on only twenty-two songs, but some of them are among the bandleader's best, including Benny's favorite "Dolor Carabalí," as well as "Babarabatiri" and "Anabacoa"—all of these deeply Afro-Cuban in origin, as is "Viejo cañengo." Other hits they did together for RCA include "Pachito e'ché," "La múcura," "La cocaleca," and "Locas por el mambo."

In "Locas por el mambo" Pérez Prado has Benny make a joke about mambo's origins by asking, "¿Quién inventó el mambo que me sofoca? ¡Un chaparrito con la cara de foca!" (Who invented this mambo that knocks me out? A sawed-off little dude with a seal's face!). It's very easy to imagine Benny throwing that in as a joke in the studio and Pérez Prado deciding to keep it.

Hits with a new major international star or not, Benny was nearly done with Mexico, even while offers poured in to the RCA Victor offices to have Pérez Prado tour the United States. Benny had been hearing about how the grand casinos back home had reopened, and new casinos and clubs were in the works.

Things between Juanita and Benny had also reached a turning point. The exact timing is unknown, but Benny fathered a daughter with someone near to them, possibly a cleaning woman or a woman who worked in their household. It is not even certain that Benny knew about this child while he was still alive, but most likely he would have.

While he was still with Pérez Prado, Benny's grandmother died in Santa Isabel de las Lajas. To keep him from returning to Cuba for the funeral, Juanita hid the telegram when it arrived. When Benny found out long afterward that his grandmother had died, he was furious and never forgave Juanita. The complete story between them will likely never be known, but in all the eight years of their relationship—including three years when Juanita, although separated from Benny, was in Cuba as well—they never conceived a child. This may or may not have contributed to their estrangement. It is also possible that Juanita didn't want to leave her family in Mexico and feared that, once Benny went home, he would never come back. She was right.

# EIGHT

Return to Cuba Voice First, 1950–1952

When Benny came back to Cuba at the end of 1950, it had changed almost as much as he had. In the five years he was away, the tourists and American investors had returned, there was much more work, and Havana would soon be one of the busiest destinations for Americans in search of those things that weren't permitted them back home. The majority of Cubans already lived in the cities, nearly 6 million in Havana alone, and more were leaving the countryside and its seasonal work all the time. At the end of 1952, gambling revenues soared, and Benny would never live anywhere but Havana again.

Mariano Mercerón had preceded Benny and begun to work in Santiago. Benny's voice was so popular now that he believed he could find work anywhere, which turned out to be not completely true. This time he bought his own ticket with his own money and flew back to Havana. After visiting with Enrique Benítez and looking around a little for work, Benny took the train to Cienfuegos, switching onto the line he had known so well from his childhood. He had more suitcases than he could carry, heavy with clothes, gifts, and tequila. Virginia said she was at home in the old house on Heredia when her neighbor Mario Triana came over.

"Guess who just got off the train with four suitcases?" is the way he put it when he found her about to go to the butcher shop to buy fifteen cents' worth of chopped meat. Presumably she revised the order upward, with all the people who would be crowded into the old house and Benny in need of some real food.

He was so thin that she didn't recognize him, she said, and "when he embraced me, I fainted and didn't wake up until five that night." The house instantly filled with people, and the party included the entire neighborhood and all the old friends and family who heard that Bartolo had come home. Plenty had his records, too.

When the sometimes dramatic Virginia "woke up," the first thing she said was "Ave Maria!" Benny must have needed sleep badly, but the rum and guitars and excited young nieces and nephews and his mother's picadillo would have given him energy to hang on while he learned the names of all the new children born while he was gone, including the ones who had grown so much that he didn't recognize them.

Benny stayed with Virginia, who would never call him anything but Bartolo, or Bartolomé when she was annoyed. After a few days' visit, he left to visit Teodoro and the remainder of the family who lived in Vertientes. The countryside looked the same, the cane workers, the little children playing along the track who looked up and waved, oxen pulling carts, the mud, the palms in the hot sun. He was excited, but he slept most of the way.

Teo thought his brother looked completely worn out and wanted to hide away and rest there. He did his best to let Benny sleep in and relax, but every day the wires arrived and the telephone rang constantly, all with offers of work in Cuba and elsewhere. "¿Dónde estabas tú?" (recorded back in Mexico with Rafael de Paz), "Locas por el mambo," "Mamboletas," "Dolor Carabalí," "Babarabatiri," and "El bobo y la yuca" all played on the radio, and each time one of Benny's songs came on, Teo told his children, "Listen! That's your uncle Bartolo!" Benny spent three weeks resting, playing with the children, and catching up with Teo and the remainder of the family in Vertientes. Although he had hoped for the right offer from a group in Havana, he decided to go with Mercerón, who had been calling from Santiago de Cuba ever since learning Benny had gone to Vertientes. Mercerón had first found Benny in Havana where he was staying with Enrique Benítez, and he was persistent.

Mercerón had a contract to play for the 8 p.m. show sponsored by Bacardi called *De Fiesta con Bacardi* on Radio Cadena Oriental, and he needed a lead singer. For Benny's chorus he hired Santiago natives Fernando Álvarez, Pacho Alonso, and Manuel Licea. Although Benny wanted to be in Havana very badly, the Mercerón position was a good one, and living in historic Santiago symbolized Benny's proper pilgrimage to the birthplace of *son*. Up in the mountains just outside Santiago is an important destination for Catholic pilgrims, the shrine in honor of the patron of Cuba, La Virgen de la Caridad del Cobre. Benny visited there several times on his days off.

Fernando Álvarez was a sheltered eighteen-year-old Santiago native, but a very good singer. Before they were introduced by Mercerón, he already knew of Benny from Mexican films shown in Cuba and from the Pérez Prado records. In 1947 he was a featured singer, along with his cousin Rudy Calzado, in Pancho Portuondo's orchestra. After Mercerón he joined the Pacho Alonso orchestra and would later work with Benny from the first days of his own big band.

For a time Benny's name was well known but, unlike in Mexico, few people recognized his face on the street. This would cause Benny lingering problems. Not long after Benny returned, and before he was with Mercerón, Pérez Prado visited Cuba for a short tour with his new singer Yeyo Cané. Either Cané called himself Benny Moré or Pérez Prado wasn't correcting the promoters and radio announcers. Benny's voice was what Cubans were looking for, and so for a time there were two Bennys in Cuba. It would take months before Benny's newer Cuban recordings and the Cadena Oriental shows made his voice very well known.

Musicians and fans who had seen Yeyo Cané impersonating Benny were indignant when they went to see live performances of Mercerón and found a "fake" Benny singing. Even after Benny had substantial hits with Mercerón, they were angry that an "imposter" was in "his" place and told Mercerón so. They even brandished autographs that the "real Benny" had signed after the Pérez Prado shows. For years Benny joked about how they insisted that he couldn't be the real Benny because he was a little too tall and a little too ugly.

Besides looking for the best singing options, one of the first things Benny did when he got back to Havana again was to visit his cousin Norayda Rodríguez. He was about to jump into a new relationship at another uncertain if exciting crossroads in his life, but at least this time he might have given more thought to the idea than the fast decision he had to make with Juanita Bocanegra. The desire to find another wife was certainly understandable in someone who came from such a big family, where being alone is foreign and unwelcome.

Norayda was a pretty teenage girl who had grown up in Lajas but now lived with her parents in Havana on avenida 33 in Marianao. Her mother was a cousin to Virginia. Norayda's mother and Virginia were as close as sisters, and Virginia often stayed at the house when she came to Havana in the years before Benny got her a little house nearby. That day when Benny visited, he wasn't there only to see the family, to eat dinner, and tell stories about Mexico. When he had a minute with his pretty cousin, Benny pulled a photo from his pocket to show her: it was taken when she was twelve years old, two years before.

Norayda was more than surprised. In her young girl's imagination, she thought he must have been deeply in love with her for a long time. She later called his marriage to Juanita "a tragedy," although her own relationship with Benny was eventually overtaken by drama, too. On a secret date he took her to the Coney Island amusement park at Marianao beach.

When Norayda spilled the news, her father, Félix, was livid and told Benny several things. One, that before he even imagined seeing his daughter again, Benny needed to get rid of the whiskers and get a job. Two, that he should get rid of the first wife before he found room for the second. And three, that he should "quit playing those damn dominoes so damn much! Otherwise," he said, "don't bother."

Norayda said that for the next visit Benny cleaned himself up, put on a nice suit, and arrived early. Félix went with him to Radio Cadena Azul, but when Benny tried to identify himself, they weren't permitted inside. This couldn't have gone over well. The Benny imposter was still causing confusion. Happily, when Benny persuaded Félix to return to the studio, he had the satisfaction of being identified as the real Benny who had recorded with so many orchestras, whose voice was heard from Radio Cadena Azul every day. Bebo Valdés happened by and vouched for him to Félix and, just as important, to the station's famous owner Amado Trinidad, a colorful character who had once hired tough guy *guapo* and conga player Chano Pozo as his bodyguard.

Even after being correctly identified, Benny had more convincing to do for Norayda's hand. Once he began the Bacardi show in Santiago, he went back and forth to Havana to record for RCA. On another visit he came straight to the house to see Norayda as soon as he could. From his jacket he pulled out a wrapped package. When he showed Félix the ring, Félix showed him a revolver.

In October 1951, Benny heard about Pérez Prado's bus crashing during a

United States tour, and crossed himself several times. "If I was still with Dámaso's band," he told Enrique Benítez, "I would have been on that bus."

The tragic wreck outside Fort Worth happened on the band's second West Coast tour with a New York group that included Mongo Santamaría. Pérez Prado's dancer Delia Romero was killed, Santamaría broke his leg and pelvis, and Pérez Prado was also injured. Despite the setback, Pérez Prado's star had risen for good. In 1952 he played a huge mambo show at the Palladium in Los Angeles, and a tour that year helped him sell millions of his instrumental hits. In 1953 Joe Loco put together a big "Mambo-USA" tour that also ran in 1954.

In late 1951 and 1952, some of Benny's Mexican recordings finally made it to market. Six of these were evidence that he had already matured into a fully formed singer back when they were recorded. Benny's composition "Rumberos de ayer" gave homage to deceased rumba musicians like Chano Pozo. His duets with Lalo Montané, "Encantado de la vida" and "Mucho corazón," as well as "Yiri yiri bom," "Mata siguaraya," and "Ensalada de mambo" were all works by an advanced singer, on a par with his better recordings through the 1950s.

Benny had recorded "Ensalada de mambo" in the same session as "Mucho corazón." It is an exciting and masterful work, filled with a mélange of against-the-grain vocals, chorus chants of "Puntillita," piano soloing with the bass, and wistful trumpet. Benny sang "la televisión pronto llegará" (television will soon arrive) and, joking, warned against the evils of not liking mambo. Though the piano solo wouldn't be a trademark of his later hits, the mixing of tempos and stops showed how thoroughly Benny had hit his stride as a writer of playful lyrics with multiple breaks and tempo switching.

With each 78 and 45 came increasing stature. Meanwhile, though Benny was having more success working steadily, he was getting frustrated with being out in Santiago. For much of 1951 he still went back and forth to Havana.

In April RCA released one of the best mambos Benny ever recorded with a bandleader other than Pérez Prado, "Bonito y sabroso" with Rafael de Paz. Appearing when he was already with Mercerón in Santiago, the song served as a thank-you and farewell to Mexico. In celebrating the dancing abilities of Mexican women, it was also a goodbye to Juanita Bocanegra. Juanita spent quite a bit of time in Havana over the next few years, but they would never be husband and wife again. The song was a huge hit and played everywhere in Cuba, and on every Victrola and often on the radio in Mexico as well. With the release of "Ah, Bárbara," also recorded in Mexico with Rafael de Paz, momentum began to build at a rapid pace for Benny.

He also began to wax fresh recordings with Mercerón at the studios RCA used in Havana, and these were released along with the older Mexican recordings. In May of 1952 RCA released the montuno "Candelina alé," the guaracha mambo "Qué bandolera" (written by Ramón Cabrera), "La chola," and "Demasiado santa." These songs still felt the influence of mambo horns, a style Benny would soon leave behind.

In August he did four tracks with Mercerón's backing. He finally recorded a first composition written by his old friend Enrique Benítez, "Esto sí es coco," singing about "la gente de Vertientes." The words to this son montuno have a narrator pleading with a girl, saying she's driving him crazy with love for her—a typical situation for Benítez in lyrics and in life. Once back together with Benny, Enrique would restart his self-initiated competition to see who could sleep with the most women. As before, Benny never felt obligated to compete, but he was happy to go along with the joke.

One evening, arriving for a Mercerón show a little late, Benny rushed down the corridor at Cadena Oriental and ran into Miguel Matamoros. After so much time, they happily caught up; they might not have seen each other since 1947, when the Conjunto Matamoros went to Mexico to record with Benny singing. Miguel congratulated him on all his Mexico recordings and asked about Pérez Prado. Miguel found him the "same old Benny, excitable and warm." When he stayed to hear him sing, Miguel already knew that Benny had reached the potential he was meant for: Miguel thought that Benny's improvisation and interpretation were better than ever.

During the time when he was still singing for Mercerón, RCA brought out another of his most lasting songs, "Mata siguaraya." The song refers to an herb used in Santería. A young Celia Cruz had already made her name with it, singing with the Sonora Matancera.

When Fernando Álvarez and Pacho Alonso first heard Benny warming up with the song before the full Mercerón orchestra—and, just as bad, after hearing it on the tremendous 78 record—the two singers were both stunned and a little depressed. Alonso asked Álvarez, "Compay, ¿tu y yo somos cantantes?" (Buddy, are we even singers?).

Celia Cruz must have wondered the same thing. She was angry when she heard the recording, and refused to sing the song again on the Hatuey Beer radio show, or anywhere else for that matter. It was a masterpiece of vocal control, and it now belonged completely to Benny. When Cruz told him he had ruined it for everyone else, he was very flattered. He thought she was joking, then realized she was angry.

"I'm so sorry, Negrita," he told her. "Mario at RCA made me do it. Send that man the bill." He told her that she would always own the best version. Then he lowered his voice and walked her away from everyone else. "If I had known that Mario was taking food out of Pedro's mouth . . . ," he said and lifted an eyebrow. Few people knew it yet, but Cruz and the trumpet player from the Sonora Matancera, Pedro Knight, were lovers. After she left Cuba, she would marry him.

"Look, I can't do 'Mata siguaraya' like you, anyway, *mi hija*." He squeezed her tight. "Everyone knows you are the best contralto in Cuba," he added.

Cruz laughed in spite of herself. She was more or less the *only* contralto in Cuba.

Benny was still with Mercerón when he first heard the composer Bebo Valdés on an RHC radio show. Valdés, house pianist for the Tropicana orchestra for many years, was one of the originators of mambo back in the 1940s, and was one of the most rounded musicians Cuba ever created, capable of nearly any kind of music. Valdés was so drawn to jazz that he was often a part of the late-night jam sessions known as *descarga*, which means "a release." The American jazz impresario Norman Granz had been claiming that Cuban musicians couldn't keep up with jazz cats because their tradition wasn't built on improvisation as much as on ensemble playing. Vacationing in Havana in 1952, Granz recognized that he was wrong the moment he heard Valdés at a predawn session. He promptly produced Valdés's "Con poco coco," the first recorded Cuban descarga.

Benny showed up in the studio one afternoon to meet Valdés. As so often with Benny, the two of them became instant friends. Benny said he was dying to sing for an orchestra, that he hadn't worked for a while. Valdés believed that Benny was putting together a show with another musician, but that it never materialized. He begged Valdés to help him, saying he was going a little crazy. Valdés was currently at work on a symphony, and a new sound he called batanga.

Valdés talked to RHC, and they didn't mind if he brought Benny into the show. At some time during the work he did with Valdés, Benny met Generoso Jiménez for the first time. Although Valdés's batanga experiment lasted only four weeks, the band may have been as good as any ever assembled in Cuba. To begin with, it was led by the genius Valdés. It contained two of the best trumpeters in Cuban music history, the best singer, and the best trombone player. Benny was just another star in the short-lived superband, and he had a tendency to not show up for some of the broadcasts, but Valdés never fired him. When asked about Benny's drinking and irregular attendance after he had begged for work, Valdés strongly defended him, saying, "Look, Benny was a really good person."

Also in Bebo's batanga orchestra for RHC was a young trumpeter who happened to be a first cousin of Benny, even though they had never met, Alfredo "Chocolate" Armenteros.

Chocolate had moved to Havana in 1949 and had played with the legendary Sexteto Habanero, then cut his first record with René Álvarez when he was only twenty. Born in 1928, he was almost ten years younger than Benny. He had played alongside the most famous trumpeter, Félix Chappotín, for Arsenio Rodríguez, who led the most important *son* group until Benny's orchestra came along. Armenteros played with the Sonora Matancera, and while on tour in Mexico with that group in 1951 he met Frank Grillo, who was always referred to as Machito. Machito led the best Latin orchestra of all time in New York, and he offered Armenteros a job on the spot.

Armenteros had to refuse that tempting offer because he and Benny were in the process of putting together Benny's first group, the Banda Gigante. Luckily for Armenteros, the offer would come again ten years later. Few musicians have logged as many studio and live gigs as Armenteros. At the same time that he played with Benny from 1953 to 1956, he was in the studio orchestra for CMQ and was a session player for other groups including Chico O'Farrill, Bebo Valdés, Nat King Cole, and singer Joseito Fernández, author of "Guantanamera." Armenteros said that around this time the Sonora Matancera wanted Benny as their new singer, but there is some dispute about this.

Before his short stint with the batanga group ended, Benny already knew that he needed to move back to Havana to get into the thick of things there. Unfortunately for his patience, he still had to finish his contract for Cadena

Azul. When that day finally came, he packed his things, left Santiago, and headed west.

In his old car with him for that ride were Chico Piquero and Ramón "Cabrerita" Cabrera in the back seat. From Benny and many others, they had heard that Havana could be a fickle mistress at times, but they let Benny talk them into going along. They had heard that unlike a smaller place like Santiago, or even enormous Mexico City, it didn't embrace you and whisper that it would take care of you. Yet Benny had a powerful voice and listeners who bought his records, many of his records. They were veteran musicians, too, and knew that through his connections they would do well.

On the highway, the setting sun came into Benny eyes and kept him from changing the station. Just as he was about to turn the dial, the DJ came on and said in his smooth diction, "In my opinion, friends, this man may turn out to be the greatest singer of our time." The DJ talking in that hip voice was Ibrahim Urbino. Without naming the singer or the band, Urbino spun the turntable, and "Ah, Bárbara" started.

No one said a word, but the guys were both wondering the same thing. Benny made a joke to break the silence, and Chico looked over at him. He uncorked the bottle of rum, and Benny took a quick pull and handed it to Cabrerita in the back seat. Chico would always remember that strange moment, watching Benny drink in the late afternoon light while he drove and chatted as if nothing had occurred. The warm wind blew through the car, and they passed the bottle of Palmita around again. After a few drinks Benny said, "I sure hope that motherfucker is right, because this shitty car needs new tires and a new carburetor. God knows you two mulattos aren't going to buy anything for me."

"We are just along for the free ride, Papi," Chico told him.

"Free? Come over here and kiss me like you mean it," he told them. They all laughed and killed the bottle of Palmita. It joined the other empties on the floorboard of the back seat. Pop! went the cork on another bottle.

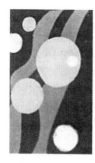

NINE

Duarte, 1952–1953

Benny's stardom didn't occur immediately just because he had returned to Havana, but it took only one adjustment to set it in motion. Once that happened, his time came incredibly fast.

Back in Havana, Benny stayed with Enrique Benítez, who had been working for the past six years as a stevedore on the docks while he sang here and there. With Cabrera they worked out a bunch of songs and then put together a little group for a gig that lasted four months at a club on avenida Dolores. This was the street where the band would spend so much time later at the Ali Bar, named after its owner Alipio García. For that first group Benny had Cabrera on piano, Alberto Limonta on bass, Chico Piquero on percussion, and Enrique and himself on voice and maracas. Two other musicians known only by single names—Palito, who played congas, and Alfonso on clave and vocals—made it a septet.

After the gig ended at the club on Dolores, Benny and a few of the others moved over to Ernesto Duarte's orchestra. Duarte was one of the best paid and most popular orchestra leaders in Havana, and he had a great deal of talent as a writer and arranger. Yet again Benny was serving in a band that didn't belong to him or play his choice of songs or instrumentation style, but it was a very good position with a major band in Havana, a level or so up from even the excellent Mercerón.

Benny and Duarte never really got along in their period of collaboration, but Duarte's skill in arranging gave Benny enough ammunition for another handful of hits. Out of the eighteen songs RCA released with Benny singing for Duarte, four or five were big hits, and two stand with his best achievements, "Como fue" and "Guantánamo." "Guantánamo," by Ramón Cabrera, was one of the songs immortalizing Cuban cities that Benny's future pianist and arranger would write especially for him. Benny had recorded another of Cabrerita's compositions, "Qué bandolera," while still with Mercerón earlier in 1952. Their relationship would last most of the remainder of Benny's career.

Benny recorded first with Duarte in September of 1952, with an afro-mambo Benny wrote called "El brujo de Trinidad" paired with the mambo "Las mujeres de mi tierra" by Justi Barreto, another writer whose compositions Benny used throughout his career. Duarte also did two other sides with Benny that month, Cabrera's son montuno "Adiós, Palma Soriano" along with "Ma Clotilde," an experimental form Duarte called a mazumba.

Sometime in 1952 Benny went to New York, possibly to meet executives at RCA. The historical record is clouded, and it is unknown if he had been invited to sit in with a group like that of Machito (whom he always visited when in New York). But he told Nat King Cole at the Tropicana a few years later how much he had always wanted to meet the star pianist. He said he had paid $200 to see Cole perform at the Teatro Puerto Rico on 138th Street in the Bronx. Enrique Benítez said he and "the group" were also along on that trip; he bought himself a nice shirt made of yellow wool for the cold, and some new shoes.

Alicia Candia was a young woman on a double date with her boyfriend who was a rabid Benny fan and had dragged her along to a show at the Palladium in New York. When the two couples arrived at the famed dance club, they found that the show had been cancelled due to "unforeseen circumstances." Although Candia didn't know anything about Benny's music, she was still disappointed that the show didn't take place after all her boyfriend and the other couple had said about Benny's singing. When they went to the nearby Liborio restaurant on West Forty-seventh Street, in walked Benny. Her boyfriend leapt up immediately and brought him over to their table. She didn't think much of Benny's looks. He was unkempt and unshaven; on his nappy hair he wore a dirty beret. He sang "Esta noche, corazón" and "Ah, Bárbara," boleros she didn't know. Her friends were ecstatic. Despite herself, she fell under the spell of the songs and Benny. He paid lots of compliments and attention to the women, and he had such a way with words that "lo que salía de esa boca era azúcar"—everything that came from his mouth was sugar. Candia later married a cofounder of *Latin Beat* magazine, Silvio Álava.

In March of 1953, Benny did one of his best-loved ballads with Duarte, "Como fue," a dreamy bolero of a man stunned by new love, who tries to explain to his lover and himself how it happened. "Was it your eyes or your mouth, your hands or your voice?" he wonders. Still one of his most memorable boleros, it was actually a B side to Enrique Benítez's guaracha-mambo "No deben de llorar." "Como fue" is a song that Miami's Cuban Americans of a certain age can never hear without singing along and feeling very, very nostalgic.

In that month they recorded two Benny Moré compositions. Then in June they went back to the studio for four singles, among them one of Cabrera's seven city songs Benny would record, "Guantánamo." Cabrera would supply five. Benny himself wrote two, and they are still among his best and best loved: "Cienfuegos" and "Santa Isabel de las Lajas."

The year 1953, when Benny did the majority of his recording with Duarte, marked an important moment for the future of Cuba. In July, Fidel and Raúl Castro led a failed rebel attack on the Moncada army barracks in Santiago de Cuba. Although sixty-one rebels were killed and many of the captured survivors tortured or executed by Batista, historically this signaled the beginning of the Cuban Revolution. The young lawyer Castro famously defended himself in court and was sentenced to death, symbolically it so happens. Batista had missed his chance to execute Castro by recently having abolished the death penalty in Cuba, so instead Castro's sentence was reduced to fifteen years' imprisonment. Two years later Batista freed the imprisoned rebels, and Castro immediately set about building more support for his next actions. The Moncada attack spelled the beginning of the end for the orchestras, even though Benny had yet to form his own.

Distractions are what artists must learn to avoid, so Benny did his best to concentrate on his singing, find new songs, and get help from arrangers like Duarte or Cabrera. He was capable of learning to read music, and would have been less tied to other arrangers, but Benny never felt that having other musicians do the arrangements took away from his control of the music. His methods were already long in place for working with an arranger, going back to his earliest days in Mexico and then with Pérez Prado—who, besides being one of Havana's most experienced orchestraters, actively enjoyed doing arrangements with Benny.

Working closely with an arranger was Benny's preference for two reasons. Since he only had to sing his ideas to be transcribed, he could drink and fool around, and let someone else take care of the hard part. He also understood that his power resided in knowing the African rhythms and percussion from the guateques, not in spending hours in front of a piano and music paper. For him a guitar was sufficient to get across the melody and rhythm he wanted, even if it had limited harmonics and a limited range of chords. His system worked as well as anything. But although Duarte was satisfied to work this way, their differences in musical ideas became apparent all too soon at the bench of Duarte's piano.

Benny sang for Duarte on the Radio Progreso show *Onda de la Alegría* and toured the nearer cities. As always, most of the work for a good dance orchestra like Duarte's remained in clubs, theaters, dances, and radio and television shows in Havana. In the first half of a show Duarte played his own music, then he brought on Benny as the star singer. Even though Benny's popularity continued to grow with each release carrying his name, it is said that Duarte hesitated to use him on all the shows, opting instead for other singers. By the time of the Moncada attack in July, Benny was already looking to abandon Duarte so that he could have much greater control over his destiny.

Thoughts differ on why Benny left Duarte when he did. In some ways it was a risky decision. A job with Duarte wasn't easy to land, and it carried considerable benefits. For one, it provided an excellent platform with the radio show on Radio Progreso. While with Duarte, Benny continued to expand his audience, sang his own hits, and kept selling his own records without the expense and trouble of leading the band himself. Duarte the musician was highly talented, and his orchestra was considered one of the best on the entire island. All the while that Benny belonged to someone else's group, his stature was growing, and he could concentrate on composing, organizing new songs, and working with arrangers for his own songs. Since he couldn't write the arrangements himself, he would always need someone who was a crack arranger, who understood the rhythms he was trying to emphasize.

The catalyst for leaving Duarte is clouded by time, but there are several possibilities.

Benny's brother Pedro said that Benny left Duarte over the bandleader's refusal to record "Bombón de pollo" and other disagreements about material. When Benny brought the Conde Negro song to Duarte, Duarte told him that it was "off." Benny carried the written composition to composer and symphonic conductor Enrique González Mantici, who had founded the Orquesta Riverside. Benny knew that Mantici's word would matter to Duarte. Mantici was adamant that it was perfectly "dentro de los parámetros establecidos de este tipo de música"—within the normal range for this kind of music. Benny asked Mantici if he should study music notation, and Mantici told him it would be the worst thing he could possibly do, that it would kill his talent. To have asked at all was probably due to Duarte's complaining that Benny couldn't read music.

Differences with Duarte over one of his old friend's songs also may have been worsened by Benny's reputation for fierce loyalty to his friends and fellow musicians. However the disagreement was settled, Duarte did record "Bombón de pollo." Being university educated and having studied at the Conservatorio Municipal de la Habana, Duarte respected Mantici's authority enough to record the song.

It is also clear that Benny was irritated with Duarte over payment for work performed. Enrique Benítez said that Duarte could be mercurial in his payment rates to Benny: he might promise a hundred pesos for a gig out on the road somewhere, but when it came time to pay at the end of the night, somehow the promised hundred turned into fifty.

The other story about why Benny left Duarte after such a short time is more complicated. According to the Naser biography, Piquero said that he and Chocolate had gone to see Benny at his house in La Cumbre, having called to say that he should stay put, they were on their way.

They told him, so the story goes, that they had learned why Duarte wasn't using him enough at dances on Saturdays and Sundays—because he was black, and the places where Duarte avoided taking Benny were dances for white clubs whose members still didn't want black musicians there. It is not known how Piquero learned this. Duarte himself was a light-skinned mulatto, but as the story has also come down through the Moré family, Duarte thought Benny was too dark and those better-paying white audiences didn't want a black singer.

Piquero goes on to say that the three of them went to see Mariano Rivera

Conde, who was then at the RCA studio in Habana Vieja. When they told him about the problem with Duarte, Piquero says, they went to Duarte's house to confront him. Duarte received them and, not noticing that Benny was angry, ordered Benny to go record with him there and then. Benny told him: "Sure, we can go record now, but after that I'm not working with you— I've taken enough of your bullshit as it is, without the fact that you won't use me at certain dances or on television because I'm black."

Duarte's answer was to let Rivera Conde decide who Benny would work with and not work with.

"Mariano?" Benny asked.

When Rivera Conde didn't reply, Benny turned to Duarte and told him that their agreement was no longer valid. Then, in front of Rivera Conde, Benny threatened that if RCA objected, he would call up Columbia Records to see if they were interested in a new artist. Rivera Conde said he didn't have any problem with Benny leaving Duarte, that whatever he wanted to do was fine. If he didn't want to finish out his contract as Duarte's singer, that was fine, too.

The story is a compelling one. However, Benny didn't move to La Cumbre until 1955, so from the outset the details of this story are open to question.

In 2007 Enrique Benítez disputed the story of Duarte's racism, and pointed out that Duarte was himself a mulatto, something Benny's daughter Hilda also said that same year in an interview at La Cumbre. Although it is true that Hilda wasn't quite a teenager at the time, it is very conceivable that she would have heard the story of Duarte's racist choice, if it were true, each time one of Benny's Duarte hits played on the radio.

Either way, it was time for Benny to lead an orchestra himself, with his own songs and arranging ideas, and with an entire career's worth of knowledge.

TEN

La Banda Gigante, 1953–1954

The day had finally arrived for Benny to take his prominent place in Cuban musical history. Through July and August of 1953 he assembled the band he had decided to call the Banda Gigante, the Gigantic Band. Things couldn't have been more favorable for him than in 1953.

The number of gifted musicians all in top form and working in Havana had never been greater than in the years surrounding 1953. Even with Frank Grillo (Machito) and Mario Bauzá gone to New York, and Pérez Prado touring the United States and living in Mexico, the concentration of talented bands working at the height of their powers was unequaled. There was Duarte's group, which had many excellent singers pass through after Benny, including Rolo Martínez, Rolando Laserie, and the Bermúdez brothers. The Hermanos Palau had been in existence for many years. There were the Hermanos Castro, Julio Cueva, the Orquesta Riverside and many other cha-cha groups, the Sonora Matancera, Arsenio Rodríguez, Arcaño, Conjunto Casino, Orquesta de la Playa, Matamoros, Bebo Valdés, Obdulio Morales, and so many others. The period is often referred to as the golden age of Cuban music, and for good reason. The number of bands working in that year, the writers, arrangers, and musicians creating an enormous variety of exciting popular music—the output was second only to the American big-band period of two decades earlier.

In 1953 Richard Egües wrote "El bodeguero" for the Orquesta Aragón, a cha-cha orchestra from Cienfuegos. When Benny would later help the

Aragón break into the Havana music business, Egües had already written one of the greatest and most delightful of the hundreds of memorable Cuban popular songs. "El bodeguero" took its place alongside the other best-known cha-cha, Enrique Jorrín's "La engañadora." In the late 1940s Jorrín created the cha-cha-cha as a simplified mambo rhythm to make it easier on American dancers who couldn't follow mambo. The tourists adored the rhythmic and lightly swinging ballroom sound played by conjuntos—a modified danzón-mambo led by flutes, pianos, and violins. In Cuba its popularity was greatest with white upper-class society. Those tourists and visiting musicians took the cha-cha back with them to New York, Chicago, and Los Angeles, where the charanga had already gotten a foothold. Even so, in a few years Benny would declare his own love for *son* over cha-cha-cha.

Charanga was then beginning to influence New York music. Of the Cubans traveling to New York then, it is said that "los Cubanos tomarían café tocando la charanga, y luego Broadway tocaría y todos sudarían"—the Cubans took charanga with their coffee, and pretty soon it had Broadway and everyone else sweating—meaning, everyone at the Palladium and anywhere else they danced to this music.

Based on jazz, *filin* was one style that never really left Havana in the 1950s. Taking its name from the English word "feeling," it was little known outside Cuba. Its syrupy nature didn't age well, although *filin* singers were very successful at the time and into the 1970s.

Despite being several decades old, *son* was still one of the leading established styles and would always remain the music of the people. Smaller conjuntos played music straight from the Santiago streets and country *bohíos*, while the larger orchestras performed through the night in Havana cabarets, social clubs, and outdoor spots like the Polar and Tropical beer gardens. From Arsenio Rodríguez to Conjunto Casino, *son* was the music that Benny wanted most to play.

When Mariano Rivera Conde gave Benny permission to leave Duarte and lead his own group, the first thing Benny had to do before anything else was register the group's name at the musicians' union. Saxophone player Roberto Barreto says that Benny had a meeting to discuss what he was planning with Chocolate, Celso Gómez, Barreto, Cabrera, and Virgilio Vixama in the Ali Bar. When someone asked him how he could leave Duarte to start another band, he said that as long as he delivered songs for his contract, RCA would let him move. Benny waited to see what they would say, grinning, with one hand on a bottle. When they all were properly enthusiastic, he broke the seal and they drank to their new band. Of those with Duarte, not one hesitated to leave him for Benny.

"Duarte is a fat little hen. Don't you want to be with the big rooster instead?" he asked them.

Saxophonist Paquito D'Rivera's father Tito (D'Rivera was a mistaken spelling that Paquito decided to keep) was a Cuban representative of the Selmer Company, makers of musical instruments, and had a little music shop at 57 calle Virtudes that stocked books, instruments, and musical supplies. A musician himself, Tito knew absolutely everyone, since all musicians had to pass through the shop in the 1950s. Everyone in jazz, and the most progressive musicians in Havana, went there. During the day it was the gathering place of the greatest musicians in Havana at any given time. Tito's good friends included Cachao, Chico O'Farrill, Bebo Valdés, Chocolate, Mario Bauzá, René Touzet, Peruchín, and Ernesto Lecuona. One of Paquito's first gigs was playing with an orchestra directed by yet another Havana musical genius, Obdulio Morales.

Paquito never saw anything unusual about being in the midst of such extraordinary artist brains; it all seemed perfectly normal. When Tito bought one of the early phonographs, a Silvertone, on credit from the local Marianao Sears, the first LP he played was Benny Goodman's all-star band at Carnegie Hall in 1939 with Lionel Hampton, Gene Krupa, Harry James, and Teddy Wilson. This was the kind of music that would lure Chocolate to New York, and the very recording that would someday lure Paquito there too.

Thus far Benny had Chocolate, one of the best trumpeters in Cuba, as band director. He had three saxophone players—Barreto, Gómez, and Virgilio Vixama—and Cabrerita for piano and songwriting. Benny had in mind the other important parts, backup vocalists to sing chorus and to cover for him if his voice failed. He was sure he could get the musicians he wanted most.

When Benny decided that he had had enough of Duarte, he certainly was ready both emotionally and musically. He had spent many hours—and years—with conjuntos of all sizes, with full orchestras. Benny had watched bandleaders, worked with arrangers, had heard his own compositions performed by full groups. By 1953 he understood a great deal about orchestration, even if he couldn't write horn charts himself. He believed, correctly, that he knew what a hit song should sound like to move the dancers, and he was now a real master of improvisation. As well prepared as he came to lead a major *son* orchestra, given that he couldn't read music, he still needed arrangers who understood the entire range of capabilities of each instrument—writers who knew theory and harmony, and the distance of one instrument from the other. Someone writing out parts had to know that the trumpet plays an octave higher than the trombone, the baritone sax an octave lower than the alto sax, and so on through the entire orchestra. His arrangers also had to transcribe from how he sang out or hummed those ideas that he couldn't play on guitar, with its limited range for composing. Finally, he also needed arrangers who could put up with unorthodox methods and habits.

All he asked of Ramón "Cabrerita" Cabrera was to play piano, write arrangements, and keep bringing him songs. Cabrera was born to a musical Oriente family in 1918, the year "when *son* invaded Havana," as he put it. His father, an army sergeant and subdirector in bands of Palma Soriano and Santiago de Cuba, taught his young son early to play and read music. Cabrera chose the trumpet. By age thirteen he began composing songs. Cabrera had first seen Benny sing in Havana in the bar Baturro on Eguido near the train station, one late night that he spent walking to clubs with another hard-drinking *son* singer, Cotán, but it was Mariano Mercerón who introduced them in Santiago.

Cabrera wouldn't remain Benny's pianist beyond the first Banda Gigante, but he would continue to write many of Benny's best-selling and enduring songs, some of them about Cuban cities or towns. Cabrera was a composer who could channel life's emotional milestones into his works. He wrote "Santiago" in a nostalgic mood for his childhood home while on a visit to the city in 1954. Back in 1940, to deal with grief over his father's death, he had written "Adiós, Palma Soriano," which Benny recorded with Duarte in 1952. While in a Manzanillo bar at the beginning of a night of drinking, Cabrera watched the moon's reflection shimmering over the water. Fully formed, the melody for "Manzanillo" came to him as if whispered by an angel in his ear. To differentiate it from the earlier "Manzanillo" that Benny recorded with Mercerón, Cabrera's song is often called "Bahía de Manzanillo."

Another of Benny's hits about Cuban cities came to Cabrera while he visited Guantánamo with the novelist José Soler Puig. Cabrera admitted he wrote "Guantánamo" not so much for the city where the United States would keep a navy base in perpetuity (for a payment of $4,085 per month), but out of a powerful desire for "una mulatica del barrio de Mamoncillo"—a little mulatto girl from the Mamoncillo neighborhood. Cabrera writing and Benny interpreting made a very effective team. Cabrera would say later that Benny put such life into his "Marianao" that "it made people who heard the song want to live there." This was especially true for men, since the song praises the beauty of las Marianenses, who still grace those broken boulevards today, as much as it does life in Marianao. Celia Cruz would also record Cabrera's "Tu voz" with the Sonora Matancera, and Tito Gómez sang a masterful Cabrera mambo-cha, "Ahora sí tengo un amor," with Riverside.

Cabrera's compositions sold many 78s and 45s for Benny, but after a while Benny told him, "Mulatto, don't bring me any more songs about cities; I'm going to write some of my own," and promptly wrote "Cienfuegos" and "Santa Isabel." Cabrera left Cuba in 1965 to live in Spain, where he died in 1993. He called Benny "un tipo muy llano, sencillo, muy natural, y nada engreído"—a very straightforward guy, simple, very natural, not at all stuck-up. Cabrera believed that Benny had no true understanding of how great he was or how lasting his music would be. He called Benny a Cuban Gardel, equating him with the Argentine who represented his country's music.

Depending on whom you ask, to build the rest of his historic band, Benny sought the help either of Chocolate or of Enrique Benítez. Likely both of his country cousins contributed, each knowing some guys the other didn't. Benny at first was in a hurry to put together a group for a two-week live radio gig substituting for the Sonora Matancera band. Chocolate claimed that Benny had come to him.

"Compadre, I want to talk to you. I want to put together an orchestra. I play with Duarte and Mercerón, but when someone calls me to sing, I don't have any of my own songs," Benny told him. Chocolate agreed to help.

Benny had already decided who his chorus singers must be. The first backup singer he asked was Conde Negro, who had never left Havana after he and Benny moved there in 1947. Enrique was more than happy to say yes, as he had continued to work his backbreaking day job as a stevedore all the time that Benny was gone. But to get Fernando Álvarez, the young kid who sang backup for him with Mercerón, Benny couldn't just wire money and a train ticket. When he called and said he was putting together a band for a guaranteed two-week job that would probably go much longer, Fernando didn't answer.

"Mulatto, you still there?" Benny asked. "Mulatto? Hey, pay attention!"

Fernando had to remind Benny about his father and how difficult he had been when Fernando first sang for Mercerón. Benny got in his car and drove down to Santiago. To get Álvarez to join his conjunto and move to Havana, Benny had to go ask for his hand by meeting Fernando's parents. He had to promise that he would never take advantage of Fernandito and that he would always help him out—as if he were a suitor of their only daughter. To be sure, Álvarez was young and the family was strict. With his pay from Mercerón, Álvarez was sure to have been contributing to the family's budget, and Benny must have stressed the higher pay in Havana. It would be a very good career move for Fernando in the end, his steppingstone.

Alfredo "Chocolate" Armenteros had grown up near Lajas, though he and Benny had never met until the day they both arrived at the RHC studios to play in the Bebo Valdés batanga orchestra in 1952. Chocolate was twenty-five and Benny was thirty-two then. The cousins did share musical interests and a hard but happy rural childhood, but their never having met as children is an indication of the size of their sprawling families and the isolation of guajiros. In his apartment in New York's Spanish Harlem in 2006, Chocolate described his first meeting with Benny. It was as exciting to hear the stories as it was for Chocolate to tell them. He smoked cigar after cigar and sipped from a tall glass filled with one of his favorite beverages, Rémy Martin cognac, which he called his "Do-Rey-Mee." The walls of his apartment were crowded with reminders of his achievements in Latin jazz and salsa. "We didn't live far apart in distance, but it's not like we had telephones, you know. And on a horse it was a long way. I didn't meet him until he came in to sing for Bebo Valdés, and he asked me to put together his first band."

One important thing that separated Chocolate from Benny and placed him on a different musical track was being taught to sight-read music when he was only a boy. By a lucky chance, Eduardo Egües (father of the Richard Egües who wrote "El bodeguero" and led the Orquesta Aragón) taught Chocolate notation and theory when he was still in elementary school. This helped Chocolate to avoid the years of manual labor and scraping by that Benny had endured.

Arguably, along with Bola de Nieve and Conde Negro, Chocolate had one of the best nicknames out there. His came from "the Cuban Bon Bon," the 1930s world champion Cuban lightweight Kid Chocolate, who had more than fifty knockouts and who would live in the Havana neighborhood where Benny someday would buy his mother a house.

Armenteros was a hot property at the time Benny asked him to join the band. He had already recorded his first trumpet solo at age twenty-one on "Para las niñas y para las señoras" for the René Álvarez group Los Astros. He played with the Septeto Habanero, Arsenio Rodríguez, and many other groups in Havana. In 1946 he even did session work on Nat King Cole's first Latin record, *Rumba a la King*, and would again record with Cole on his 1950 *Cole Español*. He had played with Mercerón in Havana, though not at the same time as Benny. In Bebo Valdés's batanga orchestra he had been part of the greatest trumpet section in Cuban music history, and stood on the bandstand beside Félix Chappotín, the first great trumpeter for Arsenio Rodríguez.

To paraphrase Gil Evans's claim that "with jazz trumpet there was everything from Louis Armstrong up to Miles Davis, and everything after Miles Davis," there was everything Chappotín did, and then Chocolate changed the face of conjunto trumpet playing thereafter. When Benny sang in the batanga group on RHC-Cadena Azul, Chocolate had played next to the other great trumpeter in Havana, Alejandro "El Negro" Vivar, who would join Benny later on.

Havana was a wide-open city then, and Benny didn't know its better secrets yet. But Chocolate did. He knew the best seafood restaurants, and who were the most desirable girls over at Violeta's. He had played with most every conjunto and orchestra in town. Although Enrique Benítez certainly knew his way around, Chocolate's success in music had given him a different path and different contacts. Paquito D'Rivera said that of all his father's friends, Chocolate was the most elegant. His style must have been sharpened by those many trips back and forth to New York, where he would have seen and acquired all the latest: silk ties, tailored shirts, a pearl gray suit, handmade Italian shoes.

Chocolate would go on to spread the Cuban trumpet style across the world and influence every Puerto Rican kid dragging a trumpet case to a party in Brooklyn, every mariachi trumpeter in Durango, even the tone of buglers who call the bullfight to order. Benny asked him to lead the band because he was a bit of a tough guy and could keep the band in line, and because he could sight-read music. Although Chocolate was too restless to stay forever, Benny was lucky to have him while it lasted. Chocolate was also one of the few hard drinkers who could keep up with Benny, and the two drank rum together like nobody's business.

At the time he was assembling the big band, Benny was living in an apartment building at Oquendo and Clavel in Habana Centro near a printing company. That apartment would soon become a very busy headquarters overdecorated with musicians, girls, music producers, empty rum bottles tipped over on sheet music, guitars in the corners. Benny never fell into his bed beside Norayda until the sun was coming directly into the windows.

Benny wouldn't be divorced from Juana Bocanegra until 1956, a fact about him that remained unknown until 2006 when a researcher stumbled across a fifty-year-old document in the Havana archives. After Benny left Mexico, Juanita had come to Cuba from time to time for one-sided attempts at reconciliation. Benny tried to go along with her visits when he was in Santiago, but he had already made up his mind when he left Mexico. He tried to get a divorce from her then but couldn't, either because a stung Juanita wouldn't grant it or because it would have meant visits to Mexican courts. One of Benny's childhood friends, Alberico Veloz Álvarez, said that an angry Juanita "pursued" Benny and once threatened to kill him with a Smith and Wesson pistol. Some of Benny's friends claim that in the latter part of the 1950s, she once cruelly punched him in the ribcage at a time when his cirrhosis was particularly painful.

After he moved into the apartment in Habana Centro, Benny had Norayda come and live with him. They were together until 1954, and in that time she gave birth to two boys, the first named Benny and the second Bebo, for Bebo Valdés. Eventually the boys grew up in Venezuela, where Norayda went to live with another man. Although Benny was warm and loving with all the children he fathered, it was a crazy time to be associated with him, from Duarte through the putting together of his orchestra and the sudden fame. With him gone so much on tour and with women in constant pursuit, Norayda suffered throughout the relationship. Even though he was involved with many women, Norayda says that he became very possessive and wouldn't let her go anywhere. He forbade her to go to the beauty salon, saying that the manicurist and hairdresser had to come to the apartment. It was a time of crushing outside pressure on the new bandleader. The relationship would last only four years, but it wasn't Norayda who ended it.

Very much like the notorious rock and roll rebel Jerry Lee Lewis, Benny had a little weakness for his kissing cousins. Benny may not have preferred them quite as young as Lewis did, but he had relationships with at least three and possibly four of his cousins. Cubans have an expression: "Las primas son para mí," the cousins are for me. Unfortunately for Norayda, Benny fell in love with her light-skinned girlfriend Iraida Castillo. Many years later Norayda was still angry about the betrayal, yet she still had positive things to say about Benny.

The first Banda Gigante held a lot of unique personalities: seventeen veteran musicians. Benny had finally gotten his wish to build a band completely to his specifications: For horns he had five saxophones, three trumpets, and one trombone to which another was added soon after. For percussion there were bongos, congas, timbales, and a jazz-style drum kit. The rest of the rhythm section consisted of an upright bass and a piano. The group was big enough to tackle any style of song Benny wanted. He was a master of mambo, *son*, bolero, and mixtures of the three, and his past and current hits with so many orchestras meant the band needed to play everything.

For someone who drank himself to death and was notorious for arriving very late to his shows, Benny turned out to be a bandleader and conductor with a perfectionist streak. He could drive his arrangers crazy with his alcoholic antics and his guajiro approach to life. Yet he had an excellent ear, and in a practice session he always noticed if a single horn player, above all that sound, was playing slightly flat. It was the legacy of the singer, who feels most acutely any disharmony of his accompaniment, and he worked very hard to keep his pitch right.

Benny had already developed his own flamboyant style of conducting, using every part of his body to direct the tempo and stops. Throwing his hat in the air meant a full stop, although sometimes he did it as a joke or at seemingly random places. In his later appearances when he arrived hours after he was billed to start, he might hurry through the crowd or from backstage and shout "Heirro!" and the band would start up, shifting gears to the introduction for the first vocal on the sheets taped to their music holders.

His fame for drinking dark rum while leading the band was no act; Benny almost never sang in front of a live audience sober. For most of the studio recordings after he became famous, Benny was buzzed if not completely drunk. Somehow he was able to function at a very high level of intoxication, and once he found his pace, he never stopped drinking until he was forced to by failing health. According to musicians and others around him, he did play-act drunk later on, when he believed that those watching expected it. The general public never knew of his illness, nor that he had stopped drinking for the last two years of his life.

In addition to the legal stimulants, marijuana and cocaine were used by some wealthy Cubans and a few foreign high rollers in the time of the mob-owned casinos. It can be presumed that some musicians of this era smoked marijuana or used cocaine to keep going through the long nights. Those few who did use cocaine were mainly upper-class Havana socialites, but in Cuba marijuana was fairly common among musicians—as it had been throughout the Americas and Europe since the 1920s. For those whose preferred drug was alcohol, there was more than enough heavy drinking to make up for any lack of illicit substances. Sicilian-American mobster Lucky Luciano did import heroin into the United States from Sicily while working from his base in Cuba, but heroin was not in common use among Cuban musicians, unlike among jazz musicians of that decade in the United States. In any case, life in Havana by the middle 1950s was lived at a very fast pace. It was at this time that Benny rocketed to prominence.

In the first orchestra of seventeen players, nearly all were black. Fernando Álvarez was mulatto, and Pibe, who played trombone, was white, as was trumpeter Pedro Rodríguez, who came to the band later. Benny often referred to his band as Mi Tribu, my tribe, in a reference to the African heritage of their music. Although most of them had broad musical backgrounds, they all shared a fluency in their Afro-Caribbean heritage. This was the lineup:

Ramón "Cabrerita" Cabrera, pianist, songwriter, arranger
Miguel Franca, alto saxophone
Santiago "El Moro" Peñalver, tenor saxophone
Cosme Peñalver, tenor saxophone
Roberto "Barretico" Barreto, tenor saxophone
Celso "Pacho" Gómez, tenor saxophone
Virgilio Vixama, baritone saxophone
Alfredo "Chocolate" Armenteros, trumpet, bandleader

Rigoberto "Rabanito" Jiménez, trumpet

Domingo Corbacho, trumpet

José Miguel Gómez, trombone

Luis "El Pibe" Outumuro González, trombone

Alberto Limonta, bass, sometime manager for second band

Rolando Laserie, timbales, drums

Tabaquito, congas

Clemente "Chico" Piquero, bongos

Fernando Álvarez, chorus

Enrique Benítez, chorus

Israel Castellanos, band secretary, agent

Besides being one of Benny's closest friends, who was there until the very end, Israel Castellanos was an *utillero* (useful one), the guy who did a little of everything. Usually Benny's driver, he acted as a roadie too, setting up the microphones and taking care of hauling and testing sound monitors. When that was done, he played guiro. His nickname was Muela, which means "molar," or someone who has the gift of gab. In Castellanos's particular case, the name was earned by his prowess with women. It was said that with the finesse of a cobra handler he could coax women out of their skirts solely by the caressing of his words. In a related skill, he was a great dancer, and would show off his moves on the bandstand or just offstage. His name is immortalized in "Qué bueno baila usted" when Benny sings "Castellano, ¡qué bueno baila usted!"

Added after Gómez to the regular lineup, El Pibe came from the police musicians band. Benny had Castellanos try to find Generoso Jiménez at the time, but for some reason the message never reached him, so El Pibe was hired instead. In 1955 Pibe went to Jiménez for help with trombone for two shows, which is how Jiménez would come to join the band.

Benny sometimes joked that his backup singers were better-looking than he was, and it was true that Enrique and Fernando had prettier faces. Álvarez's light-skinned and boyish looks balanced Enrique's handsome dark face and bedroom eyes. The older Benny got, the more handsome and even dashing he became. As a young man, he could look goofy and awkward, but once he developed his trademark way of dressing and had a little more age on his face, Benny cut an interesting figure. His style was part American hepcat and part Cuban field hand. He loved the big baggy pants of the late 1940s zoot suit, including the suspenders and two-tone Florsheim shoes, an extra long jacket, and a big beret. He was just as fond of a white suit and a large Cuban cowboy hat. Whatever way he dressed, his Palo cane was a constant.

Benny rehearsed the band at a warehouse in Cerro, a location he probably kept for years. The first time Benny led a full group in public was for the *Cascabeles Candado* show on radio CMQ on August 3. Some of the musicians were borrowed from other groups, since Benny was still building the permanent band. He was completely finished recording with Duarte, and the two stayed out of each other's way from then on.

Benny led the group for their first dance at the Colonia Española out in Placetas in Las Villas Province, not far from Lajas. Everyone who knew him or knew of him from the area was there, and Chocolate said the craziness of the reception given to Benny and his band began from the opening note. It took the whole band by surprise, and they witnessed for the first time how an audience would be so transfixed by Benny's directing style that couples stood watching instead of dancing together.

When they had practiced enough that they could bring the entire brass section and the percussion to a stop instantly, or steam along in a son montuno and shift to a mambo roar with only Benny's left hand to guide them—they all knew they were as good as any band out there. No one in Cuba had ever seen an orchestra like this one, nor a singer like this, nor music like this. Although Pérez Prado would lead his bands with high kicks and a grunting "¡Di-LO!" he was much more popular then in Mexico and the United States. The tradition of singers in Cuba had always been static, not attention-getting. Matamoros was restrained, Duarte restrained, Sonora Matancera restrained. But Benny had spent time with the very unrestrained Pérez Prado, and he knew that onstage entertainment should offer more than just music.

Benny had a unique dancing-skeleton way of directing the band, and he led them forward as if he were riding a galloping horse bareback. He used a bounce step to emphasize a horn riff just before he made a fist, dropped his elbow, and raised his knee to meet it. At the end of songs he would yell, "¡Se acabó la salsa!"—that's it, now that's the stuff!

Watching him on television was like, for an American teenager in a farmhouse, getting just enough reception to watch Little Richard for the first time in 1956: he was a bit outrageous as well, and the music was as surprising as the delivery. He would come offstage and, with no trace of cockiness, say to his singers: "That was good, wasn't it? Goddamnit, can we play! Shit!"

Live shows and radio and television broadcasts create buzz, but records can be replayed over and over at will. The band's first hit together was Cabrera's composition "Manzanillo." Chocolate said that from then on, and even from the first show in Placetas before the song was released, it all exploded everywhere in Cuba at the same time. "A musician who didn't smoke, *smoked* when he heard it. A musician who didn't drink, *drank* the day he heard it." After the records began to appear, Cubans lined up to buy Benny's 78s like they waited impatiently for hot bread at the bakery every day.

Cubans remember every single time they saw El Benny. Those Cubans who somehow hadn't yet seen the band on television were mesmerized when they did finally see a lanky black guajiro leading the band of all-black players, playing like the devil. Those who watched him for the first time realized that for all his scarecrow-jerky maneuvers and bounce step, dropping his elbow like pulling the brake cord on a speeding train—he was leading every instrument of the band with various parts of his body! They were marionettes and he was the puppeteer, and when he threw his white canecutter hat into the air, the band stopped instantly. The live audience roared, and listeners felt the pure joy in that first hit song. Even so early in the history of his big band, with so many more to come, "Manzanillo" was one of Benny's best. It embodies the breathless excitement of the time, with the horns playing a nimble, prancing rhythm. Onstage, when Benny finished the song, he brushed sweat from his eyes, bounced his Palo cane on the stage, and danced a little loose-hipped step while the horns stopped on a dime. From the moment they appeared in public, everyone who watched or participated knew the Banda Gigante was the real thing.

As a boy, Havana native Cintio Vitier initially knew of Benny from the radio and television, and then the records. The first time the Vitier family saw Benny on television, the mother, a guajira from Matanzas, said of his clothes and odd movements "You mean that's him? He looks like a mockingbird stuck up in a mango tree." She watched for a moment, then sat down. She watched the rest of the show and found she had been holding a plate and a dish towel in her hands the entire time. When Benny began "Como fue," she got up and danced in the living room in her apron with Cintio, singing along about the time she fell in love with her son, too, when she watched him nursing a few minutes after he was born. This kind of reaction to Benny's boleros and son montunos was very common, and many fans would feel an intense personal connection to him.

For writer Félix Contreras, the first in-person encounter with Benny came at a dance at the Colonia Española in 1953 when Contreras was still a boy working in a shop from five in the morning to nine at night. On his grandmother's tiny radio he had heard Benny sing the bolero "Tú me gustas" on a show broadcast from Pinar del Río. He was immediately hooked. When the group came to town for their first concert in public, Contreras and his friends eagerly went to see him. Sporting a new guayabera for the occasion, Contreras was an avid dancer. His friends from the barrio circled around him and yelled his nickname, Quimbán: "¡Baila, Quimbán, baila!" When Benny noticed, he pulled Contreras onstage to get a better look at his dance moves. At the end of the song, Benny picked him up and yelled in his ear that Contreras was such a great dancer that Benny owed him a drink. "But what does Quimbán mean?" he asked. When Contreras told him he didn't know, Benny sputtered with laughter. He told the crowd to applaud the Great Quimbán, and afterward they had a rum and Coke together.

From that first gig in Placetas, the band was booked with very little time off for the next seven years. They performed daily on *Cuba Canta y Baila* at the America theater, on *De Fiesta con Bacardi* on CMQ, and at night at the club La Campana. They played shows at the Warner and Vedado theaters, and on Radio Progreso. In between radio and nightclubs and theaters in Havana, the band performed at many outdoor dances in town plazas, theaters, and concert halls across Cuba.

In 1953 they recorded ten songs for RCA Victor, four during one session in November that included that first hit, "Manzanillo," and its B side, "Oye una canción para ti." The choice of A- and B-side songs followed the pattern that was standard in the recording industry for as long as there were two-sided 78s and 45s: usually a fast dance number on the A side, with a ballad on the flip side. From this point on, Benny's recordings were released in both twelve-inch 78 rpm and the fairly new seven-inch 45 rpm format. Through aggressive sales of its Victrolas, Victor had standardized the 78 rpm speed. Vinyl 45s were cheaper to make, were stackable for playing multiple records, and weren't as brittle and heavy as 78s, so RCA Victor began to release its 45s after 1949, with an overlap of dual releases for years.

At the end of November the band returned to the studios in Havana to construct six more songs, which included the son montuno "Semilla de marañón" and the wonderful guaracha "Tú verás, Margot." Both of these songs contain the seagull squawk "ah-AH!" that would become one of Benny's trademarks.

"Manzanillo" and "Devuelveme el coco" are the best of the group's recordings from that year. "Manzanillo" gives a taste of Benny's ability to improvise, to swing across a melody line, and contains one of his trademark "eh!" vocalizations. It is a thoroughly modern sound that still keeps its country *son* roots, and it became a standard for the band as soon as it was released. Benny's composition "Devuelveme el coco" is a bright son montuno that has an opening melody played by all the brass and a pure bop-influenced big-band jazz introduction that could have been written by Dizzy Gillespie. Then it drops into a behind-the-beat son montuno rhythm. Although many of Benny's subsequent recordings drift farther away from jazz into a more pure Cuban *son*, his earlier recordings often pay clear homage to American jazz. With its jazz-influenced horn lines, "Oye una canción para ti" contains an easy and fine trumpet solo by the versatile Chocolate. All of the songs recorded in 1953 have excellent lead and secondary vocals and arrangements.

The first group of four songs was recorded in an expensive hour and a half, but the band had faster results for its next session, doing all six songs in the same time. Some of Benny's best songs were recorded, with the entire band of seventeen or more musicians, in only fifteen minutes each, though it was not until into the next year, 1954, that Benny was able to perform such a feat consistently.

The first full year of the band wasn't as busy with recordings as later years. Although Benny would sometimes feel pressure to keep coming up with songs to fulfill his annual obligations to RCA Victor and Mario Rivera Conde, he never left them for another recording company but remained part of their enormous Latin American pool of talent. RCA knew Benny could be a bigger singer, and Rivera Conde thought he could sell him throughout Latin America. To prepare the way for tours and appearances in Central and South America, RCA brought in Pedro Vargas, a Mexican master of the bolero.

In April of 1954, Benny and Vargas recorded duets, "Perdón" and "Obsesión." "Obsesión" is a tour de force, with its brooding opening riffs played by the brass, and the saxes giving little licks behind the masterful vocals: "Amor es el pan de la vida . . . amor es la copa divina" (Love is the bread of life, love is the divine cup). The song is one of Benny's best boleros and rises well above that form on the strength of the horns and duet. "Perdón" keeps closer to standard boleros, except for moments of complex interplay in the vocals. The time allotted to get both songs, with full orchestra backing, was thirty minutes; with half a year of heavy practice, Benny and Chocolate were now very capable of maintaining excellent control over the process.

The two singers made a comical pair in television appearances—Benny the lanky and underfed-looking black man, who seemed to be barely behaving, alongside the short, stocky, and formal Mexican. But the duo was a great success, and Rivera Conde knew he could keep their momentum going by recording an LP worth of singles. Vargas's face was everywhere in Cuba at the time, owing to his role in the recently released film *Piel Canela* (Cinnamon skin).

The next year when Benny was under the gun to keep to his recording contract, RCA Victor lined up another session with Vargas, but the nine scheduled studio visits had to be cancelled, because Benny got laryngitis. By then the Banda Gigante's success in Cuba completely overshadowed everything Benny had ever done before. Even though Benny was a bigger star than Vargas, his face showed up far less often in the magazines like *Show*. Benny was black, and Vargas was a very light-skinned Mexican with Hispanic features.

The year 1954 was mostly a brand-building time for Benny's group, and his touring across the island interested him more than worrying about the harder work of collecting songs for recording. In 1954 Benny did acquire his memorable nickname Bárbaro del Ritmo. As the story goes, one afternoon he and Israel Castellanos were on a Santiago street corner when a pretty girl passed. Benny extravagantly kissed the air and sang, "Mira, que bárbara"— look, what a hot chick—in the style of his song then out, "Ah, Bárbara." A young kid heard him and said, "Compay, usted es el bárbaro"—Compadre, *you* are the hot one. (*Bárbaro* with a masculine ending means "barbarian" or "wild man" or, in slang, something really fantastic.) Later, when the radio personality Ibrahim Urbino heard the story of the beautiful girl on the street, he announced Benny as Bárbaro del Ritmo. Benny decided he liked the nickname, and it stuck.

At some time in or around 1954 Benny hired as his manager Eugenio "Tito" Garrote, who took care of bookings and contracts, and who paid Benny. Benny paid the band out of his own earnings, or negotiated their salaries separately. Someone was appointed to distribute the salaries to the rest of the band members, and the bass player Limonta had this role until he angered Benny some years later.

Of the twelve recordings that year, three besides the duets with Pedro Vargas stand out from the rest: "Santiago de Cuba," "Guajiro de verdad," and "Baila mi son."

Toward the year's end, in November, the orchestra returned for two more sides with Pedro Vargas and Benny, the uptempo bolero "Solamente una vez" paired with "La vida es un sueño" (Life is a dream). The latter is the song that Arsenio Rodríguez composed after a heartbreaking trip to New York. He had flown there with the belief that a physician would be able to restore the eyesight he had lost as a boy when a mule kicked him in the head. When Rodríguez got into the examining room, the doctor told him within minutes that they could do nothing to restore his vision. In a lifetime of struggle, it was the bandleader's worst moment. From his profound depression Rodríguez was able to write "La vida es un sueño."

Tours and engagements through the holidays kept the band working with no rest, but in January they would return to the studio after a few nights of sleep.

In those days, Benny's romantic relationships were as messy as they would be at any time in his life. Norayda had been living with him in the apartment in Habana Centro, and they now had two sons, Benny Jr. and Bebo. But Benny was often involved in public affairs with various other women. One was a professional model for Cristal beer, Marta Véliz. Another was an unnamed blond nurse. Finally and most notably, Benny began a romance with a young woman so beautiful she could have been mistaken for a model. There was no mistaking one fact, however: she was a friend of Norayda's and a cousin to Benny.

When Norayda found out, she confronted Benny, hoping to get him to end the relationship. He had come to a crossroad. One woman was the young mother of his children, the other had a combination of qualities ideal for him then: a country upbringing like his own, a sense of humor, and great patience with his peripatetic life. Iraida Castillo would give Benny three more children, the two girls Bárbara and Lázara and a boy named Robertico. The house where they lived at La Cumbre represented the most domestic Benny would ever be, but he was still gone most of the time and any woman involved with him was sure to spend much of that time as a musician's widow.

December 4, 1954. Norayda remembered the date because it was Santa Bárbara's feast day, and the night that Benny told her he was going to live with Iraida. Instead, she left with the children and went back to her mother's, where Benny would show up one night, very late and very drunk, pounding on the door to talk to her, frightening the women inside and waking the neighbors. She said that there was no reconciliation before he left to work in Venezuela. Not long after, Norayda found work as a dancer and traveled with a show in Panama over the Carnival season in February 1955. Not only was Benny also there working, but the *de-nuevo-con-Benny* (Benny's new thing) had arrived with him.

When Norayda married a Venezuelan and went out on tour as a dancer, Benny kept the boys with him for a year. He and Norayda became embroiled in a custody battle when she returned for them in 1956 and Benny told her he wanted to keep little Bebo. Norayda's mother got involved in the disagreement. Both boys were allowed to go back with Norayda to Venezuela, where they grew up. But Benny was still not childless. By the time he bought the house at La Cumbre, he had taken on his young daughter Hilda.

ELEVEN

Son Montuno and Murder Inc.

Benny didn't need to put out recordings to make money in those days. The streets of Havana glittered with the nickels, dimes, quarters, and dollars fed from American purses and pants pockets into the slot machines. That money rolled downhill to any bandleader who was able to put together a half-decent conjunto, with far more for the large orchestras. Since gambling always favors the house or the man who runs a particular game, there was a bottomless source of money that in turn paid for lavish entertainment, all the orchestras, hundreds of showgirls, luxury goods in the stores.

Because there was no government oversight, the casino comps to high roller gamblers included more than the standard free suite with a view of the water from high floors. Cuban and imported prostitutes were comped as commonly as the French champagne in ice buckets. A floor manager might notice a high roller eyeing a pretty cocktail waitress, and whether the man lost or won that night, the casino manager would send up two girls who offered a nice four-handed massage with a happy ending. It was said that, for the right visitor, room service would also send up a half gram of cocaine or a handful of marijuana joints. Cocaine in Cuba was easy to find, though not as cheap as a fifth of rum that sold for $1.25 a bottle in the clubs. Meyer Lanksy had made it all possible, with help from his friend Fulgencio Batista.

Nineteen fifty-five was the year that the film version of *Guys and Dolls* was released. When Marlon Brando playing gambler Sky Masterson brings the uptight virgin Sarah Brown (Jean Simmons) down to Havana on a bet (placed with none other than Frank Sinatra), they were playing out a joke that was enacted for real every day. Americans went to Havana and lost their inhibitions while drinking rum drinks at lush outdoor bars like the Bajo las Estrellas or the Sans Souci, flying there any day of the week on a whim.

Americans didn't need a passport to enter Cuba, and the $2.50 visitor visa was good for two years. French, Swiss, and British citizens were exempt from the visa requirement. Visitors could bring with them automobiles and trailers on ferries, up to 400 cigarettes, fishing equipment, and shotguns for hunting trips. They could return home with 100 cigars duty free and a gallon of alcohol. Once worn, that Dior gown a woman might have bought at the Encanto department store didn't have to be declared. Over the next few years the glamorous faces of Californian, European, and South American film stars were as common as the geckos. Politicians from Washington flew into José Martí airport to walk in the brilliant sunshine to the busy terminal where little bands played for their arrival.

Several radio stations broadcast in English, along with shows in Arabic, Yiddish, and Chinese for immigrants who spoke those languages. Aside from English and Spanish there were Chinese and Yiddish newspapers. Among all the foreign tourists, many Spanish workers had recently migrated to Cuba from Galicia, Asturias, and the Canary Islands.

You might possibly have gone to Havana without gambling, but it would have been pointless to go without seeing a show or visiting the glamorous cabarets. These were as beautiful as any in Paris—and the music was infinitely better. Especially for top-earning musicians and entertainers from cold climates, the winter season was when everyone in jazz and pop played in Havana. There was some tourism to places beyond Havana like Varadero beach, but few Americans traveled for sightseeing much deeper in Cuba than into a forest of one-armed bandits. Other gambling possibilities included dog tracks, horse racing, jai alai, and bolita.

From the perspective of the owners like Meyer Lansky, the casinos were the most important, certainly, but they didn't neglect the nightclubs and cabarets and any other attraction that helped bring in the gamblers.

The ultimate nightclub in Havana was without any doubt the Tropicana casino, where everyone from Josephine Baker and Nat King Cole to Carmen Miranda had performed. It was best known for its sinuous dancing girls and muscled acrobat dancers. Located in the luxurious Miramar neighborhood, the spectacular ultramodern building and tropical gardens alone were and still are reason enough to visit. The trademark marble fountain of the muses greeted guests as they arrived at the curved drive, and a facsimile of its other well-known statue, of a ballerina, graced the plastic swizzle sticks in each mojito and Cuba libre.

The five-dollar-per-person cover charge included dinner, with two or three shows nightly and usually three orchestras. Specialty drinks cost only a dollar. With the music free, it was an incredible deal. Visitors could also take a stool at the glowing Bajo las Estrellas (Under the Stars) bar to avoid the cover charge and still watch the more than fifty dancers on the high catwalks overhead. For rainy or hot nights, visitors sat in air conditioning beneath the Arcos de Cristal, a masterpiece of modern architecture. Total seating indoors and out was more than 1,500.

As in any cabaret show, the dancers' costumes concealed little. *Cabaret Yearbook* noted that Cuban chorus girls often had figures with a bit more sand in the bottom portion of the hourglass, but the writer wasn't complaining.

> Like night clubs all over the world, the gay spots in Havana present girls—but they are unlike the females seen in America or Europe. The latin chorine is more buxom, more sexy-looking than her American counterpart. In keeping with the latin standard of what is a desirable woman, most dancers have hips that would bar them from American stages. Actually latin pulchritude is closer to nature, not nearly as make-believe as some US chorines.

The Sans Souci was another nightclub casino that was not to be missed. Located a lucky seven miles (and equally lucky eleven kilometers) from Habana Vieja, it had a dramatic double arched entrance and outdoor seating in atmospheric gardens. Its casino revenues also paid for well-known international acts and several orchestras each night. Benny played there far more than at the Tropicana.

Santo Trafficante Jr., mobster and business associate to Meyer Lansky, oversaw the hotel and casino complex at Sans Souci and hired slippery Lefty Clark to manage it. Clark was also manager of the Desert Inn in Las Vegas. Back in the States he was known to the FBI by other names: William Buschoff and Frank Bischoff. Clark, who also took part in drug smuggling in Cuba, had earned his rank by work performed back at Lansky's illegal Florida casino Greenacres. Among the big names hired by the Sans Souci were Marlene Dietrich, Liberace, Susan Hayward, and—in keeping with its French name—one of the most famous singers in the world at the time, Edith Piaf. They tried anything they could think of to bring in the tourists. Lefty Clark offered champ Rocky Marciano the huge purse of $350,000 to fight black Cuban boxer Nino Valdez there, but Marciano's manager refused and so the two never fought in Cuba or the States.

The Sans Souci had a capacity of a thousand. Its gaming included roulette, craps, blackjack, and chemin de fer (the "shimmies") tables. Serious dice players could bet against themselves rather than against the house, another way to lose a great deal of money. You could listen to music acts in the Nevada cocktail lounge without a minimum, or pay the $5 minimum per person at the tables outside. One interesting way the Sans Souci distinguished itself was with high-stakes bingo with fabulous prizes. Best of all, the Sans Souci was truly family-friendly: children were permitted to play bingo, with payoffs of $1,500 and other desirable winnings like 1957 Cadillacs or Chevrolet convertibles.

The Montmartre had been around longer than either of the other two most famous cabarets. Operated by Meyer Lansky—the man who recognized in Havana a potential for American organized crime figures like himself to earn enormous sums, pay no taxes, and hide or launder their earnings in Swiss and offshore accounts—and located not far from the University of Havana in the Vedado neighborhood, the Montmartre was a completely indoor club with a $4.50 table minimum.

There was so much going on that specialized magazines, reviews, and newspapers like the Spanish-language *Show* and the English *Cabaret Quarterly* provided heavy coverage of cabarets and casino spectaculars. Daily newspapers and the newsmagazine *Bohemia* also reported on music and dance and on the clubs and casinos, while the foreign press covered the action as well. Although Benny's photograph commonly appeared in the press, musicians and showgirls weren't the only interesting characters who filled those publications. Listed sometimes as American businessmen or investors, photographs of organized crime figures well known to the FBI, CIA, and Interpol also appeared on occasion. These men posed behind cocktails while surrounded by club owners, famous faces like Frank Sinatra, and American politicians.

One important man who made sure his photograph rarely appeared was the "accountant to the mob" Meyer Lansky, who from the late 1940s not only ran the Hotel Nacional but in most respects ran Cuba itself. His closest associates in Havana included Santo Trafficante Jr., with whose father he had built a gambling operation in Tampa targeting the Cuban immigrants who had moved there for the cigar industry. Along with their rolling skills they brought with them a love for the lottery game bolita. A somewhat more unsavory associate was Lansky's childhood friend Charles "Lucky" Luciano. The U.S. government handed Luciano an intended break when it deported him back to his native Sicily. When Luciano grew bored in Italy, he returned to Havana where the action was.

No one in Cuba with the exception of President Batista, however, was as powerful as Lansky. The man never saw much need to raise his voice. He didn't have to, he was Meyer Lansky. With Benjamin "Bugsy" Siegel, Lansky had created Murder Inc. A kind of temp agency for mob hitmen, Murder Inc. was responsible for the execution of hundreds of enemies of the American Cosa Nostra in the 1930s and 1940s. By 1947 Siegel had himself been murdered for skimming money from the mob's construction funds for the Flamingo casino in Las Vegas. The meeting that decided Siegel's fate took place in the Meyer Lansky world headquarters, the great Hotel Nacional in Havana.

Born Majer Suchowlinski in Grodno, Poland, Lansky made friends as a boy on the Lower East Side of Manhattan with Bugsy Siegel and Lucky Luciano. With his pure mathematical brain, he developed gambling operations in Tampa and New Orleans, and hid much of his money in numbered offshore accounts. He kept an office and living suite on an upper floor of the Nacional, and another large suite at the Riviera. He rarely drank anything stronger than milk, and he drove an average car, a white Chevrolet convertible.

The largest and most opulent music and review clubs were usually connected to the grand hotels. Lansky's Parisien in the Nacional was three clubs in one: dinner, dancing, and shows like Benny's Banda Gigante took place in the largest portion, called the Casino Parisien; gambling tables filled the Casino International; and smaller music acts played from time to time in the Starlight Terrace bar located between the other two clubs. If prohibition created the mob problem in the United States, Havana and gambling raised organized crime to another level of power and influence altogether. Few

American politicians at the time of the Havana casinos could avoid dealing with associates of Lansky in the States, and many businessmen and politicians had direct dealings and investments themselves in Cuba, much of it in the mob-owned casinos. What formula they, meaning Lansky, perfected in Havana was then applied to Las Vegas, which thrived after the Havana casinos' time was over. Although investors would eventually lose many millions of dollars in Havana when Fidel Castro ended the party, they probably made hundreds of millions in Cuba before that happened.

To help rebuild the gambling empire, Batista enlisted Meyer Lansky—as hard as it is to believe—to clean up the crooked dealers. Lansky controlled the Montmartre at that time, but he wanted to put a casino in the Nacional with suites for high rollers. When the Nacional opened, Eartha Kitt headlined for the debut. Not far away Lansky also built the twenty-one-story Riviera, where Ginger Rogers performed on opening night in 1957. Special guests included Lena Horne, Marilyn Monroe and Joe DiMaggio, Jayne Mansfield, and Ted Williams. Another mob casino, the Capri, had opened in late 1956. Gambling profits at the St. John's and the Comodoro also benefited organized crime members. Combined gambling earnings ensured that more than $500,000 per month went to underworld figures and Batista.

Santo Trafficante Jr., who had been arrested at the Apalachin meeting in upstate New York in 1957 along with Carlos Marcello from New Orleans and Meyer Lansky, voted as part of the national crime syndicate in secret mob meetings to kill Murder Inc.'s own Albert Anastasia. Anastasia had muscled in on the gambling in Havana and wouldn't play by mob rules. Hired hitmen sent by Murder Inc. shot Anastasia repeatedly as he sat in a barber's chair at the Park Sheraton in Manhattan on October 25, 1957.

The Nacional building itself had also played a historic role in Cuban politics, when in 1933 a group of army officers barricaded themselves there and conducted a bloody action against the recent coup led by Fulgencio Batista, which had replaced Gerardo Machado. Sharpshooters on the roof killed army and revolutionary members who attacked the hotel. After a pitched battle with forces under Batista's control, the survivors inside the Nacional surrendered. Many of the officers, like others who attempted to revolt against Batista's rule through the years, were executed, even though they had helped drive the dictator Machado from power.

Not long after Batista became the real power behind the scenes in Cuba,

Batista and Lansky became friends. It was not a friendship of shared experiences and going to dinner with the wives; it was the most lucrative and parasitic relationship that Cuba would ever see. In every sense, Meyer and the American Cosa Nostra were the brains and investment behind the gambling pits and hotels, and Batista was the muscle. Together they earned incredible sums from all forms of gambling. One of the very first things that the Castro government did after seizing office on New Year's in 1959 was to heave slot machines out onto the sidewalk and take axes to the roulette tables where Benny used to ask for credit.

Lansky genuinely loved Benny and often hired him to play at the Riviera or the Parisien, but just as often fired him for drunkenness, or lateness, or unprofessional behavior. Like him personally or not, Lansky was a serious businessman. The portrayal in *The Godfather: Part II* of Lansky in the character of Hyman Roth wasn't so far from the truth: a seemingly harmless old Jewish grandfather wearing a sweater and slippers. He may have offered lunch with tea and cake, but he was still a dangerous old lion with some very sharp teeth. His only weakness was for a Cuban mistress named Carmen who lived in an apartment on the Paseo del Prado where he paid the rent.

More than once, Lansky's bodyguard Armando Jaime Casielles or a floor manager called upstairs to say that Benny was gambling in the casino and wanted a line of credit. Lansky approved the credit, unless Benny was late in going on that night. Lansky would send Casielles or his own brother Jack downstairs to move Benny along and get the show started. Benny was so popular at that point that Meyer was forced to ignore his naughtiness and rehire him repeatedly. He once asked Benny if he knew what "Moré" meant in Hebrew; it tickled him to tell Benny that *moréh* meant "teacher."

"Come on, *compay*," Benny would say, shaking his fist as if holding a pair of dice. "Just tell Meyer it's Benny who wants it."

Without looking at him, Casielles would adjust his cufflink and answer dryly, "He knows it's you, that's why he says no."

Benny had first played at the Nacional back in 1944 or 1945 with Matamoros, before he went to Mexico. There is an old story passed down by his family that he once played at the Nacional for a private audience of fewer than fifty people. He said that the audience consisted of a group of important men, all at a single table, and no else in the room. It's anyone's guess who was present then, and what year this occurred, but American investors, mobsters, Cuban and American politicians, and even President Batista are all likely to have been in meetings like that at the Nacional.

Another interesting face that would not have been present in the meetings but was often in town when they occurred was Frank Sinatra. He was said to have been in Havana when East Coast crime bosses convened at the Nacional in 1947 to decide to kill Bugsy Siegel for skimming money from the Flamingo. Benny could have played with Matamoros around then, but was already gone to Mexico at the time of the meeting when Meyer Lansky lost patience and Siegel's fate was sealed. The FBI believed that Sinatra brought two million dollars cash for Lucky Luciano in a suitcase, a rumor corroborated by recently opened FBI files. Incidentally, Sinatra may even have been in Havana around Christmas in 1958, possibly having flown there for New Year's when Castro overthrew Batista.

The most popular clubs like the Montmartre had initially put up with Benny's antics, but toward the end of the 1950s he wasn't welcome. Because of his reputation, Benny had never been hired for a long run at the Tropicana. Whenever Benny ran into Martin and Ofelia Fox, the owners of the Tropicana, at the Ali Bar, he would jokingly ask Fox why he was never hired over there, saying that his hungry babies ("mis negritos") needed a lot of malanga.

None of the excesses of the 1950s would have been possible without the permission and direct participation of Fulgencio Batista, who had been military dictator of Cuba ever since the Sergeants' Revolt of 1933. Batista's historical legacy includes countless assassinations, and the stealing of hundreds of millions of dollars (a tradition he inherited and then perfected). His racial makeup was as clouded and complicated as the various ways he held power for nearly three decades. First appointed leader of the student- and union-led coup that overthrew Gerardo Machado, then army chief of staff wielding the real power behind five puppet presidents, then himself voted president in a rigged election in 1940, then a resident of Daytona Beach, then a member of the Cuban senate, Batista firmly took power in a coup in 1952 when he found out he was in last place in a fair election.

Batista was never accepted by upper-class white Cuban society. Once in 1937 many patrons walked out when Batista and his family entered the Sans Souci gardens for a show, not as a political protest but because blacks were not allowed in the club then. Because of the narrowness of his eyes and the somewhat Eastern look of his face, Batista was rumored to have been part

Chinese, or native Indian, a rumor tinged with racism in a white society that shunned him for reasons of class as well. Never accepted by the wealthy whites of Cuba, Batista instead made friends with Meyer Lansky. The two were quite a team; Lansky, even after great losses in the Cuban Revolution, wound up with unknown millions of tax-free dollars, and Batista did the same. Batista's wife herself got a weekly skim of the profits, for her walking-around money.

Benny also became friends with Batista at this time. On occasion he drove out, for dominoes and dinner and perhaps a little baseball, to the president's ranch, Kuquine, in the country to the southwest of Havana. Although Benny was almost completely apolitical, they did have some things in common: both were mixed-race country boys with no political or social ties, who had worked their way from poverty to the highest positions in their domains. For all the distaste upper-class white Cubans felt for Batista, most adored Benny's music and forgot his skin color, even if there were white country clubs and private clubs where he was never invited to play. Benny's own lack of sophistication, as manifested in the late 1950s, meant that he never built lavish homes, never put money in numbered Swiss accounts (as many others did), and never left with bags of gold (as Batista and associates did). Money had never meant anything more to him than a gift to bestow on his family, and on the musicians who worked for him—his second family.

Batista gave Benny an interesting gift at this time—one he sometimes gave other close friends and business associates—a gold ring containing a large cut amethyst stone. He had it engraved "From F.B. to B.M." Benny wore the ring often and laughingly nicknamed the amethyst—which is *amatista* in Spanish—his "ama-'Tista," or "love [Ba]tista." He would show it off and say: "*Mira, compay,* come see my love-'Tista!"

The ancient Greeks wore amethyst in the belief that the stone had the power to counter the effects of alcohol, both drunkenness and hangovers. Perhaps Batista's gift was a defective alcohol deflector: Benny's nearly constant, superhuman drinking binges were beginning to show in his body.

Benny's unremitting alcoholism had begun in his early teens, and by 1957 his liver was already hard and damaged. He hadn't worn a belt in years. Everyone knew of Benny's drinking, but few of his fans knew that he always wore suspenders because belts hurt his belly. His reputation for lateness was certainly due to his drinking. Even though he was well known for playing for free until long past dawn at the same club where he didn't show up the night before, he was killing himself with rum. He wasn't killing himself slowly, either. The garlic he ate in bars along with hard-boiled eggs in the belief that this would counteract the effects of all the rum didn't slow down the damage to his liver any more than his love-'Tista ring.

Getting an exact estimate of how much Benny drank is not an easy task. Every day of his life he might have drunk one or even two bottles of rum, which is 200 to 400 grams of alcohol. Only 20 percent of extremely heavy drinkers like Benny actually get cirrhosis, and there is the small possibility that Benny's liver was already compromised by a case of hepatitis. But that is unlikely. He was destroying his body all on his own.

1. Benny and Banda Gigante on the *Cabaret Regalías* show for the CMQ television station. From the collection of Vicki Gold Levi.

2. El Casino de los Congos, the little meetinghouse where Benny learned music, dance, and the culture of his African heritage. The building is now a Cuban national monument.

3. Benny in the early 1940s. Photo by Ramón Fernández Morales.

4. RCA publicity photo, from around 1950. Photo by Ramón Fernández Morales.

WAIKIKI REFORMA 13

Presenta a la sensacional bailarina: *TONGOLELE*

Acompañada por el conjunto tropical mas completo del momento:

JUAN BRUNO TARRAZA
Famoso pianista y compositor cubano,

BENNY MORE
"La Voz DE ORO de Cuba"

Tabaquito y Silvestre, bongoceros, trompetistas, etc., además:

NELLY AMERICA
"El alma de Buenos Aires"

LOLITO
Un comico original

JUAN JOSE SARO
"El cantante de moda"

ROSITA ALVIREZ
Cancionera folklórica

Animador del espectáculo: **ROSITA ALVIREZ**

2 SHOWS: A LA 1.30 y 3.30.

5. A handbill from Waikiki, a Mexico City nightclub that booked Cuban acts in the late 1940s. Rumba dancer Tongolele has top billing, with Benny as "The Golden Voice of Cuba." Tarraza, Silvestre Méndez, and Tabaquito were among the many Cuban musicians Benny worked with in Mexico. Courtesy of Marcos Salazar.

6. Yolanda "Tongolele" Montes, known to American audiences for her role in the Boris Karloff movie *Isle of the Snake People.*

7. *El Rey del Barrio*, one of the movies Benny worked on in Mexico. He sang "Cabio Sile" off camera while Tongolele danced.

*Other handbills for
Mexico shows:*

RIO ROSA

Valladolid y Oaxaca.

PEPE MEDELLIN
Master of ceremonies

PRESENTS

LUPITA ALDAY
Exclusive artist of X. E. W.

EVANGELINA Y TOÑO
genuine interpreters of Mexican folklore.

PACO DEL REY
with his Spanish songs.

B. MORE
Cuban novelty

And you will dance with the modern music of maestro

NOE FAJARDO'S
Orchestra

and the orchestra from the Tropic

VERACRUZ
and its singer

LALO MONTANE
Every Sunday, after the Bullfight

Doble Floor Show!

8. Río Rosa handbill, December 1945. Benny is listed as "B. More, Cuban novelty."

SALON DE BAILE

LA PLAYA

ARGENTINA 105   MEXICO, D. F.

Viernes 19 de Agosto de 1949

Extraordinaria fecha de celebracion del

15 ANIVERSARIO
de este Salon, con un Grandioso Baile
de 6 a 12 p.m.

3 DE LAS MEJORES ORQUESTAS CAPITALINAS
Arturo Nuñez ★ Gamboa Ceballos ★ Chucho Rodríguez
con sus Cantantes
Benny Moré, Lalo Montané, Tony Camargo y Julio

Actuación Especial del Los Grandes
Interpretes del la Canción Moderna.

El Trio los Jaibos
El Fantástico Dueto de las

HERMANITAS LUNA
Y otras varias grandes artistas

Precios Populares   **No falte Ud.**

9. La Playa handbill. Benny recorded some of his first hits in duets with Lalo Montané and Tony Carmargo, with orchestras led by Arturo Núñez and Chucho Rodríguez, all of whom are listed for this show in 1949.

El Club Habana

Invita a usted y a su distinguida familia al grandioso BAILE que celebrará en los salones del

CLUB BRASIL

(Avenida Instituto Técnico número 82), el sábado 1o. de febrero próximo, de las 20 a las 5 horas.

Tocarán 4 Orquestas:

ARTURO NUÑEZ
ALFONSO TORRES
PEPE CASTILLO y
El Son CLAVE DE ORO

Variedades:

KIKO MENDIVE
CHEPILLA
BENNY MOORE

NO FALTE USTED

10. El Club Habana handbill. Benny is billed as "Benny Moore," and sang with the group El Son Clave de Oro.

El Timbero de Belén.

Guaracha-Rumba. Benny Moré.
Arr. de H. Cané.

Piano.

COPYRIGHT 1949 EDITORIAL MEXICANA DE MÚSICA INTERNACIONAL

11. Sheet music for "El timbero de Belén," one of Benny's earliest published compositions, with arrangement by Humberto Cané. Used in the 1949 film *El Gran Campeón*, the song was later recorded by Dámaso Pérez Prado. Benny has signed the page at the right. Courtesy of Marcos Salazar.

12. Banda Gigante, Benny's first band under his own direction, 1953. *Front, left to right:* unknown, Tabaquito, Celso "Pacho" Gómez, Domingo Corbacho, Alfredo "Chocolate" Armenteros, Virgilio Vixama, Fernando Álvarez, Enrique "El Conde Negro" Benítez. *Back, left to right:* Rolando Laserie, Santiago Peñalver, Roberto Barreto, Rigoberto "Rabanito" Jiménez, Benny Moré, Ramón "Cabrerita" Cabrera, Alberto Limonta, Luis "El Pibe" Outumuro González, Clemente "Chico" Piquero. Courtesy of the Cuban Heritage Collection, University of Miami Libraries, Coral Gables, Florida.

ALI BAR *Club*

Avenida de Dolores y Carretera de Lucero. Orquesta Antillana de Moisés Alfonso. Horas del Show: 12:30 y 3:30 a.m. Elenco artístico: Benny Moré, el Bárbaro del Ritmo; Orlando Vallejo, cancionero; Candita Vázquez, vedette; Roberto Faz y su Conjunto; Berta Pernas, la tanguista famosa; Ñico Menviela, cancionero y la animación a cargo del actor y recitador Ignacio Valdés Sigler.

13. Magazine advertisement for Benny, Roberto Faz, and other acts at the Ali Bar. The late-night spot was Benny's favorite and is most famous for the Banda Gigante shows.

CANDITA VAZQUEZ
actuando en el
ALI-BAR

El Cabaret "Ali Bar" estaba presentando un gran show que encabezaban dos figuras de seria popularidad en el ambiente. Benny Moré y Candita Vázquez. La foto de Santos ofrece la versión de Candita Vázquez, la estupenda vedette, en su conterno. Todo el mundo se hacía los ecos aquí preguntándose cómo era posible que en sitio pequeño, pudieran alternar estrellas de tal magnitud, dándose el caso que además participaran del show, artistas del calibre de Orlando Vallejo, Roberto Faz y su Conjunto, Sonia Pernas y Rino Mauricia.

14. Dancer Candita Vázquez backstage at the Ali Bar.

15. Onstage at the Ali Bar.

16. Benny's business manager Tito Garrote *(left)* and the owner of the Ali Bar, Alipio García.

17. Backstage at RCA studios: Benny with bandleader-violinist Rafael Lay *(left)* and timbales player Orestes Varona, of the Orquesta Aragón. Courtesy of the Vicki Gold Levi collection.

YO SOY EL BARBARO DEL RITMO

PERO LAVASOL ES EL BARBARO DE LA BLANCURA

18. Advertisement postcard for Lavasol laundry soap that reads: "I am the wildman of rhythm but Lavasol is the wildman of whitening." Courtesy of the Ramiro Fernández collection.

19. Benny and Cienfuegos Elephants catcher Rafael Noble. Noble later played for the New York Giants. Photo by Ramón Fernández Morales.

20. Benny with the Havana Lions.

21. Benny with Jack Dempsey, at Dempsey's restaurant in New York.

22. Banda Gigante at the world-famous Tropicana nightclub, December 1956. Benny was rarely hired there because of his reputation for showing up late.

23. Nat King Cole during his annual winter run at the Tropicana. With Cole is Rolando Álvarez, who would later marry Benny's widow Iraida. Courtesy of Keith A. Llorens and Theodore Leong, private collectors.

24. Benny and Iraida with fans at the Alloy nightclub.

25. Benny visiting Santiago de Cuba, just after the Revolution. To Benny's left are
Alfonso Leicea, who was also known as Juan Carón, and Gil Ramírez.

26. Banda Gigante, Benny directing, for bolero singer Olga Guillot in *No Me Olvides Nunca*, the only movie Benny filmed in Cuba.

27. Benny in a photomontage. From the collection of Vicki Gold Levi.

28. Benny and his mother, Virginia, on a visit to Rancho Luna beach near Cienfuegos. Courtesy of the Cuban Heritage Collection, University of Miami Libraries, Coral Gables, Florida.

29. Benny clowning for the camera at home, 1957. Courtesy of the Cuban Heritage Collection, University of Miami Libraries, Coral Gables, Florida.

30. Benny's house on the outskirts of Havana. Behind the little house was his *conuco*, an urban farm plot crowded with songbirds, poultry, litters of pigs, tropical fruit trees, and vegetables.

31. Benny caring for his bananas and plantains out back of his house in La Cumbre.

32. Benny, late in life.

Album cover art

33. Así es Beny (Here's Beny)

34. Pare, Que
Llego el Bárbaro
(Stop, here comes
the Wildman!)

35. The Most
from Beny Moré

36. Benny's grave in the municipal cemetery of Santa Isabel de las Lajas. Alongside are memorials for his mother, Virginia, and tributes from Iraida and the children. At the left is a memorial tribute from Enrique "Conde Negro" Benítez. Benny's headstone reads: "Lajas mi rincón querido, pueblo donde yo nací" (Lajas my beloved place, town where I was born). The gravesite is now a Cuban national monument.

TWELVE

The Hogs and the Hits, 1955–1956

In 1955 music from the Americas, both from the States and from Cuba, was as big a global presence as it had ever been. Pérez Prado scored a huge worldwide hit with "Cherry Pink and Apple Blossom White," which spent two and a half months at the number one position on the American pop charts. Promoted heavily by RCA Victor, the man who used to write Benny's checks back in Mexico had become one of the wealthiest Spanish-speaking entertainers in the world. His mambos became so famous and ubiquitous that they seemed to represent all of Cuban music, at least for many Americans now attracted to that very adult playground in the Caribbean. Benny was happy for the sometimes difficult-to-work-with Pérez Prado, and never had anything bad to say about him, even after the episode of the fake Benny.

The year 1955 was also a very busy one for Benny. It was the year of his second biggest output of releases. To be sure, some of this was due to his indifference to recording. It had been easy to avoid doing what he didn't relish, the hours spent preparing for studio dates, in the hectic months of 1954 and early 1955. In 1956 he would follow the same pattern, and then pay for it by having to record even more in 1957, the year of his highest output. Combined with touring, appearances, and now advertising endorsements, it was a load that put a strain on anyone involved.

From this year onward, every year until his death seemed to be the Year of Benny. He would slow down somewhat after 1958, and from 1960 on he was very ill, but he was still as adored as ever, on the island and off. The early part of 1955 saw him with a new common-law wife, a new house, and many new members in the band.

He was a real orchestra leader now, and not only directed and chose songs but had to deal with the hiring and firing of members, the personnel and the personal. Even so, Benny somehow managed the feat of never firing any member of his band. He was too soft-hearted to deprive a man's children of food. Besides, with his own drinking binges and disappearances to sing in far-off places or to let himself be caught in the soft net of a pursuing woman, could he ever judge the actions of his boys? He couldn't.

But a bandleader is running a business. From time to time he would gently deal with everyday issues with which normal bandleaders would never have shown any patience, such as lateness and drunkenness. The idea of fining band members for a little drinking, or reprimanding a horn player for cursing, would have been ludicrous. In one instance Benny snapped and attacked someone, but in defense of his musicians. No one he ever worked with called him a bad boss. When his manager urged him to get tougher with the band, Benny told him, "Tito—look at me. I'm not Artie Shaw," referring to the great but hot-tempered jazz bandleader.

Even before their first trip outside Cuba in 1955, Cabrerita was already hinting to Benny that he had had enough of the rigors of touring. Although he would keep feeding Benny songs, he no longer played piano or toured with the group. He remembered a time when Benny had to tell Chico to go home for showing up drunk onstage one too many times. It must have been quite a feat to get kicked out of Benny's band for drunkenness, since they had to pay kids to haul away the empty rum bottles from any practice or recording studio. And Benny, the heaviest drinker of them all, was never out of arm's reach of a bottle of Palmita. Benny got things done by finesse, not by being autocratic. His relationship with all members of his bands was always that of a big brother. In effect, telling Chico to stay home was a firing, but it was a firing Benny-style. He wouldn't let Chico play with the band until he straightened up some, but Benny still paid him his salary; he would never forget what Chico did for him in Mexico, and he knew what a toll it took on you to constantly be where someone else ordered. The impossibility of always being on time was something Benny knew about as well.

A few days after New Year's the band entered the studio, and they returned twice over the next month and a half. "Me miras tiernamente" was a bolero they released as an A side, and the B side was the exciting tribute to Bebo Valdés's short-lived orchestra, "Batanga no. 2."

Next came the guajira "Buscando la melodía" with the son montuno "Apúrate mi china," and in February another son montuno, "Mi saoco" (also released as "Me voy pa' Morón"), with the cha-cha "Celosa" (Jealous woman). Saoco is made by pouring rum into a coconut and sipping it through a straw, the kind of drink sold for pennies at the beach. Although the song's lyrics aren't much more than a chorus of "Vertientes, Camagüey, Florida, y Morón," they name places that all had significance for Benny's past, a past very connected to Enrique Benítez as well.

Generoso joined the band in April of 1955 simply to play the slide trombone, but with his skills on the instrument, he ended up transforming its place in Hispanic music from that day on. He was a very busy session and house musician, and soon replaced José Miguel Gómez. By the time he agreed to take over much of the band's arranging in 1956, there had been some turnover in personnel for the usual reasons. Many of the turnovers around this time were due to Benny's own issues as well, and the loss of good musicians never ceased to infuriate Generoso. Because he became the unofficial house bandleader and largely handled the demanding task of arranging as well, new members just meant more work for him. The only spots that never changed throughout the entire life of the band were those held by Chico Piquero (except for at least once getting "fired" for drinking too much), Enrique Benítez, and Israel Castellanos.

Benny had first met Generoso in July of 1952 while the two of them were taking the no. 58 bus downtown—Benny was on his way to work with Bebo Valdés at Cadena Azul and so was Generoso, who had just left an engagement playing for the national police band. Generoso, whose nickname in those days was Tojo after the Japanese emperor because of his slightly Asian face, noticed Benny immediately as someone dressed a little strangely, someone you avoid sitting next to on public transportation, someone he immediately thought of as "un sujeto," a character or oddball. Generoso, with a stiff and formal personality that was easily irritated, saw Benny looking at his trombone case. Benny had already noticed the police band uniform, the spit-shined shoes, the straight-backed way Generoso sat. Benny wore a beatnik's beret, a white turtleneck, baggy pants held up by suspenders, little gold earrings, and sandals on dusty bare feet. He was just the kind of person that Generoso avoided on principle. Characteristically, Benny slid over to talk, poking at Generoso's elbow and trying to catch Generoso's eye through the sunglasses that Generoso rarely took off in public. Also characteristically, Generoso ignored him. Benny persisted, saying, "*Compay*, I bet you and me are going to the same place." Generoso told him he was sure they weren't. Benny kept on bothering Generoso. Even without the trombone case to tell him Generoso was a musician on his way to Cadena Azul, he may already have seen Generoso before and known who he was. Benny never let an opportunity pass to tease, especially someone who needed a little teasing. This is how one of the greatest teams in Cuban music came to meet. They were also one of Cuba's greatest Odd Couples, complete opposites. Although their exchange would improve in monetary terms from their first meeting, the essential relationship never did change and Benny never did cease baiting the tightly wound Generoso.

Bebo Valdés was working for the Sun radio chain in those days of his batanga orchestra. Generoso said in 2000 that "the Sonora Matancera was using foreign singers like Daniel Santos, León Marini, the Colombian Nelson Pinedo, Pablo Martino, but Bebo wanted to break out of the mold a little. And so they began to hire artists. In the first two weeks we had Lucho Bermúdez, who was known in Colombia as the King of Cumbia, now gone, and his wife Matilde Díaz." For the next two weeks it was Benny's turn.

When Generoso got up for his stop, Benny leapt up and said, "Hey—I told you we were going to the same place." Generoso tried to shake him off by going into the bar Las Brisas del Maní on Morro. It was in the same block as the radio station, and he had a little time to kill anyway. An overly gregarious Benny took hold of his shoulder and said, "Hey, *compay*, aren't you going to offer me a drink?"

Generoso said he bought rums, hoping that would get rid of "this strange character," and when they had finished, he had them put on the tab he kept there. Benny said he wanted to buy Generoso one, so Generoso shrugged why not, and they had another. When their glasses were empty, Benny stood up and told Generoso that he didn't have any money, and would pay him back some other time if he put those on the tab too. Benny told him, "¡Está bien, ciao!" Like the smart aleck Bugs Bunny he loved at the movie theater, Benny put on his beret, winked at the bartender girl, and disappeared out the open door. Laughing hoarsely, Benny would forever retell the story of how he stiffed Generoso for *tragos* back in 1952, yet it's very likely that he knew he would see Generoso later and that it was all one big joke. And if he didn't know who Generoso was, he picked the perfect target to mooch from. Generoso's name was richly ironic: he was anything but generous.

When Generoso walked into Cadena Azul, there was Benny with Bebo, who said to Generoso, "Hey, come meet Benny Moré." It was still the time when no one knew Benny's face, and although Generoso's wife knew Benny's voice from the radio, Generoso didn't, though he did know that Benny had worked with Pérez Prado, Mercerón, and Rafael de Paz.

Benny cackled his laugh when he laid eyes on Generoso, now changed out of his police band uniform. He went to put his arm around Generoso, who put up his hand angrily to stop him. Benny had been asking Bebo who could help him score his hit with Lalo Montané "Mucho corazón," which he had promised to sing with Bebo's band the next day. When Bebo said that Generoso was the person he wanted, Generoso didn't respond. He was still annoyed at Benny for running off without paying at the bar.

Ignoring Generoso's glare, Bebo told Benny: "Like I said, if anyone I know can do it, this is your guy."

Generoso's wife had just arrived, and she said she adored "Mucho corazón." She told Benny if he got the score, she could get Generoso to do it by the next day. Generoso gave her a sharp look, but she too ignored him. Benny was pleased. Away from the others, he told her that if she got Generoso to rescore the song for the band, he would be godfather to their first child.

Generoso had work to do, so he forgot about his wife's offer. At home in the morning, he grumbled but took the score out of his trombone case at her urging. The original score called for three trumpets, but Bebo had six. Then there were five saxophones, and even a tuba to deal with. When he began to look over the score a little more closely, he cursed and yelled for his wife.

"I don't know the son-of-a-bitch melody, how am I supposed to score this thing?"

She calmed him down, and sang it for him. Generoso gave Benny the score the next night. Benny did become godfather to two of Generoso's daughters, Regla and Regina.

In 1954, putting his orchestra together, Benny tried to contact Generoso but never heard back from him, presumably because Generoso was still annoyed about the bar bill. When Enrique Benítez was first introduced to Generoso, he recognized him from a show he had seen years earlier, back in 1931. Generoso had come with the Las Cruces orchestra to Vertientes. Benítez and Generoso had been introduced in Havana on New Year's of 1938. In those days Generoso was still playing piano and hadn't started playing trombone in public yet.

In June the group recorded a bolero paired with "Las mulatas del chachacha." Then a few weeks later came one of Benny's most popular boleros, which is actually a beguine. "Y hoy como ayer" would be used as the A side, matched with Enrique Benítez's *son* "Nena, me muero."

The next huge bolero was produced during a recording session in August. "¡Oh, vida!" was released as the A side to "Ya llegó la hora." For unknown reasons the studio time for these two songs was two hours, a long time for Benny. By now he could finish two three-minute songs in less than half an hour, quite a feat with so many band members and with multitrack recording still not as established as it would be at the end of the decade. Later in August Benny recorded another duet, this time with Alfredo Sadel and the Aldemaro Romero orchestra. "Y hoy como ayer" and "¡Oh, vida!" remain two of his better-known boleros, with lush horn arrangements and expert vocals.

In the same month of August, Cuba and the Latin American world heard the sad news that, two days after returning to Beverly Hills from a two-week engagement at the Tropicana, Carmen Miranda had dropped dead. Just after an appearance on the Jimmy Durante show, she died of heart failure brought on by pregnancy-induced hypertension, at forty-six. Benny had first met her in South America, and likely in Mexico. He liked her shtick and loved her movies. The "Bananas Is My Business" Portuguese-Brazilian, who was only five feet tall and more famous for her balanced fruit hats than for her samba singing, was a major contributor to keeping the tropics in the world's cultural landscape. Benny would be another of those contributors.

In November Benny recorded one of the few merengues of his career in the A side of "¡Ay! Cómo me gusta" by Chiquitín García. With all his touring to the Dominican Republic, Benny was very familiar with that country's contribution to Afro-Caribbean music, but he would return to the form just once more in the recording studio, with "El santo de tía Juliana" two years later.

The day after Christmas Benny recorded two of the greatest songs of his musical career, including his first composition to celebrate a Cuban city. Fittingly devoted to his birthplace, this great son montuno was "Santa Isabel de las Lajas." With ingenious arranging by Cabrera, the first bar of the song contains a son montuno's chunka-chunk marching beat accenting eight syllables of the town's long name, with three more syllables contained in "queri-da." The horns charge forward with several spectacular riffs. Benny sings soaringly of "my favorite place, where the men are all gentlemen and the women are all proud" and mentions all the neighborhoods of the town. As a lasting work, the song remains as brilliant as any *son* created in the 1940s or 1950s.

Another terrific song from that date contains a tongue-in- cheek public declaration, something that Benny loved to do. In "De la rumba al chachacha," the chorus "no quiero rumba, yo quiero chachacha" (I don't want rumba, I want chachacha) embodies a popular call for Benny to perform cha-cha. The song was Benny's way to proclaim his preference for *son* and rumba. The deeper significance was Benny deliberately identifying himself with his African heritage and all it did for him, by placing himself on the side of the Afro-Cuban percussion versus more European-influenced dance music. The song begins with Afro-Cuban rumba percussion and lyrics sung in Lucumí, and glides into a slinky cha-cha with one of the great Cuban trombone riffs of all time. That dizzying riff is one that Generoso wrote and would return to with his own band in 1965 in *El Trombón Majadero*. While Benny chant-sings, a chorus keeps intruding on his trance with "I don't want rumba, I want chachacha." In his teasing way, Benny manages to leverage the cha-cha's own power possibly better than any of the orchestras that specialized in that music, which at the time were most popular with upper-class white Cubans. The form's tempo is derived from ballroom danzón and its own French and Spanish ballroom origins. It is the complete opposite of the chaotic and African drumming accompanied by sexually suggestive dance moves of the three types of rumba: the guaguancó, the yambú, and the columbia.

At the time of all this new recording, Miguel Matamoros took a lady friend out for an evening of music and ended up at the Sierra, where Benny happened to be playing. Matamoros had seen him many times on television, and said that already he was the greatest singer in Cuba. When Benny found out he was in the club, he asked Miguel up to do their old duet "Olvido." The band didn't have an arrangement for it, so they sang with the piano, Miguel taking the first part and Benny the second, then swapping on the next chorus. The crowd rose for a standing ovation.

By 1954, impatient to be out of the apartment building on Oquendo, Benny had started looking around for another place to live, farther away from the action. Sometime in 1955 he bought a little two-story concrete-block house located nearly at the southern limits of Havana, in a neighborhood of modest houses called La Cumbre. For the rest of his life he never lived anywhere else.

La Cumbre was still slightly more country than city. Along with the Ali Bar, also on the farthest edge of the city, the house in La Cumbre would become synonymous with Benny. It was no accident that both locations were about as far away from the center of Havana as you could get. The Ali Bar was a good car ride away, and La Cumbre up on the heights of San Miguel del Padrón was where Benny could find peace and quiet when he wanted it. He spent a lot of time in the shade of his banana trees, and instead of taxicabs, streetcars, and city noise, he wrote to the sound of canaries singing and children playing in the neighborhood. A white concrete horse at the entrance to the barrio gives it its unofficial name, Caballo Blanco.

Benny kept a Lázaro shrine at the front entrance, with poor Lazarus leaning on his cane and the dogs beside him. The rooftop water tank lay hidden by a wall covered in colored tile, and Benny added a cross for good measure at the top of the tank frame. Off Benny's second-floor bedroom was an expanse of flat roof where he could sit on a chair and watch the sunset, or look out at the neighborhood dogs down the street chasing a car they didn't like, or kids on a bicycle. To the side of the house was a carport, but Benny's Cadillacs were too long and too wide for it, and had to be parked on the street. Benny called his prized blue Cadillac "mi pupú." The house had tile floors and, like all other casitas in Havana, could be opened from the front to the back to let the sea breezes through the iron gates. When it got too hot during the day, Benny would take his shirt off and lie on the tile floor, the coolest place in the house, and listen to the wild pigeons cooing through the window. On warm nights, they opened the side shutters to help the breezes through.

At La Cumbre the quiet and distance from the city lasted only as long as it took to raise a litter of pups, a brood of chickens, a clutch of turkeys, and a litter of pigs. Benny chose the house because it came with a yard big enough to build pens and cages, and to grow vegetables and plantains. He realized how much he had missed the happiness of his country childhood, and so he set about building his own miniature farm. After he moved into the house with Iraida, he would sit out on the patio, completely happy, listening to the songbirds he had brought from the apartment. He sipped at his rum, stubbed out a cigarette, and went inside to get paper to write down all the things he would need, while the coffeemaker hissed on the stove. Through the little window he could see the old mango tree, heavy with fruit, at the back of the property.

When deliveries of chicken wire and lumber came, Benny built cages himself for the farm animals, with a fence that could keep in a little horse or donkey. He installed boxes for the laying hens, though they would leave eggs all over the property, and sometimes the dogs would find them before he could. He bought piglets, chicks, ducklings, and got puppies from farmers in the area. He dug the long mounded rows for the cassava, potatoes, squash, and malanga. He would turn it into a proper *conuco*, a little country plot that poor guajiros worked for kitchen vegetables, and he often referred to it half seriously as Mi Conuco.

Food was an important element in this domestic phase of Benny's life. Iraida learned that he hated leftovers, but if she roasted duck in a sauce, there wouldn't be any leftovers. He loved lobster and ajiaco, a stew made with malanga, and would complain if there wasn't any tamarind juice on hand. Sometimes when he came home from a trip in the country, he would bring a wild pig to roast with sugarcane, and the scent of its rich skin brought visits from dogs and cats and neighbors. He also made *cerdo asado en púa*, spit-roasted pig done in the African manner. Another weakness was Chinese fried rice.

From his time in Mexico he had acquired a very un-Cuban taste for cayenne, and cooked an oxtail dish called *rabo encendido*, tail on fire. He grew several types of hot peppers, alongside the bananas, plantains, tomatoes, yucca, citrus. And the flowers. He raised so much in the narrow yard that it ceased to be a patio garden and became more a small farm of crops and livestock.

With Benny, leg-pulling came with the territory, especially at his house. Although his friends and music associates were long acquainted with it, visiting journalists added to his public portrait as a guajiro in the big city. More than one journalist wrote stories about how he raised animals, giving names to a litter of piglets, pointing them out and saying, "This one is Celia Cruz, that one Celeste Mendoza, and see the little fat one that's half black? That's my favorite, little Rolando Laserie. Too bad his time has come, though." He would laugh hoarsely at his own joke until he cried. Benny's country habits always played well in Cuba in the 1950s because much of the population was still new to Havana.

Benny continued to be a follower of Santería, and when something reminded him of home or his childhood, he would launch into stories about the Casino de los Congos. When he felt especially nostalgic for home, he would make a point to visit Ta Genaro in Santa Isabel de las Lajas to ask for his blessing. If the band were anywhere near Cienfuegos, he would run up to Lajas and visit everyone he had time to see at home. He looked after his Lázaro shrine, and he made offerings of tobacco and rum to his patron Bartholomew the Apostle on August twenty-fourth.

Killing the poultry to grill for guests was a relatively simple operation for a guajiro like Benny, but bleeding a young pig or a larger hog was a bit more involved. Luckily Iraida had grown up hearing pigs being slaughtered or she never would have lasted in that house. Benny did try to kill an animal when the youngest children weren't home, if possible.

When it was time to slaughter a pig, Benny did all the dirty work himself, devoting the time it took to butcher and then slowly roast the animal, adding wood to the fire for many hours. The unfortunate pig that was the center of the party may or may not have been named after one of the guests, but Benny did once invite Celeste Mendoza to a pig roast in her honor. Although Benny considered her one of his dearest friends, she was certainly more uptown than he was. When she asked him in the late 1950s why he didn't leave "this," meaning La Cumbre, and buy an apartment closer to the action as she had done, maybe one of those sleek new buildings in Vedado or on Quinta Avenida in Miramar, he told her, "Now, *mulata*, how would I raise my pigs and plantains in Vedado?"

Benny was as dedicated to the happiness of his children as he was able. After he moved to La Cumbre, he decided that he wanted to send for his first child, a girl named Hilda whom he had never met until she was nine. She had known him only from clippings sent from Mexico, and a movie publicity photograph on the living room wall where she lived with her mother, Celia Ponce, in Lajas.

Just as it had before, a nightly party followed Benny home. Before, it had been visitors stopping by for a late-night drink, artists ringing the bell, singers, editors, producers, and drinking buddies out in the front hall with the shutters open. Now at La Cumbre visitors could stay as long as they wanted, and sometimes they slept over—if they slept at all. The bedrooms upstairs lay in the direct line of noise, guitar playing, singing, smoke, and smells from late-night cooking Benny would do when the urge hit. And once the animals were old enough to add their noise, La Cumbre turned out to be as chaotic as living in the city. With all the noise and lights burning, the roosters often crowed late at night from their roosts. The pigs squealed and argued, the turkeys gobbled. Of course the dogs were noisy, anytime someone arrived, and fought over bones someone threw in the yard. Or if a strange dog from the street made the mistake of peeking in the front gate, a torrent of noise poured through the house. And as time went on, increasingly La Cumbre was where Benny slept off the rum from the night before, rarely rising before early afternoon.

In July the band played out in Santiago and then, after returning to Havana, left for their first full tour outside Cuba. Cuban *son* was still very popular throughout the Americas, and music fans in many of the somewhat isolated countries like Colombia, Venezuela, and Panama were hungry for any outside music, especially big bands from Cuba. American big-band jazz was still popular, but rock and roll had yet to enter the popular culture of Latin America and the Caribbean. These were Spanish-language songs and rhythms they knew, and Central and South American fans were very excited to see the man who had sung with Pérez Prado. Benny took twelve of the musicians from the band, but not Cabrerita, who was replaced by Felipe Llanes. The first stop was Kingston, Jamaica. There—as everywhere they went in the Caribbean, in exciting colonial cities or impossibly beautiful tourist destinations—people already knew all of Benny's records and packed every venue.

Benny and the Banda Gigante went next to the black republic of Haiti, which had become a tourist destination under the dictator Paul Magloire, who had seized power in 1950. Nearing the end of his reign, Magloire threw endless parties and was a lavish entertainer. On another tour to Haiti, Benny is said to have made Magloire and his ministers wait at a big party at his farm while Benny played a guitar for young children in a very poor neighborhood. Barreto, Celso Gómez, and Rabanito had to go find him. He told them that he couldn't leave such "poor things" and, so the story goes, they didn't see Benny again until the 6 a.m. flight back to Havana.

The band took a Braniff flight down to Panama, where the other great Cuban singer, Cascarita, was also playing. Benny's old friend met them at the airport and the two posed for press photographs. Benny was well known in Panama from his tours with Pérez Prado and from records going as far back as the 1940s. The band's first dates were in Colón. In a city that loved Benny as much as he loved to be there, the band appeared at the same types of venues as back home: live radio, outdoor concerts, large dances, and theaters. The tour then proceeded to Panama City.

At this point in his professional life Benny had taken many airplanes, beginning back in 1945 with Matamoros, but from the beginning he was frightened of dying in a plane crash, and he would never cease to dread each flight. Granted, flying in those days was glamorous and not within the budget of average travelers. For male passengers anywhere in the world, flying had its "coffee, tea, or me" allure: pretty stewardesses in pencil skirts and heels, who carried cocktails and bumped seductively against the wealthy, jet-setting men who made up the majority of passengers. This certainly helped relieve the fear of flying somewhat, but Benny still loathed air travel. Glamorous or not, flying in the early days was loud and not particularly comfortable, and pilots were less able to avoid the violent effects of storms. Benny once told his brother Teo that he had been in three airplane accidents, one in California, another in Jamaica, and the last in Manzanillo. During the one in Manzanillo he was certain he would die. Very shaken by the experience, he said that at least that would have occurred on Cuban soil, and not over water where his body would never be found.

The band continued on to South America, first to the coastal city of Cartagena, Colombia, where they played live at the Riomar radio station, the theaters Miramar and Padilla, and the Tahiti restaurant. Next they traveled up the coast to Barranquilla, and then inland to the mile-high city of Medellín, nestled in an isolated valley in Antioquia. The seventeenth-century city was decades away from being known as the dangerous cocaine traffic base, and was still a sleepy town. On August 4 they played an early evening radio show. That night before the show at the Club Campestre, Benny went AWOL for the second time on the trip. As everywhere, he could never turn down a party, and with so many people excited by his music, he never said no to another drink or another drunken request to sing with a borrowed guitar. Several weeks of this had taken its toll, and that night Fernando and Enrique had to cover as best they could with Benny either catatonic drunk or off on an adventure.

Finally they arrived at Caracas, capital of Venezuela. Although the shows there went as well as everywhere else, Benny was about to have the worst moment of his entire career. This came at a time when it seemed that nothing bad would ever happen to him, and unfortunately the incident had an effect on the band itself. In some ways, he would never have as good a band as he had before the run-in with Max Pérez.

Pérez was the promoter for the shows in Venezuela. When Benny went to collect the band's share of the proceeds of the concerts, reportedly Pérez had altered the receipts and offered him a far smaller amount than was promised. Pérez, whose real name was Max Jordan, had a history of pulling the same stunt on other Cuban groups. He was said to have been a boxer, and if so, he certainly would have intimidated those he cheated. Benny returned the next day and asked again, saying that with such popular shows there must have been plenty in the take to cover his contracted rates. Again Pérez refused. Benny said that if Pérez would just pay the band what they had earned, he would forgo his own share. Benny was already known for paying his musicians scale rates or better; he often paid more against the advice of other bandleaders. Because of the way he treated them, his band members were extremely loyal, and most forgave him his lateness and disappearances. His own loyalty to the guys went deep. It was the protectiveness of a big brother who rushes out angrily to fight a bully who has picked on his younger siblings.

With this resolve and a little something extra, Benny returned the next day. Under his arm he carried a metal rod hidden in gift paper. The menacing Pérez may have expected the wrapping paper to contain conciliatory flowers, but instead he received a rather nasty little gift. When he again refused to pay, Benny ended the disagreement by attacking Pérez with the rod and knocking him unconscious with several blows to the head and ribs. Benny admitted later that he had fractured Pérez's skull in four places and sent him to the hospital. His status as a rising international star notwithstanding, the local police arrived at his hotel a few hours later and took him into custody. According to his brother Teo, Benny had only "defended himself," but the police regarded the matter very seriously. It was almost completely out of character for Benny to be violent, but he was Cuban, and Cubans themselves often say that, while they are slow to anger, they are loyal to a fault and, once their temper is aroused, they make bad enemies.

Local and Cuban newspapers covered the incident for some time. While Benny sat in custody for a week, the guys went without pay. Luckily the pianist Bola de Nieve, whom Benny had first met in Mexico, was in the country at the same time and heard the news. Apparently he knew the national chief of police and appealed to him for help, as well as to the secretary general of the national musicians' union, Alfredo Sadel. In what happened next, the entire band may or may not have taken part, but Benny was pardoned by Venezuelan president Marcos Pérez Jiménez after playing a private show at his residence.

Benny's version is simply that Pérez wouldn't pay and had the reputation of stiffing his artists, and Benny was determined not to be one of those artists. He called it the worst experience in his entire life as a musician. In the end Benny wasn't proud of it, but the incident put other promoters on notice for the rest of his career and added to his popular image in the media.

It is unclear whether the band members had to fend for themselves or had return tickets to get home. Benny does seem to have gone back to Cuba after the others, and he may have paid a short visit to the United States after the Venezuela episode.

When Benny made it back to Havana, he fielded several interesting offers to go out on tour as a solo artist. Late in 1955 he did so, reportedly for lucrative appearances as a singer with pickup local bands.

The Banda Gigante lost several well-paying shows during the holidays as a result of Benny's absence. Many of his musicians were angry. Most had families to support, so they had to look for other work. The way Benny had talked about how he loved his time in Mexico, and with the crowds adoring him, some of them wondered if Benny would come back at all—wherever he had gone. They already knew his tendency to disappear. Wherever he went in Latin America or South America, he could find work through his connection to the all-important RCA Victor, so he had ample means to stay away indefinitely. When the guys had trickled back to Havana after the episode in

Venezuela, Generoso took over control as music director from Chocolate, but he didn't have a group to direct for long.

In February Benny resurfaced in Havana. Full of stories and excited, he called Generoso one afternoon out of the blue and yelled to pack his bags and call the guys because he had a great gig for the band, Carnival in Caracas, with all kinds of radio and dance shows. The best part? They were booked on a live Venezuelan television show called *Manteca Carnaval*. When Benny realized that Generoso hadn't responded, he said, "Come on, Negro, call up the band, we have to get ready!" Generoso asked him what band he meant, since he didn't have one anymore. In his unexplained long absence some of the horn players had left, and there wasn't a rhythm section either. When Benny finally understood, he told Generoso to find everyone who was able to go in two days. He was sure that they could put together enough of a group to play the gigs in Caracas. Players would jump at the chance, he said, and hung up abruptly.

In the end, Generoso was right. Benny no longer had a Banda Gigante. Not only that, but most other likely musicians in town with orchestra experience were long booked into bands with so many shows they couldn't play them all. It was Carnival season, after all, and that year was the busiest Havana had ever been.

Benny wasn't so worried about finding new musicians, but the loss of key players did cause disorganization for some time. Fernando Álvarez had left for what was to be a fine solo career with the Conjunto Casino. Rolando Laserie didn't just leave Benny's group but left drumming completely and had a much bigger career as a singer. Cabrerita had left as piano player, though Alberto Limonta, Chico Piquero, Tabaquito, and Conde Negro remained. Limonta took over for Chocolate as band spokesman.

They found a full enough band to tour with, but few of the new musicians knew the charts for the live shows. They were all seasoned musicians and were more than adept at loose playing of *son*, son montunos, and Benny's hits, but the group that they assembled didn't get a full practice before they had to leave. It took longer than Benny had anticipated to get replacement players who could commit. One standout they were very fortunate to get was the virtuoso trumpet player Alejandro Vivar to take the place of Chocolate. Nicknamed El Negro, Vivar was the next best lead trumpeter on the island and was an excellent veteran of the jazz descarga scene. Generoso's brother

Pedro Jiménez, José Aníbal "Mayía" Martínez, and Domingo Corbacho (who stayed from the original band) made up the rest of the trumpets. Santiago, one of the Peñalver brothers, played alto saxophone. His brother Cosmito on tenor stayed with the band, and so did Celso Gómez. René "Musiquito" Aiyón joined them, and Roberto Barreto. They no longer had the baritone sax in Virgilio Vixama. Felipe Llanes was still the regular pianist, but he couldn't leave a job when the time came for the the shows in Venezuela, so Rolando "Plomito" Colombié was hired for that spot. Miguelito Cuní came along as a guest singer.

They flew to Caracas on February 8, the day before their shows, so that they could practice, but they were delayed either by weather or by the search for musicians, so the six songs Generoso had set aside never got properly practiced by the assembled band. They played successfully in shows at the Coney Island, Club Claro de Luna, and Los Palos Grandes, but on the live television show *Manteca Carnaval*, not expecting to go so long, they ran out of Generoso's arrangements. They had already played their entire prepared repertoire twice. In this case, it was an embarrassing bad surprise, but it had a very good ending.

With the cameramen frantically waving their arms and signaling that they should play ten minutes more, Generoso walked over to Rolando Colombié and told him to play something in F, anything, just to play. Columbié improvised a little melody. It wasn't even a real *guajejo* that a Cuban pianist plays as a repeated line to add texture for a rhythm section, but it was enough to work with. Limonta came in with a bass line in step with the piano. Benny had moved off camera for a moment, and the percussion section automatically began: congas, timbales, Enrique on claves, and Muela scratching his guiro. Generoso signaled the horn section, and the trumpets and saxes played along with Colombié's riff. Generoso fell in with the horns, and Benny began to improvise with the first thing he thought of to buy a little time: Castellanos, how good you dance!

"¡Castellano,' qué bueno baila usted!"

Muela moved into the center-stage light and did a few of his famous dance steps. Then Benny looked around at Generoso and called into the microphone:

"¡Generoso, qué bueno toca usted!" He pointed his chin at Generoso, who replied:

"¡Benny Moré, qué banda tiene usted!"

The chorus picked up Generoso's line. Like a dixieland jazz band, they all improvised in a loose but forward motion. The next thing they knew, the credits were rolling in the monitors and sound guys were clapping and yelling and slapping Benny on the back.

They didn't record the song until a year and a half later. By then they had played it as a part of their live shows for so long, and to such overwhelming enthusiasm from every person who heard it, that they changed hardly anything from the descarga it had always been. In the studio Generoso added a few colors here and there, a trumpet solo and his own magnificent trombone solo, but little else. The chorus echoed Benny's calling of the "qué bueno" lines.

While Castellanos's and Generoso's names would be remembered throughout the world of Hispanic music because of this song, it was the muscular and lithe solo Generoso played that would influence trombone players in Latin music and jazz for the next fifty years and more. The released version of the song swings with such breathtaking joy that it leaves you lightheaded.

On all of their frequent trips to San Juan, Puerto Rico, the band stayed in the lovely Condado neighborhood. On one of those trips Benny did a radio interview, and the next afternoon he went with some of the guys to see Viejo San Juan, which in some ways was even more beautiful than Habana Vieja because the Spanish built the Puerto Rican old city on the heights of an imposing set of hills. The following day Benny went to see the fort called El Morro, where in the strong trade winds children fly hundreds of kites every Sunday afternoon on the vast plain in front of the fort where cannons still point downward to cover the harbor.

"Damn! Isn't this better than church?" he told Castellanos, who was trying to bribe a kid to let him use his kite. "These people just know how to use a perfectly good Sunday, right?"

For the rest of the tour the band lost El Negro Vivar, who had to fly back for other obligations. They traveled to Florida to play for cigar rollers in the Keys. Everyone was amazed by the drive up from the Keys, the views of blue-green water and mangroves from the Seven Mile Bridge. Although Miami wasn't the center for Cuban culture it would become very soon, they played a full show at the Miami auditorium and then drove up through the snake and cowboy country and palmettos along the Florida Gulf Coast to play a show at the Círculo Cubano in Tampa. Generoso had been able to get away from his duties with the police band to go to Venezuela but couldn't travel to Florida.

Also sometime in 1956 Benny went before the cameras in the only feature film he ever shot in Cuba, *No Me Olvides Nunca*, starring Rosita Fornés and Luis Aguilar, directed by Juan José Ortega. A publicity shot shows bolero diva Olga Guillot with arms outstretched and singing "Vete" in front of the full band. Benny meekly directs the band with a little conductor's baton. Although he would soon leave the band, Chocolate was still with him and appeared in the film along with the other band members. Guillot sang like a Cuban Dinah Washington, with full range and powerful delivery, and her *Vete* was a treat for the moviegoers who saw it.

One thing that no one in the band, or even Benny's closest friends, knew at the time was that Benny and Juana Bocanegra had gotten legally divorced in the Havana city court at the beginning of 1956. A connection with Benny's mysterious absences in the period after his return from the misadventure in Venezuela seems inescapable. Yet somehow the news of his divorce apparently didn't make it into the newspapers, and neither his friends and bandmates nor Norayda ever heard about it, though Iraida may well have known. Benny didn't feel in the least bittersweet over the divorce, and knew it was better for everyone involved. Juana had given him the legal status to remain in Mexico, and had supported him through the lean times until he began to work, but then she had kept from him the news of his grandmother's death. Although many people were under the impression that Benny and Juana were still married because she spent so much time in Havana, and even acted as a kind of stepmother to young Hilda, they divorced quietly on January 13. Benny was so happy over his release from her drama that he didn't at all care if he went to Venezuela with half a band.

Like Generoso, Chocolate was one of those musicians left behind when Benny went off by himself to Venezuela who didn't suffer for lack of work. He had been very busy with studio jobs with the CMQ orchestra, was also working with the great Chico O'Farrill, and participated in many of the descargas led and recorded by Cachao. O'Farrill, Cachao, and Bebo Valdés, like Chocolate, were at the forefront of the greatest Cuban musicians who leaned a little farther over toward jazz. By the revolution, all four would leave Cuba. But at that time, the descargas went on every single night and included dozens of musicians. The only competition for RCA Victor was Panart. Its Cuban owner, Ramón Sabat, had made a good amount of money on the recordings and spread the gospel of Cuban music far and wide. In 1957 Sabat sold a million records around the world, even though inside Cuba the descargas were known only to the musicians who played in them. Julio Gutiérrez, tres player Niño Rivera, José Fajardo, and others were also involved. Cuban American producer and filmmaker Nat Chediak would later say of the Panart recordings that "those jam sessions are five of the finest Cuban records of all time." Sabat believed that these were the best records he ever made.

Benny did at times show up at descargas, but generally he stuck to dealing with his own shows and hanging out afterward. Although most nightclub owners knew it was worth putting up with Benny, his drinking and fooling around cost him some gigs, most notably at the Tropicana, where he never had a long run until that November. He had played the Tropicana for one-night shows many times, but the club's booking manager Alberto Ardura assumed that Benny would never be able to keep to the demanding on-time schedule.

Finally in November 1956 Benny did get to play a two-week run at the Mambi Room of the Tropicana. The owner's wife, Ofelia Fox, interceded on Benny's behalf after he promised her that he wouldn't let any misbehavior get in the way of doing the shows. The acts manager Ardura gave in and booked the band for three nightly shows, at 10:30, midnight, and 2 a.m. After the last show, Benny would unwind with a drink or two for the road at the open-air bar. Back in March in that same spot, Benny had had a longtime dream fulfilled: to meet Nat King Cole when the American star paid his annual late-winter visit to the Tropicana. Benny, Enrique, and other musicians had a drink with Cole at the Bajo las Estrellas, where everyone knew him. Benny was dying to tell Cole how he once paid $200 to see his jazz show at the Teatro Puerto Rico in the Bronx.

Ofelia Fox loved Benny's music as much as she loved her own exotic pets: an African lion, a succession of monkeys, and a cat named Negrito. For her thirty-fourth birthday in 1954, her husband had given her a white Cadillac Eldorado with its own 14- carat gold key. Martin himself wore a 13-carat diamond ring. The cheap buffets in the Las Vegas casinos would never be able to compete with the glamour and energy and creativity embodied in a place like the Tropicana. When Benny had his first long run at the Mambi Room,

Martin Fox was completing plans for a partnership with Cubana Airlines for his Tropicana Special. A custom-designed airplane fitted with a miniature Tropicana stage and featuring dancing girls and daiquiris, the Tropicana Special left Miami every Thursday for the one-hour flight. For $68 you got entrance with dinner and drinks at the Tropicana, one free night at a hotel with breakfast, and the return flight.

On New Year's Eve of 1956, the extraordinary bingo prizes over at the Sans Souci were six brand-new 1957 automobiles, some of the most desirable models sought by collectors to this day: a Cadillac, an Olds, a Buick, a Mercedes, a Pontiac, and a Chevy. At the Nacional, the Parisien casino and nightclub had finally opened, and the noise of the slots competed with the music.

Unfortunately, on that New Year's Eve bombs went off in the Bajo las Estrellas bar of the Tropicana and in other cabarets around town, detonated by guerrillas working for the revolutionary cause headed by Fidel Castro and Ernesto Guevara. A seventeen-year-old girl lost her arm in the explosion at the Tropicana. In October, radical students had assassinated Colonel José Blanco Rico, the head of Batista's feared military intelligence service, at the Montmartre.

These and other attacks around the country shook those who were directly affected by them, but others who should have been paying closer attention, like Meyer Lansky, were certain that their investments were safe. Still, just in case, mob members and club owners like Martin Fox at the Tropicana were secretly giving money to Castro guerrillas.

Benny's irregular schedule, and his disappearances for parts unknown, occasioned continuing personnel changes. By the end of 1956 the band consisted of the following musicians:

Lázaro Valdés, piano
Mauro Gómez Suárez, saxophone
René "Musiquito" Aiyón, saxophone
Fernán Vincent, tenor saxophone
Diego Loredo, saxophone
José Aníbal Martínez, trumpet
Jorge Varona, trumpet
Pedro Rodríguez, trumpet

Pedro Jiménez, trumpet
Generoso Jiménez, trombone
Ramón Caturla, bass
Jesús González, drums
Clemente "Chico" Piquero, bongos
Jesús López, congas
Enrique Benítez, chorus
Gil Ramírez, chorus
Delfín Moré, chorus
Alfonso Eliseo, chorus
Israel Castellanos, guiro, various

All those band membership changes couldn't have helped Benny's record output for that year. In all of 1956, he was able to manage only three or four songs. All were hits, but he got behind in his contract to RCA. He had also lost Chocolate by the time he arrived for the only session of the year in August, and so he had no one to crack the whip anymore.

Generoso began to work as Benny's main arranger in the wake of a Benny-induced emergency. With Cabrera gone, Benny had been able to get Rolando Columbié to take piano, but he now had no dedicated arranger. One night Benny screeched his brakes in front of Generoso's place on San Indalecio in Cerro, and banged on the door in a panic.

"Compadre, what's more blood to the man who's already committed murder?"

Generoso opened the door and asked Benny what hell he was talking about.

"Those motherfuckers! I owe them eighteen new songs! You gotta help!" Benny told him, pushing his way in. He dropped a huge file of song material on the table.

Generoso lifted the cover with a finger. He wasn't about to promise anything. He knew Benny's lack of concern for his RCA contracts, so if Benny thought he was in trouble, he was probably in a real bind.

Already well aware of what Benny's work methods meant for arrangers, Generoso would only commit to looking at the folder, which contained fifty songs in various stages of completion. After Generoso looked over the pile of sheet music that night, he told Benny he would help him, but only for those songs he thought were worth his time and effort. Eighteen songs was a lot, and Generoso couldn't find that many in the pile, which meant looking for more—yet another crapshoot.

In a nightclub in Marianao they went to meet Alberto Barreto, a writer Israel Castellanos had told Generoso about. From Barreto they got "Corazón rebelde." They also found "Elige tú, que canto yo" by Joseíto Fernández after an all-night party in front of a fire station. They ended up collecting songs for much of 1956 and into 1957, and recorded them as fast as they could. In addition to all that Castellanos did with the band, he also acted as a talent scout and had been responsible for Benny recording several important songs, the two they got from Barreto and "Dolor y perdón."

On an afternoon in August the band recorded the next of Benny's Cuban city tributes, the guajira "Cienfuegos," as well as the son montuno "Compay José," the bolero "Mi corazón lloró," and one other track that has become a bit of a mystery. The song was the Tony Martínez composition "Bacalao con papa." Instead of the usual music rights ownership by Peer International, publishing rights for the song were owned by Mills Music, since Martínez was the author. Intriguingly, although the Benny Moré orchestra is listed as recording the song, RCA recording notes mention "From the film *Rock Around the Clock*." For that soundtrack released in March of 1956, New York bandleader Tony Martínez provided several other compositions, and he had an acting role in the film. The Puerto Rico–born Martínez had a long Hollywood career as Pepino in the television series *The Real McCoys* and he played Don Quijote's sidekick Sancho Panza on Broadway in *Man of La Mancha*. Martínez had also led a salsa group in New York and was a good singer and vibes player. It is unclear what plans RCA producers had for Benny's "Bacalao." Unfortunately, all other information about this cut has been lost. Even if "Bacalao" had been released in Cuba as a flip side to one of the other three songs from that year, surviving copies of original 78s or 45s of "Cienfuegos" or any other release from this time are extremely rare. However, "Cienfuegos" was released as the A to "Mi corazón lloró" in both 45 and 78, and "Cienfuegos" also was released as a B to "Compay José." This suggests that rights issues didn't permit a release of Benny's version of "Bacalao," or that the cut was never meant for release at all.

THIRTEEN

Recordings, Tours, 1957–1959

It wasn't only legal gambling opportunities that in 1957 attracted 300,000 tourists across the Florida Strait and from Europe. They arrived ready for the vice and sin they had heard so much about. The music and the exquisite clubs served as atmospheric backdrop, and as one evening's entertainment for a man down visiting with his wife. Men who came alone or with buddies were much more interested in what went on in the many houses of prostitution, the live sex acts, and the naughty burlesque shows.

There were more 1956 Chevrolet sedans on the road in Cuba, it seemed, than donkey carts pulling loads of cut cane. Wealthy white Cubans frequented many of the best-known clubs and shows, but unlike the North American visitors, they went to dance to the orchestras. Americans jammed the most famous locales like the Tropicana and Sans Souci but didn't often dance, except for shuffling along behind a drunken conga line. Finding most basic Cuban dance steps beyond their skills, many American visitors went home to enroll in lessons for their next visit. Whether they danced or not, Americans down for a weekend still got an earful of Cuban music and an eyeful of the female Cuban form at the major clubs—both in the long-legged chorus girls and in much racier shows.

The houses of prostitution were busy offering up everything a 1950s husband or bachelor couldn't possibly find back in uptight postwar Eisenhower America. What those men wanted as a warm-up was strip shows like those at the Shanghai Theater in Chinatown where, after the fully nude burlesque acts, hard-core porn films screened at a charge of $1.25 for the most expensive seats and 65 cents for sharing a bench in the balcony. The films were quite shocking by 1950s mores—so shocking, in fact, that it was standing room only for three shows every night while the hushed and sweating audiences watched transfixed. Up to a thousand people filled the Shanghai for each show. Women visitors, too, couldn't resist the whispered stories about the films and the acts beforehand, which were vaudeville-style skits and gags, but with nudity. From time to time, brave and curious women off the cruise chips arrived in groups. They wore masks while they sat in special seating at the side of the theater.

Cuban José Orozco García, who ran the Shanghai, complained that his biggest problem was finding enough women to dance and perform in the pornographic live show before the blue films ran. Little did he know, when he crowed in 1956, "We only close for revolutions," that the revolution would soon ride him out of town on a rail.

The Shanghai filled every night with all races, and not only tourists. Most of those men stumbled out afterward and tumbled directly into the cathouses. Havana alone had at least 270 houses of prostitution, offering more than 11,500 girls and women. The largest and most expensive was Casa de Marina, but if a man wanted an encounter with a black girl, he went to Casa de Violeta. Just off the main tourist artery of Prado was the Colón red-light district where men on a budget strolled along streets named Trocadero (place of commerce), Animas (souls), and Virtudes (virtues—or, in slang, penises) to choose from the women who beckoned from doorways and windows. Another, newer red-light district was Barrio de la Victoria, where, as a *Stag* magazine article put it, everyone wins. For women visitors who themselves wanted a little adventure with a handsome Cuban man, gigolos were commonly employed as "dance partners." Many women who arrived alone or with other women friends on cruise ships yearned for an experience with the fabled Latin Lover. Plenty did more than yearn. Americans who visited Cuba acted like bears at a salmon spawning run.

Other places where men could watch racier shows than at the Tropicana or the Sans Souci included the Colonial and the Palette Club, the latter of which had private rooms in the back.

For tamer entertainment, tourists in mixed company might go to the Bambú, the Panchín, the Pennsylvania, or the Southland Club. These had excellent music and often food as well, and usually slot machines. Benny and most other conjuntos and orchestras played all of them from time to time. For the food and wine of Spain, tourists went to the Taberna San Román, El Colmao, and the Tasca Española. The Sevilla-Biltmore's little piano lounge called the Carnival Room was good for a quiet drink and music. Its lovely interior courtyard with fountains and palms was a welcome place to get away from Prado, and a good spot to watch for celebrities.

The tourists packed famous bars like the Floridita on Obispo, whose secret ingredient for a frozen daiquiri was a tablespoon of grapefruit juice. Much of its fame came from Ernest Hemingway, who went there often while he was living just outside Havana in the 1940s and 1950s. Hemingway also made La Bodeguita del Medio famous; there he reportedly wrote on the wall: "mi mojito en La Bodeguita, mi daiquiri en El Floridita." Another famous writer, Graham Greene, was also partial to the crabs and daiquiris served at the Floridita.

More adventurous tourists went to Johnny's Dream Club, in a pleasant location along the Almendares River, or to Mes Amis when they wanted to get off the beaten track. El Dorado on Prado had its own attraction: an all-woman orchestra. Quite a few of the open-air cafes along Prado like El Dorado or El Mirador had all-woman orchestras; the most famous was Anacaona, which once had Graciela Pérez as a singer.

January of 1957 began as a month of bombings, sabotage, kidnappings, and train derailments all across the island. Brutal crackdowns followed. In March came an attack on the presidential palace itself, in the middle of the day. It became dangerous to travel outside Havana, but the casinos and pleasure houses were as busy as ever, and no place that separated tourists from their dollars ever closed.

In 1957 Benny really picked up the pace of recording and, with the help of Generoso and other arrangers, cleared much of the backlog he had built up in his contract with RCA Victor. As he always had, he worked with Cabrera, Pedro "Peruchín" Jústiz, and Generoso the way the Beatles would later with classically trained musicians, humming parts and knowing exactly what he wanted but needing a translator to get the ideas from his head onto paper.

Regardless of where he played as a "last show," Benny's favorite place to end up was Alipio García's Ali Bar far out on avenida Dolores, practically outside the city and known to very few tourists. It was a very late-night place, the kind where musicians hung out after their own gigs and foreign musicians went when they wanted to see Benny play. Both Frank Sinatra and Nat King Cole had visited, and the pretty "vedette" Candita Vázquez sometimes performed on the bill with Benny. Across the road was the Cuatro Ruedas, another bar that also served food. Benny said often that the Ali Bar was his favorite place to play, and he is synonymous with the club. It was a bit rustic, had a thatched palm frond roof, red and green lights on strings around rough-sawn columns, and plank tables that probably seated no more than twenty groups. The club is now called El Rincón de Benny. It books music again, and contains a small collection of artifacts Benny owned.

A normal weekend run might include the Ali Bar on Saturday night, El Sierra on Sunday, Night and Day, or a matinee at the Cristino Naranjo. At the Ali Bar, Benny gave a hand to Ibrahim Ferrer, then a struggling singer who had relocated to Havana from Santiago. Not only had Benny helped Ferrer get work by talking to Alipio García but, Ferrer said, Benny had defended him against his own bass player, Alberto Limonta. Limonta, who was responsible for paying the musicians, stiffed Ferrer for a night's singing. Ferrer was young, but Benny knew he had children at home and needed the work, so Benny, who always paid well, was very angry when he found out. He gave Ferrer money from his own pocket and then told Limonta he no longer was the paymaster. Although the punishment for cheating Ferrer was merely to give the slightly better pay to another band member for taking care of band business, it was the closest Benny had ever come to a firing. By 1957 or 1958 Limonta seems no longer to have been a regular band member.

In 1957 the Mexican screen actor and singer Pedro Infante was killed in a plane crash. Benny had known him in Mexico City. When he heard the news, it only gave him more reason to be nervous about flying.

After several trips with José Fajardo to the Teatro Puerto Rico in Manhattan, Chocolate was able to play again with Machito, and he saw the two mambo kings Tito Puente and Tito Rodríguez. He moved to New York in April and, after going back and forth, stayed there for good from 1960 on. And why wouldn't he? Machito had hired him, and "Choco" sat next to Doc Cheatham, one of the greats of American trumpet. He got to know Miles Davis, Dizzy Gillespie, John Coltrane, and has since recorded and played with every salsa musician of note. Whenever their schedules permitted, Chocolate would go see Benny when he came to New York.

If Benny hadn't been so afraid of flying, he might have become nearly as well known around the world as his old boss Dámaso. Intercontinental flights were an established fact of world travel. Although he could have taken an ocean liner to Europe to tour there, and promoters often invited him, he never crossed the Atlantic. Actual tours across the United States would have been unlikely, since the markets for his music were concentrated in New York, with its populations of Cubans and Puerto Ricans, and in California, with Cubans and Chicanos. Miami in the 1950s was largely undeveloped and had few Spanish-speaking fans of Cuban music. Other cities like Denver, El Paso, Chicago, and elsewhere could have supported a few days of shows of the Banda Gigante, but this never happened. For most Americans, Benny was someone you were lucky enough to have seen while on a visit to Havana. Unfortunately Benny never said yes to offers to go to France and England, and Franco's control over Spain meant that Benny wouldn't become famous there until after Franco's—and his own—death.

Around this time, Benny had also become friends with Kid Chocolate, the Hall of Fame featherweight boxer who had retired in 1938 and returned to Havana from the United States. Known as a heavy drinker, he lived on avenida 58 near calle 17 in the Marianao neighborhood close to where Benny got Virginia a little house on avenida 44. Born Eligio Sardinias Montalvo and nicknamed the Cuban Bon Bon, Kid Chocolate held world titles at junior lightweight and lightweight, and he and Benny had a lot to talk about. Alfredo Armenteros's nickname Chocolate had come from the boxer, and the trumpeter Chocolate wasn't about to complain when someone once mistook him for Kid Chocolate. When Benny came by to see Virginia at the house on avenida 44, he and Kid Chocolate would drink in a bar next to the Ambassador Theater, or in a very small bar upstairs on avenida 29. By 1957 Kid Chocolate and Benny were the two most famous black men in Cuba.

No matter how big he got, there were some places that Benny would never be contracted, including the Vedado Tennis Club, the Miramar Yacht Club, and the Havana Country Club. Nor was he asked by the Club Atenas, a social club formed in 1919 for blacks and mulattos, because they considered *son* an embarrassment to the race. Things had loosened up since the night in 1937 when audience members at the Sans Souci walked out as Batista and his family sat down for a show, but some things in Cuba would never change. Racism still hung on in Cuba long after Castro rode into town in a jeep with a Thompson submachine gun on his lap.

For recordings in 1957, Benny was able to manage a very ambitious number, twenty-nine in all. Even if he had only recorded his splendid "Qué bueno baila usted," it would have been good news for the future of Latin music. He also finished at least ten of his best songs, including the Enrique Benítez guaracha "El Conde Negro" and another by Benny called "Se te cayó el tabaco." "El Conde Negro" is Benítez boasting how he is surrounded by "un mar de pollos," a sea of chicks, and how women call him Conde Negro. Another by Benny was the intricate and irresistible son montuno "Caricias cubanas." His old writer and pianist Cabrera provided him with "Marianao," a son montuno that made men want to move to that barrio of Havana for the beautiful women celebrated in the lyrics. Cabrera's "Manigua" was yet another brilliant song from that year, celebrating "el tresero de manigua," the tres player who comes from the bush, meaning the best there is.

One of the most unusual *sones* Benny ever did was "Mulata con cola." The lyrics speak nonsensically about needing to find money "to buy a delicious suckling pig" and other "tasty things" like shrimp, "like a lobster tail." Maybe a "nice little mulatto girl," all the better if she's a rumba dancer and "has a nice lobster tail." Tatyana Praino, daughter of singer Rudy Calzado and former road manager for Mario Bauzá, once mock-complained that "Cuban music is all about two things—sex and food!" "Mulata con cola" managed to contain both subjects at the same time.

Among the songs identified with Benny, "Francisco Guayabal" also came from 1957. Written by Pío Leyva, the stirring son montuno featured an arrangement by Bebo Valdés.

Another driving guaracha, "Trátame como soy," came from Pedro Brunet. Benny even recorded a plena, the Puerto Rican form, and sang with the Benítez brothers on "Dolor y pena." He also recorded a bolero with them on the flip side of that song, "No te atrevas."

Benny would never equal this output again, though he would manage a few more of his best-known songs after 1957. Through 1958 the band in various forms continued tours outside the country, first to Panama and then to the Dominican Republic, Jamaica, and Peru.

The English writer Graham Greene saw publication in 1958 of his comic novel *Our Man in Havana*, but the movie didn't appear until 1960, when the atmosphere in Havana described in the story was already history.

This was a period of apocryphal stories about Benny. One goes that while on tour in Colombia at a show that few people attended, Benny decided they would play for themselves. Seeing a bottle of whiskey, Benny told the audience that he was a rum drinker and nothing else. Another story has Benny in Placetas, the town of the Banda Gigante's first public appearance, luring people out from a casino into a bar where he was playing guitar to spite a manager angry that Benny hadn't shown up until very late. Benny, so the story goes, attracted so many people that the manager told him he could give the concert after all, but Benny now said he would play only if all his new friends from the bar could come in free of charge. A final story, which probably contains the least truth, comes from Naser's book. It relates that Benny was playing a show in Sancti Spíritus when Batista was present, and Batista asked for a song, but Benny refused. Eventually he sang "Es mi madre," which Batista assumed Benny was singing for his wife. Benny "firmly corrected" him and said that he was only playing that song for his own mother, Virginia.

One thing that couldn't be exaggerated was the menace Benny posed to society when he got behind the wheel of an automobile. With all the drinking that went on, and Benny's habit of not looking at the road while he drove, he was much better off with someone else driving. But Israel wasn't always available. It was a miracle that Benny didn't get in any major accidents. People who recognized him or knew him personally were constantly shouting out, especially when he was in the convertible, so he would wave and yell back. He also slowed down for anything that caught his eye. He gave many karate chops to Generoso's elbow to take notice of a woman walking along the sidewalk, or a car he liked. One morning sometime after Generoso began arranging, as they were returning from the Ali Bar after a very long night of power drinking, Benny crashed the convertible into the front of the hospital's emergency room. The two of them were seeing double from rum and exhaustion. Luckily neither was injured, and the solid Cadillac had only to visit the body shop to be made new again.

In the course of 1958, Benny was able to finish twelve songs. In April he did four sides, including "Camarera del amor" and "Maracaibo oriental." On October 13 he recorded only two songs, but they were "Soy campesino" and the stunning "Mi amor fugaz." Then a week later the band recorded "El santo de tía Juliana," notable for being a good merengue, "Tumba tumbador," "Así es la humanidad," and three boleros including "Mi padre," the father's version of his song from the year before, "Por una madre."

Of Benny's many successes that year, "Camarera del amor" and "Mi amor fugaz" remain two of the greatest songs ever recorded by a big band in Cuba. Along with "Maracaibo," they still sound as exciting and contemporary as the afternoons they were recorded at CMQ studios. "Mi amor fugaz" has a darkly beautiful breakneck introduction that sets up Benny's soaring, dizzying, and completely operatic performance. It is arguably his finest bolero out of the sixty or so he recorded, followed by "Encantado de la vida," "Como fue," "Y hoy como ayer," and "¡Oh, vida!" Not only is "Mi amor fugaz" among his personal best, it is possibly the best performance on any bolero in the annals of Cuban music.

In the same session as "Mi amor fugaz," Benny recorded another song that is often overlooked in the many collections of his music, "Soy campesino," written by Senén Suárez. The exuberant son montuno is a breathtaking and fitting vehicle for Benny. It can be taken as a bit of a swan song, since he recorded only a handful of times after this. Written from the perspective of a farmer who no longer lives in the country, the first verse tells how he is a product of the countryside and can never forget the place where he was born. The second verse reminisces about some of his early life: the corn he ate, the malanga he grew, the guateques that he led and that made him so deeply happy.

> El maís del que he comido
> la malanga que he sembrado
> los guateques que he formado
> como allá me he divertido.

After the final verse, Benny begins to improvise lightly over the repeated chorus of "Soy guajiro" and introduces "regreso de mi poblado" to his "montaña querida"—I am returning from town to my beloved mountain.

Although the story was never corroborated, Benny may have played for an Oscars party in Los Angeles back in 1956 or 1957 with the Luis Alcaraz orchestra. However, in 1958 he did fly to Los Angeles by himself, invited to perform at the Hollywood Palladium by DJ-turned-promoter Lionel "Chico" Sesma. The band hired to back him was led by none other than the Nuyorican timbales player and Juilliard graduate Tito Puente, who was making a name for himself playing hard mambos back in New York. Benny arrived carrying a small case filled with rum. When asked where his luggage was, he lifted up the case and grinned, already halfway high from ordering drinks on the plane and a couple of quick belts in the airport. Apparently he hadn't brought another suit, or even a change of clothes, expecting to get new things in LA.

The Palladium, with its windowpane art deco façade, was located next to the CBS Columbia Square building on Sunset Boulevard. Also on RCA at the time, Tito Puente, with New York energy and a jazz musician's discipline, had already recorded more full LPs in three years than Benny would in his entire career. Since 1950 he had achieved the unbelievable output of twenty-eight albums. Granted, he was one of the most prolific recorders in American popular music, often raising producers' eyebrows with his enthusiasm for yet another record of jazz standards done in clave. An expert arranger and timbales player, Puente took a great deal from Cuban musicians like Arcaño and Arsenio Rodríguez, but he was just as obsessed with jazz and followed the footsteps of Machito and Mario Bauzá, leaning even more toward the jazz side than those two trailblazers. When Benny sang with Puente at the Hollywood Palladium, Mongo Santamaría had just left the group, and Willie Bobo, who would figure in the boogaloo trend, was there when Benny sat in. Sesma was very proud of having brought Benny to Los Angeles, but that was the only time Benny ever appeared there.

Sesma was not at all shy about proclaiming his preference for Benny's music over that of Pérez Prado, whom he had also brought to the Palladium. To Sesma's ears Pérez Prado was "un creador de ruido," a maker of noise. He acknowledged that Pérez Prado had been one of the first Latino musicians to make really serious money, but he preferred listening to Benny's band and playing his records when he was a radio DJ. Sesma tried to get Moré back again, but the Cold War and U.S.-Cuban relations "had already lowered the sugar curtain."

Puente worked hard, but he played hard enough, too. His own love of partying made for a good match with Benny's singing and personality. Sometimes, however, Benny's wild country ways didn't quite fit with Puente's expectations. No joint recordings of the two are known to exist, although they played together numerous times in New York and at least once in Los Angeles.

Life back in Havana in the remainder of 1957 was as busy as it ever would be for Benny. One of many friendships he was able to maintain was with

Bebo Valdés. Valdés would bring over his daughter Francia and her mother Carolina to La Cumbre so the children could play together. Benny, always a sought-after *padrino*, stood godfather to Francia at her baptism. In fact, any attempt to count all of the children at whose baptisms Benny stood up would be impossible. His godchildren numbered in the several dozen at least. He was said to have a hard time refusing the request of any friend to be godfather to a child, but Benny wouldn't have been awake or sober enough for an early morning mass, so he usually said yes as long as he could arrive late in the afternoon. Benny couldn't always be counted on to wake up until early evening, but it was a risk many thought worth taking.

When at home, Benny's schedule made it difficult to catch baseball games and keep up with his hometown team, the Cienfuegos Elephants. Whenever he had time, he would watch the afternoon cartoons with the kids in the front room. He howled and hooted at Bugs Bunny, but he especially loved Woody Woodpecker, which that year was being shown on television for the first time. Benny tried his best to catch Woody Woodpecker because of a short cartoon called *The Sliphorn King of Polaroo*, which ran on the show. Released in 1945, the animated story featured a lion trombone player shipwrecked on the Arctic island of Polaroo. The hard-drinking Texan Jack Teagarden supplied the trombone solo. Teagarden was one of the greatest blues players in American music and Louis Armstrong's favorite collaborator. Teagarden's characteristic virtuoso trombone solos were enough to make Benny jump up from the couch with excitement every time he heard them. Benny knew the entire cartoon and all the solos by heart. The kids yelled "¡Pinguino, pinguino!" at the cute little penguin in the cartoon who keeps trying to play the lion's trombone. He finally succeeds after being filled with the ingredients for a martini and being shaken by a bartender behind an ice bar.

Although there were explanations for Benny's periodic lateness, his drinking at this time contributed as much as anything else. He often complained that dishonest promoters would advertise the band at a dance but never sign Benny to a contract. Since the advertisements promised Benny at the show, those who had paid for tickets were bound to be angry when he didn't appear. But Enrique Benítez and Generoso remember how Benny often arrived very late while the band played to kill time. José Castañeda also spoke of Benny's lateness as common knowledge.

The year 1958 was Benny's busiest, and he applied himself in the studio and on the road like the condemned man he was. The pressures of grueling touring and recording often exhausted him and certainly contributed to his body's disintegration, as did his increasingly heavy drinking. The band played the Liceo de Consolación del Sur, out at the Colonia Española de Pinar del Río, and both white and black clubs. In Havana they had regular shows at the Campana, Sierra, Montmartre, and Ali Bar. That year Benny angered the booking manager at the Montmartre with no-shows. In March the sleek Havana Hilton opened in Vedado. With a Trader Vic's and several nightclubs, it promised to be another good cabaret for work, yet there isn't any record of Benny having played there. A victim of Cuban history, the hotel did not make money for the Hilton owners for very long, certainly not long enough to pay back the investment in the property and building.

The full Banda Gigante made regular television appearances on *Show del Mediodía*, and on *El Cabaret Regalías* on CMQ TV. Since Regalías were Benny's favorite cigar, he was certainly well taken care of by that tobacco manufacturer. Partagas, another famous cigarette and cigar maker, sponsored *Jueves de Partagas*, a Thursday show that booked a great deal of music talent. The band continued its regular radio shows at Radio Progreso, and also played dances in the Martí Theater and in the America and Tosca dance halls.

In October Benny's younger sister Isadora died in Santa Isabel de las Lajas. While at the funeral, Benny took Teo aside and told him that if he were ever to die outside Cuba, Teo must promise to go get his body and bring him back to Lajas. Benny certainly knew by now that his health was failing, but it's uncertain if other family members knew, aside from Teo and Delfín, who was now singing with the Banda Gigante in Benny's chorus along with Enrique and various other singers. Teo was president of a colored benevolent society in Vertientes and asked Benny to do a fundraiser there. Benny gladly complied, joined by the Orquesta América.

That year Capitol Records released Nat King Cole's *Cole Español*, which he had recorded at the Panart studios in Havana, with the great Armando Romeu, leader of the house orchestra at the Tropicana, providing arrangements. Until the Beatles came along, it was one of Capitol Records' biggest-selling LPs.

Armando Peñalver fondly remembered how some of the guys would meet for afternoon drinks in El Canal bar near plaza Cuatro Caminos throughout 1958. He remembered that Benny had a girlfriend then and would go meet her at the Marianela, where she worked. Sometimes she would join a group with Benny for drinks at night. It was in the Marianela that Benny talked about how he had hit Max Pérez with the iron bar. Once when José Maracaibo was along at the Marianela, Benny had the owner close the shutter to keep newcomers from entering. He filled the jukebox with nickels and sang a breathtaking duet with himself on all his hit songs.

As happened with many of the better-selling songs, the band had no clue that "Maracaibo oriental" had become such a hit, since they had left for shows in the eastern provinces just before a hurried release. Between recording sessions that began as a rule after midnight, the early show at Radio Progreso, and all the dances, it was getting harder to make an appearance at the Ali Bar. Once, having missed a show to spend an extra night in the studio, Benny sang at the Ali Bar the next night after essentially no sleep for days.

When the band's tour dates took them to Oriente, they found that the rebels had diverted attention from music and everything else with their attacks on police stations and bridges in the area. After the reports died down, Benny found out that "Maracaibo oriental" had become a hit by hearing it on the radio of the Caddy as Israel drove them down from the mountains to the hot plains around Havana late that spring. RCA had tested the release on CMQ first, as Rivera Conde did routinely.

In that same session the band had recorded the masterpiece "Camarera del amor," about a particularly kind and charming girl with whom the narrator has fallen in love at first sight. That song had a propulsive rhythm, with Benny hitting sharply just behind the beat, and featured Generoso's perfectly sculpted charts. But still the one that dancers found irresistible at the time was "Maracaibo."

The simple song had its origin at a fiesta in Jutinicú, where José Castañeda was playing with the Orquesta Maravillas de Beltrán at an outdoor dance. A drunken kid without a dance partner kept trying to get Castañeda's attention. When every song ended, he pestered Castañeda to play a maracaibo so that he could show off his moves. Finally, to get the persistent kid to stop grabbing the microphone stand and bothering the band, Castañeda composed a song on the spot and huddled with the singers to let them know where to come in. He sang, "So you think you can dance Maracaibo?" and the singers filled in the response chorus "Maracaibo!" and the band made something out of it. After the dance, the kid returned with a case of cognac to thank them. This is how Castañeda first gave shape to the song, approaching it like an improvised descarga. Once Benny recorded the song, Castañeda would forever be known by the name Maracaibo.

Benny and Castañeda first met in Santiago de Cuba, where Benny headlined a show of several bands in the barrio of Santa Teresa. Benny had heard him and during a break asked Fernando Álvarez to introduce them. Over a bottle of Palmita they discussed one another's star players, and admired each other's orchestras the way men admire one another's motorcycles. After getting his courage up with several glasses of rum, Castañeda pitched his version of "Maracaibo" to Benny. Benny liked the melody immediately but couldn't promise anything. He told José that he wanted to take it home and let the full band loose on it. He also needed Generoso's opinion on what they could do with this one, if anything.

A few months later when Castañeda was in Havana, he followed up by visiting Benny, who kept a room at the Hotel Boston at the time. Castañeda was introduced to Columbié, but because he didn't have the song written out, Benny told him to come out to the house the next day with notation. Before he went back to his own hotel, Castañeda helped Benny kill a bottle of Peralta. The next day when Israel brought Castañeda to the house, Benny got drinks first, then made sure Castañeda saw the farm, how he had named animals after all his friends. He teased Castañeda that maybe he would name a pig after him.

After more rum, Benny passed Castañeda a guitar and told him to play the song for Columbié. He had made it a rural changüí, a rhythm that came from around Guantánamo, a very old *son* that didn't use clave to anchor its rhythm section but did use call and response and often ended with a sped-up break. Dancers who knew it used slides, quick hip movements, and small steps that followed the tres. José called it a maracaibito, but it still fell beneath the shadow cast by *son*. The song was open enough to make it easy for Benny to modify to his swinging delivery across the changes, but he wasn't completely satisfied with the format as appropriate for the band. He loved these country rhythms, so he told Castañeda, "Let's hope we can do something with it." After they worked, the men ate a dinner of ropa vieja with congri and ripe tomatoes from the garden.

Castañeda noticed that everyone else at the table drank beer with their dinner but Benny.

"You don't like beer?"

"Mouthwash is for rinsing and spitting out," Benny told him, "not for drinking."

Preoccupied with the recording session coming up, Benny wasn't sure that Castañeda's was the song they needed to finish it. He hoped Generoso would be able to shed some light on where brass solos would go. Maybe they could have El Negro play a trumpet lead right off the bat just after the first chorus—which is what in fact happened. Benny would rely on Generoso's ear and sense of harmony, and Generoso always could be counted on to give him more than merely an arrangement.

Later that week as they were getting ready to go into the studio again, the whole band learned a little something about the secretive Generoso Jiménez. It was after 7 p.m., and everyone had assembled in the backstage area at Radio Progreso except for Enrique Benítez and Generoso. They were due to go on for a three-song set, and the nervous producer had already been by repeatedly, when Benny realized that Tojo hadn't arrived. The door flew open and in came Enrique, but he was alone. Benny looked at the clock; less than ten minutes to go. Without Generoso they had no charts, as he had sequestered himself to work on the new songs and they hadn't spoken in almost two days. Benny wondered if he would have to call for only old hits. This would please the producer and audience, but they needed to test new songs on a live audience, and the place was packed with an excited crowd. Just then, reflected in the glass of the sound engineer's booth, he saw the end of Generoso's trombone case preceding Generoso through the doorway.

Tojo himself had yet to enter the room when the entire band behind Benny burst into laughter. It was as if a mariachi band had suddenly started up behind Benny's back, so unexpected and so loud that he jumped. Whatever they were laughing at Tojo for, Benny knew by the way the boys snickered and then kept erupting again that this was one time he had better investigate.

While Generoso fumed as he unpacked his charts, Benny motioned for Israel Castellanos to come and tell him what was going on. Muela said one of the guys knew a pretty girl that Tojo had taken a liking to back last summer. It was the middle of August, and Generoso made a date with the girl for twelve noon. She must have thought he was taking her to lunch. He wasn't. For some reason Generoso insisted that she walk with him in her heels and tight dress through the endless streets of Vieja Habana for hours under the broiling midday sun of the tropical summer. Not until then would he take her to a hotel.

There he asked her if she wanted a beer, and of course she said yes. He called room service and started to order. While he was still on the phone, he heard a noise from the bathroom, water running. When the woman came out in a towel, he lost his temper.

"You didn't take a shower, did you?! Goddamnit, I just walked you all over the city and now you ruined it! Get dressed, woman!" Incredibly, he took her back out to walk around and get all sweaty again before he would touch her.

Benny whistled softly and grinned. "How could we not know about this until now?" he whispered.

It was precious for the simple reason that they now had something on Mr. Secrets. Plenty of times the guys in the band thought him a bit imperious. Some called him the traffic cop, in reference to his days with the police band and to the times when he led the band in his own songs.

Benny narrowed his eyes, took a peek at Tojo, and kept quiet. He would be able to use this on Generoso forever, and wouldn't even need to think up tricks to play on him anymore. All Benny had to say was "Do you want some nice ripe papaya?" or even just mouth the words "ripe papaya" to take a good dig at Tojo anytime he wanted.

"What would you bet Tojo only does it with the lights on, too?" someone whispered. When Generoso passed out the charts, Benny wagged his finger for quiet. They had forty seconds until curtain.

The relentless teasing lasted a few days. Generoso, always a bit tightly wound and hence a target of practical jokes, had to put up with it, eventually coming to accept it as he accepted his nickname Tojo. There was a method to Benny's method, as usual. Letting guys have their personality issues focused their irritations away from an increasingly erratic Benny. This let him appear to play the clown, yet still have a tight-enough grip on personnel. He also didn't mind being the target, especially if it was a good joke.

Soon Benny got Generoso involved with José Castañeda's maracaibito, and he worked hard on the arranging. When they prepared to record the song at the studio that night in April, Generoso went to pass out the charts but couldn't find them in his music case. He had written for the entire band, with three trombones, six trumpets, and three saxophones, and those musicians needed their scores. Benny drove the convertible all the way back to Generoso's house while the band waited. Generoso searched for an hour with no luck. He was so uncharacteristically flustered that Benny took pity on him and never said a word.

With the clock ticking on studio costs and fees for the full band, Benny decided to wing it instead of rescheduling. Back they went downtown.

Benny directed how he thought the piano should go and sang it from memory. In two takes they recorded it that way. The version they settled on has few chord changes, and contains only an introduction and a second section that feels not quite connected. After the sung introduction, Generoso takes a quick solo and then El Negro plays figures in response. The conversation between the two of them goes on for a few bars, but then the song ends without summing up or balancing anything that came earlier. The tempo and quick vocal responses make it sound something like a merengue, relentless and driving. It manages to be new music altogether. In the accident of Generoso losing his charts, it's as if the song returned to its roots as a dashed-off thing born in a sunny field.

Those were strange, exciting, and yet bewildering days. The mob, oblivious to the impending end of its ownership of the island, was still spending millions on construction of the thirty-story Hilton hotel complex that would someday be renamed the Marina Hemingway. The diamond pinkie rings, the fussy custom suits, the slots, and the Cadillacs that still came in on barges every day were artifacts of a time nearly over, a body that didn't know it was already dead. The torture and political murders increased as Batista grew more fearful. But Santo Trafficante Jr. didn't seem afraid that he might lose his $20 million investment, let alone be imprisoned and nearly executed by Castro. He may not have known it just yet, but Meyer Lansky was about to flee and never return, losing untold millions, far more than Trafficante. The houses of prostitution, numbers rackets, lotteries, jai alai parlors, bookmakers, horse and dog tracks—it was all a giant tree just sawn through, the instant before it crashes to the forest floor. When Lanksy fled, the days of the big bands and casino shows were over forever.

It is an understatement to say that Benny's own problems were growing. He looked for distractions to let him ignore how sick he was feeling, and he was beginning to feel the claustrophobia that can come with living on a Caribbean island. His worries about the shows caused him to drink all the harder. The ache below his right ribcage was the one constant in his life now. Taking sips of rum onstage had always been his trademark, but now sharp-eyed journalists were writing about no-shows and his constant state of drunkenness.

Benny desperately needed a break from the impossible pace and all the attention, and he looked forward to the tour in the Dominican Republic and Peru in June, but "Maracaibo" was a hit in both countries, too. Only when they arrived in Jamaica could he walk down a country road and, when the yard dogs barked, not be recognized by anyone who looked out. In New York that winter he had a show coming up with Tito Puente's orchestra at the Palladium, and already he was dreading the cold.

When not touring, Benny went home to check on his mother's house in Lajas and see the family as often as he could, though not as often as he would like. When he felt stressed, he usually realized that he hadn't been home in too long, and so he got Muelita and out they went. Whenever they were to do shows anywhere near, he tried to make sure they built in a show in Lajas or at least some time in Cienfuegos.

In 1958 the newspapers and radio news shows always led with stories about bombings, executed bodies found, police stations attacked. Because of a bombing, one of the Lajas shows was suddenly cancelled. This gave Benny time to spend with his brothers and sisters and let the children pull him around to show him their toys and treasures, a new puppy or kitten. As good with a tough crowd of hard-to-please children as he was with 20,000 in a fancy theater, Uncle Benny always became the night's entertainment. If there were a power outage from a thunderstorm or a guerrilla attack, his little solo shows might have been lit by flashlight, but dozens of children still crowded in to hear him sing.

# FOURTEEN

Revolution and Death, 1959–1963

Although some orchestras did record in 1959, Benny didn't release a single record, nor is there any indication he was in the studio at all. RCA likely suspended his recording obligations for the year, if he had not already renegotiated their terms. His failing health may have had something to do with this lack of recording, too. The increasing skirmishes between Castro's rebels and Batista forces caused a great deal of chaos the entire year, but no day was more surprising and chaotic than the first morning of 1959.

When Fulgencio Batista escaped the country at 3 a.m. on New Year's Day, a continuous line of self-enriching Cuban leaders who had held power militarily with the help of the United States came to a shockingly abrupt end. When Batista went, the entire gambling industry collapsed almost immediately. Warned by his old friend Batista, Meyer Lansky flew out at dawn. Then fifty-seven, Lansky would never have another birthday party in Cuba. Other mobsters wouldn't take the hint, and didn't leave until some months later. Without the gambling money that had always paid for the lavish spectacles and supported full orchestras, there was no way bandleaders could continue to earn enough to pay large bands. Many bandleaders did attempt to continue, but most would be gone within a few years. When those who had connections in New York and Florida saw what was happening to artists under the new regime, they took their bands and families and left too.

Even as American investors still hoped that they could make money with the new government, the party had ended.

Cubans had tired of Batista lining his pockets, and letting the Americans do the same. Even those who had indirectly profited by Batista's years in office were glad to see him and his brutal methods and murderous police go. Those closest to Batista escaped the country as quickly as they could, taking anything they had of value. So much money had been taken out of the country at the end of the 1950s, and so little had made its way to legitimate government accounts, that the new administration found it would need to raise money quickly. In March, *Time* magazine reported that Castro had reopened the casinos because so many workers had lost their jobs. But because of a new policy that forbade known mobsters from operating the casinos, they wouldn't stay open for long.

Fairly soon, the new government made demands of musicians that not all of them were willing to fulfill. Benny didn't like the new world, but unlike Celia Cruz and Bebo Valdés, he didn't want to leave it, either. If he had, he would have had an easier time than Cruz did in New York or Valdés did in Europe. In 1960 Valdés moved with his Swedish wife to Mexico and then on to New York and finally Stockholm. He wasn't heard from again for nearly thirty years. Celia Cruz had a long, hard road as a salsa singer in New York, even though she and the entire Sonora Matancera band had escaped the country together.

On April 17 the band left for a quick U.S. tour about which little is known. They played that night at an outdoor square in Miami. Always searching for good Mexican food, Benny and the guys ate at Don Julio's on NE 20th in Miramar. Benny most likely went to New York after the show in Miami.

Benny was back in New York at the end of the year. He flew to the city just before Christmas to discuss business matters at the RCA offices, and to appear with Tito Puente at the Palladium. Puente was, at the height of the mambo craze in New York, as famous as Machito.

At the airport, Tito had Benny picked up in a limousine driven by his own driver, a man named Pepsi. Immediately Benny noticed a strange and powerful scent in the car. He lowered the window, but then quickly shut it against the frigid air.

When Benny and Puente met and had embraced, the timbales player asked him how he liked the ride from the airport.

"Very fast, great, I loved it. Pepsi too. But you know what?" Benny said, putting a finger beneath his nose. "The car smelled weird, like flowers or something."

Puente hooted with laughter. He laughed so long and hard that someone else had to tell Benny why the car smelled so strongly of flowers: because it had just been used to transport funeral arrangements to the Fernández home, the famous funeral home in the Bronx that buried so many Puerto Ricans.

"Was there a Puerto Rican stiff in the back, too?" Benny asked.

Puente laughed like crazy again. "No, that smell was Pepsi's socks." He yelled in to Pepsi, "Boricua, I told you to change those dirty things! They look like elephant skin now, and they used to be white!"

That night when it came time for Benny to go on at the Palladium, he was nowhere to be found. Benny's old bandleader and cousin Chocolate was in the group. Chocolate, known in New York for his punctuality, shrugged when Puente asked him where the fuck Benny had gone. The show had started at 10 p.m., and at midnight they took a break.

Puente was understandably furious. When someone in the band came in from the alley where he had gone to smoke a joint, he told Puente that he had seen Benny outside. Puente marched out to confront him.

"Hey, you country motherfucker, where have you been?" he said when he found Benny leaning against a car parked at the back entrance, drinking from a bottle of Bacardi and just as high as a Georgia pine.

"I'm on vacation, Papi," he told Puente, "but goddamnit it's cold out here. Why don't you move to San Juan? A winter like this is pointless."

No one and especially not Puente could resist Benny's humor and warmth, and for another hour Puente kept him company, while sharing the rest of the bottle. Benny had wandered off to Birdland and along Broadway, he told Puente. They talked about all the times Puente had gone to Birdland to see Charlie Parker and Dizzy Gillespie. Benny had also gone over to Jack Dempsey's bar on Broadway and Forty-ninth, across the street from Madison Square Garden, and had had a staged photo taken of the two of them with their fists up, facing off. Puente had done the same thing over at Dempsey's! "Give me a little kiss on that bottle," he told Benny. They ended up staying yet another hour, blowing into their hands to stay warm. Puente knew that Benny was sick, but he also knew from experience that the Palladium dancers would get their money's worth. In the end, Benny took the stage at 2 a.m. and sang until almost dawn.

As he always did on his trips to New York, Benny visited Machito's apartment uptown. He helped Machito shop, clowning while the snowflakes fell on the busy sidewalks. Even though his face was known in Spanish Harlem, because of the crowds in New York Benny could help shop and be recognized only a few times. They fooled around in the grocery store and the meat market, and then Benny helped make dinner later. For Christmas that year Machito's family and Benny went over to Mario Bauzá's apartment at 944 Columbus Avenue. Well-known photographs of the Christmas dinner show Bauzá and his wife, Machito and his two girls and his little boy, Machito's sister Graciela Pérez, and lots of happy friends.

Sometime that following spring Teo had come to Havana to visit Benny and see the children. At the time Benny had a room at the Hotel San Luis, and there Teo found him looking very ill. Teo insisted that he see a doctor, and for once Benny was too weak to argue or joke it away. The doctor who made the house call certainly knew who he was examining: he told Benny that it was no big deal, he probably had a little flu, and gave Benny some narcotics to make him feel better. Outside the room, he took Teo aside and told him that it wasn't just a flu, that Benny was gravely ill. He needed more than a handful of medicines, and he needed to see a specialist immediately. Despite Benny's fears, Teo did get him to promise he would see a physician, but only if Teo returned for the appointment. When Teo came back, Benny consented to see Dr. Luis Ruiz, a physician who had grown up in Lajas and gone to the same grade school as everyone else. He and Benny became friends, but it was many months before Benny would let him put a stethoscope on his chest.

Luis Ruiz first met Benny at La Cumbre on a very hot summer day. Benny was cooking in the back of the house and wasn't wearing a shirt when Ruiz arrived. When Benny shook hands with him he took note of his white shirt. He told Ruiz that he was wearing a shirt so beautiful that it would be a terrible shame to ruin it. It was such a hot day—why didn't he just take the shirt off? Ruiz was a guajiro too, so he took his shirt off. Benny liked that he didn't have any airs about him, and was probably testing him. He told Ruiz that if he would agree to being his personal doctor, he must promise to always be very quiet about treating him. Benny made his belief clear: doctors were for sick people only.

"So then church is only for sinners?" Ruiz asked.

"Ha, very good. I can't speak for your church, but mine is for congueros and dancers," Benny said, holding up his index finger for emphasis. "And women with nice thighs," he added. "Your church have any hot chicks?"

Instead of patient and physician, they became lunch partners and often met at the Chinatown restaurant El Pacifico. Although frustrated in his attempts to treat Benny's illness, Dr. Ruiz had plenty of good if bittersweet memories of those days, too. Benny did relent and listen to his doctor, but by then it was too late. In the meantime, the two of them went to lunch a lot. Dr. Ruiz would do his duty and suggest that Benny watch his sodium, and Benny faked an extravagant refusal to eat his usual saltier dishes, or avoided adding too much soy. Lunch with a celebrity was an interesting diversion, but because it often included many table visits and requests for Benny to sing, it didn't make for good digestion. After Benny was persuaded to sing for two hours at the Rincón Criollo, Ruiz could see why he never put on weight even though he loved restaurants.

That fall of 1960 Dr. Ruiz no longer had to chase Benny around to see when he would give in to a full examination. In November, the walls came crashing in on Benny. On a visit to Lajas he got very sick after a foolish tequila drinking contest. When Israel drove Benny back to Havana, Benny was in such a weakened condition that he finally consented to a full examination with laboratory tests and X-rays. That examination only confirmed what Benny had guessed and Ruiz had understood from what he knew of Benny's habits and history.

Ruiz told Benny very pointedly that he was in terrible shape, and what damage had already been done to his liver was permanent. He warned him that from that day forward he could no longer drink.

"Not only can you *never* tie one on again, but any amount of alcohol is liable to kill you very quickly," he warned.

He couldn't promise how long Benny would last, but he could promise that going on another bender would tip him into an early grave. Ruiz gave him a final warning: the pain of quitting would be excruciating, but dying of cirrhosis would be far worse. Ruiz didn't leave Benny's side until the horrible withdrawal symptoms passed, but that was the easiest part; Benny's now-official physician spared him the details of what must happen someday to him after he had done a lifetime of irreversible damage to his liver.

At the beginning of 1960 the Banda Gigante played at Night and Day and El Sierra. They did dance shows in Matanzas, Santa Clara, Camagüey, and Oriente. In May Benny recorded material for an LP that was never released while he was alive, including Enrique Benítez's masterpiece "El cañonero." Other songs from the session were "Conocí la paz," "Me gusta más el son,"

"No lo dejes para luego," "Mi amor, mi fe, mi ilusión," and "Te quedarás." All seem to carry significance for Benny's last years in their titles. He would never record again after "Mi amor, mi fe, mi ilusión."

Félix Contreras, who was the boy Benny brought onstage to dance nearly ten years earlier in Placetas, finally saw the band again live in 1961, in Guantánamo. He had gone to the show with a pretty girl he liked named Nora and several other young women friends. When Benny saw the women, he came and sat down before the show and paid great flirting attention to Nora. As much as he loved Benny, this pained Contreras because Benny appeared to have taken a liking to her. Nora was understandably very flustered by the attention. Suddenly Benny recognized Contreras.

"Hey! Aren't you that great dancer I saw in Pinar del Río? I remember you! Come on, you skinny motherfucker, quit being so modest!" Benny said while squeezing Contreras. "I'll never forget you, buddy, you were unbelievable!"

Contreras was profoundly relieved and moved by Benny's kindness in front of Nora. But he was newly depressed when he had taken a good look at Benny's face. They could all see that Benny was very ill and deteriorating. His skin was ashy, and managed to be gray at the same time it was yellow with jaundice.

Benny was already beginning to disappear behind the mists, physically and historically. In December he seems to have gone to New York, though the reasons for his visit are unknown, and whether he went with the band. There is a rumor that RCA Victor offered to sponsor his leaving Cuba to move to New York. Because they couldn't promise to move the entire band, Benny is said to have refused.

Sometime early in 1961 he was in Florida. Among the fast-growing number of Cuban exiles in Miami were Martin and Ofelia Fox, former owners of the Tropicana nightclub. When Benny called them to see how they were doing, Martin suggested they meet at the restaurant El Toledo. Benny went happily. Martin asked him to carry $40,000 in hundreds as emergency money to Ofelia's sister Fara. Benny told Martin he would be more than happy to do him the favor, and he knew just how he would get the money into the country.

Benny was hardly antirevolutionary, and he tried to keep out of the way of the authorities, except when it came to doing favors for friends. Although he hadn't been hired to play at the Tropicana as often as he could have been,

Benny wasn't about to turn down Fox's request. When he reached the airport, he faked being drunk by weaving along on the tarmac. When bystanders yelled that it was Benny and rushed up to him, the customs agents let him through without examining his luggage.

The revolutionary government had several reasons to be wary of money being taken out of the country, since hundreds of millions had been siphoned off from public and private funds that could have been seized. The new government had found the treasury emptied out. And large sums being smuggled in were equally suspect. Castro's enemies were more than capable of mounting coup attempts. Any substantial funds could potentially be used against the revolutionary government. Benny would have been imprisoned immediately for bringing that kind of money into the country, regardless of his stature.

The new government still had strong support among average Cubans, but Castro's seemingly paranoid fears of being invaded by a U.S.-backed counterrevolutionary army turned out to be anything but imaginary. The Cuban intelligence service had quickly developed to help defend the government. After the disastrous Bay of Pigs invasion in April, the importance of Cuban intelligence in protecting the revolution meant a much harsher clampdown on all activity that could pose any threat.

Unfortunately it was well known that Castro had no interest in music and the arts unless they served the revolution. For the artists who were used to making their own decisions about most aspects of their careers, those musicians with enough money to move and start over began to leave just as quickly as the wealthy Batistianos had the year before. The musicians scattered to the winds, hoping to maintain the momentum in their careers. In 1960 the Sonora Matancero with Celia Cruz left for New York. By 1961 José Fajardo had gone, Cachao too. Bebo Valdés left for Mexico, as did Olga Guillot. Before leaving, both Guillot and Cruz went to Benny to urge him to leave. He told the women, and anyone else who tried to get him to leave, the same thing—that he couldn't leave his country or his children behind. No musician who did leave Havana was able to step onto a moving sidewalk with any of the success of the great years back home. Cachao and Cruz eventually became very successful again, but only after decades of struggle. Valdés didn't regain much of his former recognition and success until he was nearly eighty years old. Of all the musicians who might have directly translated some of their success in another country, Benny Moré would have had the best chance. He had built a large fan base in Latin America, and could have lived in Mexico if he didn't find New York or Los Angeles to his liking. Europe was beginning to take an interest in him, and living in New York would have aided European tours and sales.

Although Benny told his friends that he couldn't leave because of his ties to Cuba, the real reason was that he knew he was dying and any attempt to continue elsewhere would be wasted. But even if he weren't ill, it is doubtful that he would have left. Benny couldn't have been more Cuban, nor better received than in Cuba. He was a star in Medellín and Mexico City but was *understood* in Marianao. As Paquito D'Rivera explained about all the musicians and artists who fled Cuba, including his own father, "If you take a fish out of water, he can't survive. A frog, maybe, but a fish, he's not gonna make it." Benny wasn't just a Cuban fish, he was one very sick fish who knew that his sea was the only place he belonged.

It's not known if this was their first meeting, but sometime after the revolution Fidel Castro visited Benny to ask if he would help by playing benefits in Varadero for the countrywide literacy program. After introductions, Castro sat on the couch and watched Benny, who was very under the weather that afternoon.

"Will you be able to help? I need to count on you, and know that you believe in me," he told Benny. He paused. "The revolution needs you now, but you look weak."

"I am just a little hung over," Benny told him in an attempt to laugh it off. "Don't worry, I believe."

The sharp-eyed Castro studied Benny for a beat, and then continued with his request.

When he asked what Benny needed to be paid for his trouble, Benny said that he would do it for free. He politely asked that the band's transportation be paid by the government. It was a shrewd response, and Benny certainly knew his place now; he had heard what was being asked of other artists.

Later, Iraida asked how he could do anything for no money, aware that he couldn't last forever and she had four children to take care of. His response was that he had done this many times before. "A charity show is still a charity show, and this new government has no money," he told her.

"Do you really believe in Fidel?" she interrupted him.

"You know what I believe in. I believe in Bacardi white. Okay, sometimes in Matusalem black, but Havana Club is something to believe in, too." He turned with a drink in each hand. By now he only sniffed at rum and didn't actually drink it. Iraida needed a drink, and took both glasses from him.

In some unconscious way Benny may have taken a little revenge on the rigid regulations of the new government and its leanings toward Soviet-style rule. He had once had a brief romantic interlude with the wife of one of the revolution's best-known heroes, Camilo Cienfuegos, who had just died in a plane accident in October. Cienfuegos, whose face adorns the 20-peso bill, had sailed in 1956 in the yacht *Granma* with Castro and Guevara, and fought against Batista long before that. It was Cienfuegos himself who had introduced Benny to his very attractive wife. When Cienfuegos found out whom she had slept with, he laughed with relief and immediately forgave her and Benny both, since he was a huge fan and loved Benny's music. On every anniversary of Cienfuegos's disappearance, Cuban children cast flowers into the sea.

Benny took four months off for what has always been assumed was a resting period for his vocal cords, yet the chances are that the respite was ordered by Dr. Ruiz, or that Benny was simply too sick to appear. When he returned to working, he did a show at the Sierra, reportedly singing without any amplification to prove that he hadn't lost his voice as had been rumored. Celeste Mendoza also sang at this show, which was hugely successful. He sang at his usual spots at Night and Day and at the Ali Bar. He summoned the energy to resume touring outside Havana, taking the band out to Pinar del Río, Bahía Honda, and Consolación del Sur.

Benny had recently begun building a house for Virginia, who wanted to return to Lajas. Construction was under way on their old street, Heredia, on the corner of calle Labra in La Guinea, where he had grown up.

After the disastrous attempt by U.S.-funded counterrevolutionaries failed at the Bay of Pigs in the second week of April, the government began to tighten freedoms in Cuba and continued to improve its military. Cuban military intelligence rose to greater prominence, and leaving Cuba became more complicated from then on. It was even more difficult after the Cuban Missile Crisis in October of the following year.

Benny was asked to play a benefit in Palatino to raise money for new arms and planes damaged in the Bay of Pigs attacks. Now bearing a rather outmoded name, the Conjunto Casino also played at the benefit.

Just before the extremely dangerous Cold War standoff in the missile crisis in October of 1961, Enrique Benítez noticed that Benny's eyes were very yellow and his skin alarmingly jaundiced. It was an unmistakable sign of a failing liver. Hilda Moré remembered Dr. Ruiz telling Benny that he needed to stop playing late-night shows and get to bed much earlier. Benny complied as best he could and spent more time at home now than in the past, among his animals and watching the children play. He had little energy to chase them, but they clamored for his attention. They called, "Papi, Papi, mira! Come look!" constantly while they played with the pile of yucca roots he had sweated to dig up a few days before.

Benny's last days were painful and unpleasant in the extreme. Liver failure is among the more awful ways to meet your end. The liver performs some of the body's most vital functions, and a sick liver means a very sick person. Often called the body's filtration unit, the liver scours the blood of toxins. When it no longer works, they build up quickly and cause complications that ultimately prove fatal. For years his liver had been working at less than capacity, yet somehow Benny was able not only to function but even to survive further poisoning. His capacity to ingest alcohol was far beyond that of most people, but once the scale tipped against him, it would lead to just one place.

You can feel your liver by taking a deep breath and placing your fingertips lightly against your belly just below the edge of the ribcage on your right side. The liver's location within the rib bones protects it well against most outside trauma but does absolutely nothing to protect it from the owner of its body.

The effect of alcohol on the liver is highly variable, and only 20 percent of heavy drinkers ultimately get cirrhosis. A drinker dying in his early forties, as Benny did, usually means an extraordinary consumption of alcohol over time. Benny was certainly an alcoholic by genetics and cultural conditioning. It may be assumed that he began to drink in his early teens, which means some three decades of drinking. Because he was alcoholic, there was no way Benny consumed only one or two drinks a day. To be among the unhappy 20 percent of heavy drinkers who develop liver damage and hardening of liver tissue, you would likely have to drink more than 60 grams of alcohol per day over many years. If Benny drank one 750-ml bottle of rum a day, and the rum was about 40 percent alcohol, this amounted to more than 200 grams of alcohol. Even if Benny drank only eight or nine drinks (a dozen shots, or half a bottle) per day, it would have been more than enough to cause cirrhosis by his midthirties.

Late-stage cirrhosis brings rising ammonia levels, which make the sufferer lose touch with reality. Thereafter, behavior can become sluggish and even demented. Eventually the ill person becomes totally withdrawn from the outside world.

Toward the end, blood stops clotting well and large bruises become commonplace. A man's testicles shrink. For both women and men, the breasts swell from rising estrogen levels that the liver no longer metabolizes. The belly swells grotesquely with distended veins around the navel, as fluid builds up in the abdomen from the hepatic veins becoming backed up. As the liver can no longer clear bilirubin, the whites of the eyes turn bright yellow. In Benny's case, as in most, the risk of bleeding from the esophagus becomes very high. As Dr. Ruiz knew, when Benny had heavy blood flow from his throat, the end would come not long after.

If liver transplant technology had existed in 1962, no transplant surgeon would have permitted Benny to receive a new liver. For an alcoholic with tendencies toward extremely heavy drinking, the risk of relapse would be too great. There was no bilongo that could save Benny now.

Benny got a call from his manager Tito Garrote, who described an excellent offer to sing at the Olympia in Paris.

"Tito," he said tiredly.

"You can sleep the whole flight, Benny. This is a lot of money for you. Especially for your children," Garrote said in a knowing tone of voice. They had only lightly touched on the topic of what would happen after Benny was gone, but Garrote had been able to get Benny to set up a corporation.

"I am going to lie down now, mulatto," Benny said and hung up.

Benny's fear of flying had kept him from taking these important tours in the past. Now he had the willingness to see Paris, and perhaps a little bit of the rest of Europe, but his health had left him too weak for an extended tour. If he could do only a week or two of shows and could go via ocean liner, he would do it. As for flying there, he wasn't about to tempt fate. He had lately felt rather mortal, and had such a fear of dying in an airplane that he never went on another flight.

On January 3, 1963, a reporter doing an interview for *Revolución* came out to the house and got to see what close friends and family members saw of the private Benny. It wasn't a pleasant sight. Benny had a swollen chest, large bruises on his limbs. His hands looked bright pink and his eyes alarmingly yellow. Dr. Ruiz had taught him to give himself shots, but the injections caused huge bruising in his thighs and a great deal of pain. During their conversation, the reporter gingerly asked Benny how long he would like to live.

Benny replied calmly, "I would like to live many more years. I want the stories to keep coming. But none of us knows when death will arrive and say, 'Get your things, we are leaving.'"

Benny had accepted a contract to play a show in Bayamo before the end of the year along with flutist Richard Egües. The pair met for lunch, but Benny uncharacteristically didn't have an appetite and wouldn't eat a thing. Egües didn't understand until later what that meant.

Benny's sense of humor was still intact. He toyed with more than one person by pretending that he was going to take a drink. When he said, "Come on, Negro, pass that damn bottle over here," those not in on the joke froze. They knew that no one was to permit him anything to drink, and no one wanted to be known as the guy who killed Benny. Benny would pour a little on his hands and smell it, or feign opening a bottle, but he never drank.

Even though he was fading fast himself, Benny still found the strength to help friends who needed it. Castellanos became very ill and his doctor told him he had to rest for two months. When Benny heard, he summoned the energy to go over and talk to Castellanos's landlord. He paid the back rent, plus several months in advance. He then went to the bodega, paid what Castellanos owed there, and told the grocer that he should send all bills to La Cumbre while Castellanos was sick. Benny even had Alipio García continue to pay Castellanos for the shows at the Ali Bar. Castellanos always considered Benny his best friend on earth, and was very moved by Benny's latest generosity.

The holidays hadn't been as exciting as in the past, but Benny still managed to enjoy himself at Nochebuena and bought plenty of presents for the children for Christmas Day and Three Kings. He even killed the big tom turkey for the Nochebuena dinner. For Iraida those were very sad holidays, but the children were as excited by their gifts and treats as ever. Benny also rested as much as he could out in Lajas. Feeling weak, he nevertheless played a show on Christmas Eve and another on New Year's Day in Fomento, in Las Villas. The family stayed with Virginia between shows.

When they returned to Havana, Benny rested for several weeks, slept a great deal, played a lot of dominoes with Dr. Ruiz. On Sunday, January 5, they had a birthday party for Castellanos's daughter at his house in Vibora Park, and Benny played a little guitar. Dr. Ruiz asked him to sit, but Benny didn't listen and insisted on standing up to play.

Dr. Ruiz was with him most of the time now, and when they went back to La Cumbre that night he taped Benny playing in the front room on his new electric guitar. The tape, never released to the public, is unbearably sad, the sound of a doomed soul facing death, afraid and in terrible pain. Benny had ruptured a hepatic vein, which leads from the liver to the heart. His body was beginning its sequence of shutting down, and there was nothing Ruiz could do now but try to keep Benny as comfortable as possible. This meant using morphine to help the pain, and to keep Benny calm.

That same night Benny still was able to muster the energy to play an early show at the Tropicana. There were very few tourists, mostly Cubans in attendance, but he surprised everyone near him with his infectious happiness and a surprisingly energetic show. Castellanos said for a moment he almost forgot how sick Benny was. Any exertion took a great deal out of him, and he needed to sleep for several days to regain his strength.

Fidel Castro no longer visited Benny to ask for help with the revolution, but he had letters sent out to request that Benny continue to play benefits. Benny still complied whenever he was able. Even though he should have rested, he and the orchestra played the second Paper and Ink Festival downtown on January 6. Benny had only a few weeks to live, but he sang very hard, amazing the few people who knew how sick he was. Those who didn't know thought he looked pretty good, but his thinness was hidden by a vest and tie with a scarf against the unseasonably chilly weather of that week. Prado had been closed off, from Monte all the way to the Malecón. Huge crowds in front of the Capitol called out deafeningly when they saw him appear with his stick and hat. Aragón and Riverside also played, but any musicians near enough could see he wasn't doing well.

Benny's old songwriter and arranger Cabrera came out to the house to have lunch, spending the day and staying through to dinner like old times. That afternoon Benny told him that this would be his end. "Benny, lots of people get sick and then get better," he argued. "No," Benny said calmly. "This will take me, and I'm not going to get better." It was the last time Cabrera saw him alive.

Benny was able to play another show at the social club José María Pérez on February 15. The next afternoon they left for a dance out in Palmira, the town very near Lajas with such Afro-Cuban roots. It was a return for him to where he began, and a return to the culture that had created him and given him to the world.

In Palmira Benny somehow found some spiritual energy to infuse his rapidly failing body. From the night of the sixteenth, they played into the morning of the seventeenth, to the incredible hour of 4 a.m.

When they had left Lajas to go to Palmira, Benny complained to his brother Pedro that he didn't feel so good, and lay down in the back seat. As Castellanos was about to take the turn at the town of Colón, Benny suddenly told him to stop the car, opened the door, and vomited blood onto the ground. Castellanos jumped out when he heard Benny getting sick and ran around the car to see. In the light from passing cars, he was horrified to see the blood on the ground. It wasn't the first time Benny had spit up blood, but Castellanos had a bad feeling about it.

At the show in Palmira, Benny still went onstage, but he was moving in what seemed like slow motion. Someone ran to call Dr. Ruiz. After the first set Benny began vomiting blood in the bathroom, yet he still went onstage after it stopped. Ruiz was in Lajas at dinner with his family, and when they finally found him, he drove over as fast as he could. He arrived for the last set, but Benny wasn't onstage; he had gone out to rest in the car. When Ruiz asked Benny how he was doing, he told him, "Good, pretty good." Ruiz watched sadly as Benny got up and went back onstage. In his final public performance, Benny was astounding, treating the crowd to "Dolor y perdón," "Maracaibo," and "Qué bueno baila usted." Ruiz and the others had never seen anything quite like it.

Afterward, Benny needed help to get into the back of the Cadillac. Those who saw him lying in the back seat knew it was bad. His face had swollen grotesquely, and his stomach looked huge. His palms were a frighteningly bright pink, like a rooster's comb. When he opened his eyes, they could see only yellow where the white should have been. "I don't want to die in the hospital," he told Dr. Ruiz. "I want to go home." Ruiz asked him if he meant Lajas. "No, La Cumbre. Take me to see my babies. I want to hear their feet running around again."

Castellanos looked at Ruiz, who shrugged. He said they should follow

Benny's wishes. Dr. Ruiz was having car trouble, so Castellanos in the lead drove slowly on the back roads. Miriam Aguilera and her husband, who sometimes drove Benny, pulled out behind Ruiz. Up in the Cadillac with Benny were Pedro and his wife Nieves, with Castellanos at the wheel. In Central Washington, Castellanos turned his head when he thought he heard Benny say something, but it was Benny retching blood again. Miriam and her husband saw the Cadillac up ahead suddenly pull over.

Dr. Ruiz was there in a flash. Benny's pulse was weak, and Ruiz wasn't sure Benny could make it all the way to Havana. They all got back in the cars again but kept having to stop. In Jovellanos they asked a lady for rags and a bucket to clean out the car. An alarming amount of blood had collected in the back seat and on the floorboards.

When they left Jovellanos, a gray dawn began to illuminate the sugarcane fields. This time when they got in the cars, Dr. Ruiz caught Castellanos's eye and pointed at his watch. The caravan passed Limonar, where they entered the national highway, and drove at high speed all the way to Havana—except for Dr. Ruiz, who had bad brakes and had to drive more slowly.

When they finally arrived at La Cumbre, they got Benny on the couch and made him as comfortable as they could. He was still conscious. Ruiz had warned them beforehand to let him have only a little water, and no food. Before he slept, Benny told them, "No hospital, I don't want to die in a hospital."

Dr. Ruiz had no illusions. The end for Benny Moré had come. On the way to La Cumbre, he cried for Benny and the family. When Ruiz finally arrived at the house, he called to have his wife send over clean clothes. He spent the rest of Sunday at the house. Uncle Teo was there helping out Iraida. The children didn't have to be hushed, since they sensed that something was the matter, too. When Benny became unresponsive, Iraida panicked and told the doctor that they had to take him to the hospital, no matter what he made them promise.

Benny regained consciousness when Domingo Veloz came to help get him to Emergencias for an urgent plasma infusion. When Veloz arrived with the ambulance, Benny told him, "Man, I think a big fat woman fell on me and won't get up."

Ruiz followed in Benny's car, and supervised the blood transfusion. By 1 p.m. Benny had slipped into a coma. They moved him upstairs to room H, bed 22.

The transfusion had helped his blood pressure slightly, but he barely had any pulse. Besides Iraida, his final visitors were Lázaro Peña, Tania Castellanos, the actor Pedro Álvarez, Fernando Álvarez, and Mario Escalona.

Benny's heart held out until the next evening at 9:15. The children were brought to the hospital from the house to say goodbye to their father. At midnight he was moved to the musicians' and performers' union local on Prado, where he lay in state, and many thousands of mourners viewed the body all night long.

In the midst of such political unrest, it was a time of constant rumors. Cubans woke the next morning to see the news in *Revolución*, "El Benny Dead at Age 44." The news spread across the country, but many of those like Enrique González who heard the bad news at a party in Bejucal refused to believe it, imagining it was a false and particularly cruel rumor. Those who could, traveled to Santa Isabel de las Lajas for the funeral.

In Lajas all businesses closed for the day. Benny lay in state for many thousands more mourners to view the body at the Lajas *liceo*, his old elementary school. His Palo cane and white hat lay at his side in the coffin. At the Casino de los Congos and in the homes of believers, members began the last rites.

The drums played the announcement of a member's death, while believers wore red and chanted in Lucumí to the Yoruba orisha Ogun, the wounded warrier whose syncretized counterpart in Christianity is St. Peter. All members of the Casino walked to the *liceo* and performed Palo rites. They covered the coffin with a white cloth, and danced the ritual makuta. While they chanted, a Casino member repeatedly waved the Cuban flag over the closed coffin—a clever way to use the holy color of red in the ritual. It was a very solemn moment for them, because the dance symbolized that the soul had taken leave of the body. That day, a goat was sacrificed. To the altar at the Casino they carried offerings in jicara gourd cups that included rum, stews, okra, corn, yucca, meat, and sugarcane. All Benny's brothers and sisters were believers, and they and Virginia made offerings as well.

At 4 p.m. a musician from the municipal band played taps while the mourners lined up in the streets. The coffin bearers included Siro and Cueto from Matamoros, and the entire Banda Gigante walked along behind the hearse. The flowers completely filled eight cars. Hundreds of Young Pioneers and government officials marched slowly. The funeral cortege proceeded along the main boulevard, Simeón Armenteros, out to the edge of Lajas, where mourners packed the cemetery and waited while the municipal band led hymns. The hearse turned slowly off toward the town cemetery. Hundreds of thousands listened intently to the live radio broadcast and the rest of the funeral service. Listeners in Las Villas, Camagüey, and Matanzas heard the eulogy given by Professor Francisco Agramonte. Pedro Álvarez and then the president of the musicians' and performers' union spoke.

After Ramón Cabrera sang a final song, they placed Benny's casket in the shallow grave.

Benny's old friend Enrique Benítez took Benny's death harder than even those of his own mother and father. He was able to resign himself to the loss of his parents, but not the loss of Benny Moré. The grieving Enrique had a permanent marker placed beside Benny's grave: In Memory of My Friend, Beny Moré.

Although most of Benny's sisters and brothers would remain in Cuba after his death, some relatives made their way out when they could. Rolando, a boy Benny had fathered with a woman named Sophia Secundina Morejón, made plans to leave Havana in 1970. When Rolando had the money, he bought airplane tickets immediately for his pregnant wife María and their young daughter. They said goodbye to their families, each took a single suitcase of clothes, and boarded a jet in the international terminal at José Martí field.

Just before takeoff, Cuban national police went down the aisle, found Rolando, and asked if he were Benny Moré's son. They warned him that he belonged to the State and, as part of the Cuban patrimony, would not be permitted to leave. Rolando insisted that his wife take the children on to Florida. As hundreds of thousands of others had done, Maria and her daughter and unborn son Roly Jr. lived at the Freedom Tower building in downtown Miami. After a time in Los Angeles, the family resettled in Miami, but they never saw Rolando again. After Iraida died, Benny's daughters Bárbara and Lázara left Cuba for Miami in 2000.

Although the Banda Gigante did continue with various singers, the time of the orchestras was over forever. Rock and roll had already made its appearance while Benny was still alive, and bands like Los Zafiros rose in prominence.

Generoso Jiménez remained in Cuba most of his life. In 1965 he recorded his masterpiece, *El Trombón Majadero*. Even though he had fallen into obscurity for the rest of the world, Jiménez received a visit from a fervent

American fan in April 1977. It was none other than the jazz saxophonist Stan Getz, who insisted during a tour to the island with other jazz players that there was only one musician he wanted to meet: Jiménez. It was a nice surprise, but Jiménez remained all but forgotten in Cuba and elsewhere until *El Trombón Majadero* was reissued by Bembé Records in 1997. He was permitted to leave in 2000 for health reasons, and was reunited with a son and daughters in Miami. After the 2002 release of *Generoso Qué Bueno Toca Usted*, which received a Grammy nomination, he also recorded on Gloria Estefan's *90 Milles*, and died in Miami in the same year of 2007.

Enrique Benítez never left Cuba. After the group dissolved, he went back to his old job as stevedore on the Havana docks until he retired.

Estimating the worth of Benny's estate is nearly impossible, given the tangled nature of U.S.-Cuban relations. Although RCA has continued to release Benny's recordings, the American government policy imposing a Cuban embargo has tied up most of the earnings, and almost none has ever reached Benny's family. Even when revenues do enter Cuba, they are largely seized by EGREM, the Cuban government agency that handles music royalties.

A lawsuit has also tied up revenues from thirty-three songs Benny recorded in Mexico, along with rights for all the films he worked on there. That lawsuit, instituted by his ex-wife Juana Bocanegra, will not prevail in the long run, but has continued to muddy the waters. There are many Moré family members in a handful of countries who could someday lay claim to income from his continued worldwide sales, and the full value of the estate is sure to be in the millions.

# FIFTEEN

Influence

Since Moré's death, there have been hundreds of releases of his recordings in the Americas and Europe by RCA and its subsequent owners. After the Buena Vista Social Club recordings and Wim Wenders film brought renewed interest in Cuban music, two recent documentaries—one Spanish, the other Cuban—have newly illuminated Benny's life and recordings. In 2007 the Cuban government issued a postage stamp bearing Benny's likeness, and plans are under way to declare Benny's grave and the Casino de los Congos national monuments. The first full-length film about Benny's life was released in Havana in 2006. Called *El Benny*, the heavily fictionalized biopic was enormously popular during its first run in Cuba.

Benny's influence on world music is evident on several levels. Most important, Benny and his contemporaries had a profound impact on ballad singing and up-tempo music played by salsa bands around the world. His hits have been covered regularly by nearly every major salsa group in New York and beyond. Many Cuban musicians claim that contemporary salsa is Cuban music of Benny's era, with little change made to the *son* and guaracha played in Havana in the 1950s.

Cuban orchestras had an enduring though lesser-known impact on Caribbean music in Jamaica and Haiti. In Jamaica, ska was directly influenced by Cuban big bands and their arrangements. Then when American soul music traveled around the world in the early 1960s, musicians like Toots Hibbert, Bob Marley, and Jimmy Cliff took their love of Motown and grafted it onto ska and rocksteady music to create reggae. But you can still hear the clave beat in a great deal of calypso, ska, and the music of other English-speaking countries in the Caribbean.

Not very widely known is how Cuban music entered the musical culture in Haiti. Cuban-style conjuntos sprang up in Haiti from the 1920s on. Chocolate Armenteros played there for extended periods in the late 1940s and fondly remembers players like Issa El Saieh, who led his own orchestra. Groups like l'Orchestre Tropicana have a clear *son* influence in large-scale arrangements and melody. Haiti also had its own French and African traditions to rely on, and by the 1950s *compas direct* began to radically transform contemporary Haitian music. Again, Cuban music still casts a shadow across that part of Hispanola, though to a lesser extent in the Dominican Republic.

French Caribbean beguine and European music also influenced French-speaking African countries like Congo, but after the 1950s, Cuban *son* was the dominant foreign influence on popular music in Western African countries, far more so than American rock and roll. The habanera had enormous impact on the music of Africa from the time RCA Victor began to sell records on the continent. Referred to by African musicians as the GV, after the Victor music series number, the major *son* groups like Matamoros, Septeto Habanero, and Septeto Nacional profoundly influenced urban African music from the 1920s onward.

Other singers around the world continue to carry the torch. Panamanian salsa star Rubén Blades vividly remembers seeing Moré with the full orchestra in Barracas, Panama, when he was six years old. Blades remembers how the Banda Gigante members were all dressed in beautiful white suits. No one in Panama had ever dreamed of a horn section like that. Blades's father lifted him up to see, and Rubén shook Benny's hand.

So many groups and singers have recorded Benny tributes, but one stands out from dozens of others. In 1978, joined by Celia Cruz and many salsa stars, Tito Puente recorded *A Tribute to Benny Moré* (or *Homenaje a Beny Moré*), which won Puente his first Grammy award in 1979. That year Puente released a second volume, and a third in the series in 1985.

Each year Moré family members and friends, along with fans from foreign countries and those who can travel inside Cuba, make a pilgrimage to Santa Isabel de las Lajas in August on the anniversary of Moré's birth. In

September, usually every other year, an international music festival is held in Lajas. Participants have included all major Cuban musicians and groups, and despite the difficulties ordinary Cubans face in traveling around the country for such a festival, attendance grows each year.

NOTES

Prologue

p. 2:   *The stunning and capricious Ava* . . . Summers and Swan, 162.

Chapter 1. La Guinea, 1919–1935

p. 10:   *On the feast day of St. Anthony* . . . Naser, 95.

p. 10:   *Because the moon was full* . . . Film *Al Bárbaro del Ritmo*; Naser, 21.

p. 11:   *He said that Bartolo was already organizing* . . . Naser, 21.

p. 11:   *By 1932 Virginia was forced to move* . . . Naser, 23.

Chapter 2. Rumba, *Son*, and the Orchestras

p. 15:   *In 1928, the year Bartolo turned nine* . . . Sublette, 370–72.

Chapter 3. Sugar, Guitars, Vertientes, 1935–1940

p. 19:   . . . *the Maduro Company in the town of Jaronú* . . . Robinson, 63.

p. 21:   *He stayed with Virginia's brother* . . . Naser, 27.

p. 21:   *Benítez was a second cousin to Bartolo* . . . Benítez, author interview, Havana, February 2007.

p. 23:   *They had both been afflicted by one of the cane cutters' many hazards* . . . Naser, 26.

Chapter 4. Havana Apprenticeship, 1940–1943

p. 24:   *For a country boy, to think of going to Havana* . . . Galaor.

p. 24:   *Benny told* Bohemia *magazine* . . . Galaor.

p. 25:   *Originally written by Moisés Simons.* . . Leymarie, 89.

p. 25:   *Although a Latin tinge had first seeped into jazz* . . . Roberts, 7; Sublette, 396.

p. 26:   *Both he and Enrique pushed carts* . . . Benítez, interview.

p. 26:   *We had our trio in Havana* . . . Benítez, interview.

p. 27:   *The writer Eduardo Robreño* . . . Robreño, 47.

p. 28: *Sometimes Bartolo went to the club Panchín* . . . Naser, 29.

p. 28: *Bartolo's first composition was a bolero, "Dime que sí."* Pagano. Enrique Benítez sang the lyrics for Eduardo Rosillo in 1967:

> No me explico por qué tú no me quieres
> Cantando como canto mis canciones
> Canciones que nacen de mi alma
> Solamente para tí, mi dulce amor
> Quisiera adivinar tu pensamiento
> Leer el futuro de tu vida
> Y ver si es que me quieres
> O solamente te diviertes
> Con verme padecer
> Dime que sí, quítame esta pena . . .

Another early bolero by Benny was "El bardo":

> Es mi vida un crucigrama
> No sé como resolverlo
> Por eso voy a la barra
> Allí me pongo a cantar
> Y beber para olvidar
> Las penas que se interponen
> Durante mi caminar
> Que no puedo remediar
> Yo soy fatal en el amor
> Mi situación me causa horror
> Perdí la fe, no sé que hacer
> ¡Dios mio, ten compasión!

p. 28: *Another station had a similar show* . . . Naser, 27.

p. 28: *. . . a very determined Bartolo went back* . . . Naser, 28.

p. 28: *By now he was living in the Belén barrio* . . . Naser, 28.

p. 29: *In 1944 Bartolo was thrilled* . . . Naser, 30.

Chapter 5. Conjunto Matamoros, 1944–1945

p. 30: *Miguel Matamoros's biggest hit was "Son de La Loma."* Leymarie, 63.

p. 30: *. . . he had worked as a miner, farmer, . . .* Figueroa.

p. 31: *. . . their soft style was perfectly suited to the new format of radio . . .* Sublette, 368.

p. 32: *Reportedly, Bartolo had also been singing with blind tres genius and modern son pioneer Arsenio Rodríguez.* Leymarie, personal communication. Also, in a March 2007 e-mail David García said he believed that Rodríguez's brother told him this in an interview.

p. 32:   *All three of the original band members were immediately impressed . . .* Naser, 33.

p. 33:   *One of the first engagements when they used Bartolo . . .* Bladimir Cespedes in *Ofrenda Criolla* liner notes.

p. 33:   *In 1962 he told a reporter . . .* Naser, 174.

p. 33:   *Bartolo had a relationship at this time with a woman who called herself Inés Moré Armenteros.* Pagano, 158.

p. 33:   *. . . Bartolo had been living in an awful flophouse . . .* Eduardo Robreño, *Bohemia*, February 12, 1982, reprinted in Naser, 193.

Chapter 6. In the Land of the Aztecs, 1945–1948

p. 35:   *In the late 1700s . . .* Martré, 113.

p. 35:   *. . . Cuban danzón is still popular in the dance halls of Veracruz . . .* Thompson.

p. 36:   *Under contract with Mexican radio and television pioneer and RCA talent scout Emilio Azcarraga Vidaurreta . . .* Marcos Salazar, e-mail, 2007.

p. 36:   *Lafayette also claimed later to have been the one who bestowed Bartolo's new name . . .* Lam, "Esther Karula Lafayette," 29.

p. 38:   *Bartolo first met Clemente "Chico" Piquero . . .* Naser, 33–34.

p. 40:   *Rafael Cueto believed that Bartolo left the group simply because he had learned all there was to learn . . .* Naser, 35–36.

p. 41:   *Siro Rodríguez said that when Bartolo told them he was going to stay . . .* Muguercia, 27.

p. 42:   *In their eight years of marriage . . .* Lam, "La boda mexicana," 33.

p. 42:   *. . . Benny stayed in the busy border town of Tijuana to work.* Lam, "La boda mexicana," 35; Salazar, e-mail, June 2007.

p. 43:   *. . . Lafayette said she pulled a slip of paper bearing the name "Benny" from a hat . . .* Lam, "Esther Karula Lafayette," 29.

African art and music expert Robert Farris Thompson strongly believes that someone must have standardized Benny's name. Mexican historian Nicolás Argamasilla, who has studied Benny's early life in Santa Isabel de las Lajas in probably more detail than anyone else, believes that "Beny" is the true original spelling and that the name doesn't come from Benny Goodman at all. Argamasilla, who over several decades has interviewed all those who knew Benny as a child in Lajas, claims that the name comes from Virginia's family name Benítez.

Why did I choose the spelling "Benny" for this book? I tend to believe, like Cristóbal Díaz Ayala, that Benny wasn't very important in the first days of his contracts with RCA, and so the "Beny" of some of those earliest RCA Mexican recordings was probably due to carelessness on the part of RCA and a lack of concern on Benny's part. This is something that family members have also told me.

p. 43:   *... a page of sheet music for the 1949 song "El timbero de Belén,"* ... This sheet music, in the collection of Marcos Salazar, shows that Benny had already been working with other arrangers to transcribe his songs, as he had done with Pérez Prado. Identified as a guaracha-rumba, the song contains a brass introduction, then voice, and a "mambo" toward the end. Rights for this song were owned by Editorial Mexicana de Música Internacional.

p. 43:   *Other tantalizing questions include these* ... Sergio Santana, e-mail correspondence, April 2007.

p. 44:   *... Manuel "Cocaina" García, who got his* ... Sublette, 553.

p. 44:   *... Mexican singer Marco Antonio Muñiz said* ... Interview in film *Al Bárbaro del Ritmo*.

p. 44:   *Chico helped Benny find them a cheaper place* ... Naser, 37.

p. 45:   *As soon as Benny got the forms taken care of, the two of them went to see Pancho Aguirre* ... Naser, 37.

p. 45:   *Sometime in December of 1945 they formed a successful duo* ... Naser, 37.

p. 46:   *Gonzalo Martré remembered a show at Club France* ... Martré, 124. He called it a "locura reunión de etiqueta," a mind-boggling full-dress assemblage.

p. 46:   *Rivera Conde had Benny record* ... Martré, 64.

p. 46:   *... "in Benny's hands that guaracha-mambo was tremendous palo."* Martré, 59. This statement by Méndez is a fascinating affirmation of Benny's semi-secret religious following of palo. Méndez was heavily influenced by the Afro religious beliefs and was happy that someone who sang his songs like Benny had an understanding of their meaning and importance.

p. 47:   *On any recordings Benny did for Columbia at this time, his name had to be hidden* ... Notes in Moré discography, Díaz Ayala Collection; Salazar.

p. 48:   *RCA Victor offered Benny a contract for a three-month trial* ... Lam, "La boda mexicana," 33.

p. 49:   *In 1947 he invited Havana bongo player Armando Peraza* ... Fernández, 174, citing Merry Mac Masters, *Recuerdos del Son* (Mexico: Consejo Nacional para la Cultura y las Artes, 1995).

p. 49:   *Benny had landed smack in the center of the golden era of Mexican cinema* ... Agrasánchez.

p. 50:   *With Juan Bruno Tarraza's conjunto he sang "Ya son las doce"* ... Salazar, e-mail, September 2007.

Chapter 7. Locas por el Mambo, 1948–1950

p. 51:   *The doomed Austrian Maximilian I* ... Fernández, 73.

p. 51:   *... mambo is "danzón that was irradiated with son that was irradiated with a little jazz plus Toscanini plus anything."* Thompson.

p. 52:   *One Colombian bishop called the music "devilish inventions . . ."* Leymarie, 161.

p. 52:   *Although he did work with other singers, Pérez Prado . . .* Unpublished materials, p. 2284, Díaz Ayala Collection.

p. 52:   *. . . the "crucible of rumba," . . .* Sublette, 267.

p. 53:   *He told Max Salazar in 1954 that in the 1940s he was under contract to the Cubaney orchestra . . .* Sublette, 509.

p. 55:   *As she had done for Benny, the Cuban actress Ninón Sevilla helped Pérez Prado . . .* Giro, 217.

p. 55:   *When sound engineer Juan Pedro Rivera asked Pérez Prado . . .* Rivera, http://members.aol.com/PerezPrado/index.htm, accessed in 2007.

p. 57:   *. . . Benny fathered a daughter with someone near to them . . .* In the 1980s Juanita claimed to Hilda that she and Benny had a daughter. The Moré family believes that Juanita later adopted the child of Benny and the other woman as her own. Her name is thought to be Virginia, after Benny's mother.

Chapter 8. Return to Cuba Voice First, 1950–1952

p. 58:   *"Guess who just got off the train . . ."* Film *Al Bárbaro del Ritmo.*

p. 59:   *When the sometimes dramatic Virginia "woke up," the first thing she said was "Ave Maria!"* Naser, 43.

p. 59:   *Mercerón had first found Benny in Havana . . .* Naser, 130.

p. 60:   *For years Benny joked about how they insisted that he couldn't be the real Benny . . .* Naser, 45.

p. 61:   *When Norayda spilled the news . . .* Rodríguez, 37. Benny played with Valdés in 1952, but had already come to Havana before then while still with Mercerón.

p. 61:   *Norayda said that for the next visit . . .* Rodríguez, 38.

p. 61:   *Bebo Valdés happened by . . .* Rodríguez, 39.

p. 62:   *Pérez Prado's dancer Delia Romero was killed . . .* Fernández, 90.

p. 62:   *In 1953 Joe Loco put together a big "Mambo-USA" tour . . .* Giro, 221.

p. 63:   *. . . Miguel already knew that Benny had reached the potential he was meant for . . .* Naser, 46.

p. 63:   *Alonso asked Álvarez, "Compay, ¿tú y yo somos cantantes?"* Naser, 44.

p. 64:   *Celia Cruz must have wondered the same thing . . .* Film *Al Bárbaro del Ritmo.*

p. 64:   *Valdés believed that Benny was putting together a show . . .* Film *Al Bárbaro del Ritmo.*

p. 65:   *Benny was just another star in the short-lived superband, and he had a tendency to not show up . . .* ["Bebo lo usa y es un éxito, aunque a veces no aparece para las transmisiones, me cuenta Bebo"]. Sección 4 (M) 1615–1882, discography notes, Díaz Ayala Collection.

p. 65: *When asked about Benny's drinking and irregular attendance. . .* Valdés, author telephone interview, October 2005.

p. 65: *Chocolate had moved to Havana in 1949 . . .* Armenteros, author interview, New York, November 2006.

p. 65: *Armenteros said that around this time the Sonora Matancera wanted Benny as their new singer . . .* Naser, 48. Chocolate also claimed in *Al Bárbaro del Ritmo* that Benny told that band he would join only if they used four saxophones and added another trumpet. Héctor Ramírez Bedoya, who wrote *La Historia de la Sonora Matancera*, responded that the band never asked him to sing for them, nor did Benny ask for four saxes; see Loyola Fernández.

Chapter 9. Duarte, 1952–1953

p. 68: *. . . an experimental form Duarte called a mazumba.* Asked what a "mazumba" might be, John Storm Roberts wrote in an e-mail in September 2007:

> I think what you have here is an example of a phenomenon that was fairly common in the 1940s and 1950s, and may have started earlier for all I know. The success of Afro-Cubanisms genuine and bogus—from "Babalu" to (and especially) the conga—led to a fairly general search for the next Big Rhythm. I would guess that the mazumba, both rhythm and name, was born in a rehearsal room or recording studio in a fit of optimism. In form it is, or at the least sounds, Bantu. If indeed mazumba existed anywhere out in the world it would be likely to have to do with one of the Congo-Angolan palos. This tendency to create rhythms with a life span of a gnat isn't confined to Latin musicians. I sometimes think that every Nigerian percussionist who trips over a pile of pans gives the result a name in the hope that it will be the next Fuji!

p. 68: *Sometime in 1952 Benny went to New York . . .* Benítez, interview.

p. 68: *Alicia Candia was a young woman on a double date . . .* Candia, 15. Candia's meeting of Benny may have occurred in another year.

p. 71: *Mantici was adamant . . .* Naser, 50.

p. 71: *Benny asked Mantici if he should study music notation . . .* Naser, 53.

p. 71: *It is also clear that Benny was irritated with Duarte . . .* Benítez, interview; Hilda Moré, author interview, Havana, 2007.

p. 71: *The other story about why Benny left . . .* Naser, 55.

Chapter 10. La Banda Gigante, 1953–1954

p. 73: *Through July and August of 1953 he assembled the band . . .* Martínez Rodríguez, 18.

p. 74:   . . . *"los Cubanos tomarían café tocando la charanga, y luego Broadway to-caría y todos sudarían"* . . . Loza, 139.

p. 74:   *When Mariano Rivera Conde gave Benny permission to leave Duarte* . . . Naser, 56.

p. 75:   *Saxophonist Paquito D'Rivera's father Tito* . . . Paquito D'Rivera, personal communication.

p. 77:   . . . *Benny put such life into his "Marianao"* . . . Ramón Cabrera, in Contreras, 91.

p. 77:   *He called Benny "un tipo muy llano, sencillo, muy natural, y nada engreido."* *Bohemia,* November 2000.

p. 77:   . . . *to build the rest of his historic band, Benny sought the help either of Chocolate or of Enrique Benítez.* Armenteros, interview; Benítez, interview. Each said during the interviews that he was the man Benny asked to put together the band.

p. 77:   *Benny at first was in a hurry to put together a group for a two-week live radio gig* . . . Fernández, 135.

p. 77:   *"Compadre, I want to talk to you. . . ."* ["Compadre, quiero hablar con usted"] Interviewed in *Al Bárbaro del Ritmo,* Chocolate says "usted" when telling the story of how Benny came to him. This is a rather formal way for two Cuban musicians from the country, especially cousins, to talk to each other.

p. 78:   . . . *Chocolate described his first meeting with Benny.* Armenteros, interview.

p. 79:   *Paquito D'Rivera said of all his father's friends, Chocolate was the most elegant.* D'Rivera, telephone conversation, 2007.

p. 80:   *Benny wouldn't be divorced* . . . Argamasilla, e-mail, 2007. Because she had been his only legal wife, Bocanegra has continued rancorous estate battles over recording royalties and film residuals that still continued into 2007. Argamasilla stumbled across the divorce certificate in 2006 in Havana. It states alimony amounts and other details of the divorce.

p. 80:   . . . *Alberico Veloz Álvarez, said that an angry Juanita "pursued" Benny* . . . Argamasilla.

p. 81:   *The relationship would last only four years, but it wasn't Norayda who ended it.* Rodríguez, 37.

p. 84:   *At the end of songs he would yell, "¡Se acabo la salsa!"* Andrés Castillo, *El Crisol,* September 2, 1957.

p. 85:   *"A musician who didn't smoke, smoked when he heard it. . . ."* Armenteros, in *Al Bárbaro del Ritmo.*

p. 85:   *The first time the Vitier family saw Benny on television* . . . Cintio Vitier, quoted in Contreras, 198.

p. 86:   . . . *Benny sputtered with laughter and told the crowd to applaud the Great Quimbán* . . . Contreras, 199.

p. 86:   *They performed daily on* Cuba Canta y Baila *at the America theater,* . . . Naser, 57.

p. 88:   *The next year when Benny was under the gun to keep to his recording contract, RCA Victor lined up another session with Vargas* . . . Liner notes to *Grabaciones Completas.*

p. 88:   *In 1954 Benny did acquire his memorable nickname Bárbaro del Ritmo* . . . Naser, 35.

p. 89:   *. . . Benny's romantic relationships* . . . Rodríguez, 37.

Chapter 11. Son Montuno and Murder Inc.

Background for much of this chapter came from http://www.cuban-exile.com. Most of the material related to the Tropicana is based on Rosa Lowinger and Ofelia Fox's *Tropicana Nights.*

p. 93:   *The five-dollar-per-person cover charge included dinner* . . . *Cabaret Yearbook* 1 (1956?): 62, viewed at http://cuban-exile.com/doc_176–200/doc0188 .html.

p. 93:   *Cabaret Yearbook noted that Cuban chorus girls* . . . Ibid.

p. 95:   *He rarely drank anything stronger than milk* . . . Cirules, 112.

p. 96:   *Combined gambling earnings ensured that more than $500,000 per month went to underworld figures and Batista.* Pérez, 197.

p. 97:   *His only weakness was for a Cuban mistress* . . . Cirules, 114.

p. 97:   *More than once, Lansky's bodyguard Armando Jaime Casielles or a floor manager called upstairs to say that Benny was gambling* . . . Roly Moré, telephone interview, September 2007 and other dates. When Roly Moré was a boy playing in Miami Beach, he and his friends knew Lansky as Uncle Meyer. Lansky would send boys out to get him the paper, and would answer their questions about his dogs that he walked every day while he searched for different telephone booths to use for his illicit conversations. Roly and his friends never knew until they were much older why so many people recognized Lansky and why strangers often took his photograph in public. Lansky liked Cubans very much and certainly missed living in Havana. He spent the remainder of his days annoying J. Edgar Hoover's FBI agents as they attempted to record his conversations.

p. 98:   *. . . Sinatra brought two million dollars cash for Lucky Luciano* . . . Summers and Swan, 134–35.

p. 98:   *. . . Sinatra may even have been in Havana around Christmas in 1958* . . . Summers and Swan, 448.

p. 98:   *Whenever Benny ran into Martin and Ofelia Fox* . . . Lowinger and Fox, 258.

p. 98:   *Batista was never accepted by upper-class white Cuban society. Once in 1937* . . . Argote-Freyre, 124.

Chapter 12. The Hogs and the Hits, 1955–1956

p. 102: *In effect, telling Chico to stay home was a firing, but it was a firing Benny-style.* César Pagano to Fernando Álvarez, in Contreras, 159.

p. 103: *Benny had first met Generoso in July of 1952 . . .* Vázquez.

p. 104: *Generoso said in 2000 that "the Sonora Matancera was using foreign singers . . ."* Jiménez, author interview, Havana, 2000.

p. 105: *. . . he would be godfather to their first child.* Generoso had six children, all named with R's: Regla, Regina, Rubén (Tuti), Raquel, Raúl, and Ricardo. Most of them are musicians in Cuba and Miami.

p. 105: *In 1954, putting his orchestra together, Benny tried to contact Generoso . . .* Vázquez.

p. 106: *In the same month of August, Cuba and the Latin American world heard the sad news . . .* Lowinger and Fox, 258.

p. 109: *. . . he hated leftovers . . .* Rodríguez, 43.

p. 110: *"Now,* mulata, *how would I raise my pigs and plantains in Vedado?"* Contreras, 90.

p. 110: *She had known him only from clippings sent from Mexico . . .* Hilda Moré, interview. Unfortunately, Hilda was mistreated by Benny's brother Pedro after Benny died. Juana Bocanegra also appeared in Hilda's life for many years, and Hilda thought of her as an adopted stepmother. Eventually their relationship soured when Bocanegra began to speak of a child she claimed she had with Benny, and initiated a rights battle over Benny's estate, suing for song royalties and movie residuals.

p. 111: *. . . Benny is said to have made Magloire and his ministers wait . . .* Naser, 66. With Benny's personality, this is a likely story that comes with a caveat. It pays to be aware that any Cuban publication that discusses dictators outside Cuba can sometimes contain a bit of spin influenced directly or indirectly by government censors.

p. 112: *. . . he had been in three airplane accidents, one in California, another in Jamaica, and the last in Manzanillo.* Naser, 177.

p. 113: *Under his arm he carried a metal rod . . .* Armando Peñalver, in Contreras, 100.

p. 114: *According to his brother Teo, Benny had only "defended himself," . . .* Naser, 64.

p. 114: *He called it the worst experience in his entire life as a musician.* Naser, 65. Pérez later emigrated to Miami. When Roly Moré met him in the 1990s, Pérez said he had long forgiven Benny and had no hard feelings, and even admitted that he had deserved the beating.

p. 115: *In February Benny resurfaced in Havana.* Martin.

p. 116: *With the cameramen frantically waving . . .* Delgado.

p. 118:   *. . . they divorced quietly on January 13.* Argamasilla, e-mail, 2007.

p. 119:   *. . . Nat Chediak would later say . . . "those jam sessions are five of the finest Cuban records of all time."* Cantor.

p. 119:   *Finally in November 1956 Benny did get to play a two-week run at the Mambi Room . . .* Lowinger and Fox, 286.

p. 119:   *Benny was dying to tell Cole how he once paid $200 to see his jazz show . . .* Benítez, interview.

p. 119:   *Ofelia Fox loved Benny's music as much as she loved her own exotic pets . . .* Lowinger and Fox, 62.

p. 120:   *On New Year's Eve of 1956, the extraordinary bingo prizes over at the Sans Souci . . .* Ibid., 286.

p. 120:   *. . . mob members and club owners like Martin Fox at the Tropicana were secretly giving money to Castro guerrillas.* Ibid., 300.

p. 121:   *"Compadre, what's more blood to the man . . ."* Cantor.

Chapter 13. Recordings, Tours, 1957–1959

p. 123:   *What those men wanted as a warm-up was strip shows like those at the Shanghai . . .* Mallin.

p. 124:   *. . . "We only close for revolutions," . . .* Ibid.

p. 124:   *Most of those men stumbled out afterward and tumbled directly into the cathouses.* Pérez, 167.

p. 124:   *Another, newer red-light district was Barrio de la Victoria . . .* Fortune.

p. 124:   *Many women who arrived . . . on cruise ships yearned for an experience with the fabled Latin Lover.* Pérez, 192.

p. 124:   *For tamer entertainment, tourists in mixed company . . . Cabaret Yearbook* 1:68.

p. 125:   *January of 1957 began as a month of bombings, sabotage, kidnappings, and train derailments . . .* Lowinger and Fox, 294.

p. 126:   *He gave Ferrer money from his own pocket and then told Limonta he no longer was the paymaster.* Film *Al Bárbaro del Ritmo.*

p. 127:   *When Benny came by to see Virginia . . . , he and Kid Chocolate would drink . . .* Author interviews in the neighborhood, February 2007.

p. 127:   *Nor was he asked by the Club Atenas, a social club formed in 1919 for blacks and mulattos, because they considered* son *an embarrassment to the race.* Faget, 136.

p. 128:   *This was a period of apocryphal stories . . .* Naser, 131–33.

p. 129:   *. . . Batista asked for a song, but Benny refused. Eventually he sang "Es mi madre," . . .* Naser, 133. Stories like this, written under the gaze of state censors, show how the Castro government would often directly or indirectly influence historical writings. Since Bastista and Benny were known to be friends, it can be assumed that this story contains little truth.

p. 130:   ... *Benny may have played for an Oscars party* ... Naser, 68.

p. 130:   ... *in 1958 he did fly to Los Angeles by himself, invited to perform at the Hollywood Palladium* ... Raúl Fernández, telephone conversation, August 2007.

p. 131:   *To Sesma's ears Pérez Prado was "un creador de ruido," a maker of noise. He ... preferred listening to Benny's band* ... Loza, 150–51.

p. 132:   ... *he especially loved Woody Woodpecker* ... Hilda Moré, interview.

p. 132:   *But Enrique Benítez and Generoso remember how Benny would arrive very late while the band played to kill time.* Chocolate Armenteros disagreed and saw that time differently. About Benny's lateness to shows: "[*makes a sound of irritation*] People always complain about that, but they don't understand how a band works. You have the first set. That's when Rolando Laserie and Conde Negro would sing. Benny wasn't supposed to sing until the second set. People got used to seeing him on the television shows, and hearing him on the radio. They never understood that a dance or concert is different: the main singer doesn't just go on at the moment the music starts."

p. 133:   *The band continued its regular radio shows at Radio Progreso, and also played dances* ... Naser, 74.

p. 133:   *Teo asked Benny to do a fundraiser* ... Naser, 75.

p. 133:   *Until the Beatles came along, it was one of Capitol Records' biggest selling LPs.* Epstein, 294.

p. 135:   *This is how Castañeda first gave shape to the song, approaching it like an improvised descarga.* Film *Al Bárbaro del Ritmo.*

p. 136:   ... *the whole band learned a little something about the secretive Generoso* ... Paquito D'Rivera, telephone interview, 2000.

Chapter 14. Revolution and Death, 1959–1963

p. 141:   ... *Castro had reopened the casinos because so many workers had lost their jobs.* "The Mob Is Back," *Time*, March 2, 1959.

p. 141:   *On April 17 the band left for a quick U.S. tour* ... Delgado.

p. 141:   *At the airport, Tito had Benny picked up in a limousine* ... Roly Moré, telephone conversation, February 2007.

p. 142:   *That night when it came time for Benny to go on at the Palladium, he was nowhere to be found.* Ibid.

p. 143:   *As he always did on his trips to New York, Benny visited Machito's apartment uptown.* Frank Grillo Jr., e-mail, July 15, 2007.

p. 143:   *When Teo came back, Benny consented to see Dr. Luis Ruiz* ... Naser, 77.

p. 143:   *He told Ruiz that if he would agree to being his personal doctor, he must promise to always be very quiet about treating him.* Naser, 77.

p. 144:   ... *often met at the Chinatown restaurant El Pacífico.* Naser, 78.

p. 144: *After Benny was persuaded to sing for two hours at the Rincón Criollo, Ruiz could see why he never put on weight.* Naser, 80.

p. 145: *Félix Contreras . . . finally saw the band again live . . .* Contreras, 206.

p. 145: *There is a rumor that RCA Victor offered to sponsor his leaving Cuba . . .* Liner notes to *Grabaciones Completas.*

p. 145: *Martin asked him to carry $40,000 in hundreds as emergency money to Ofelia's sister Fara.* Lowinger and Fox, 409.

p. 147: *"If you take a fish out of water, he can't survive. A frog, maybe, . . ."* Paquito D'Rivera, telephone interview, 2000.

p. 147: *. . . Castro visited Benny to ask if he would help . . .* Naser, 81.

p. 148: *In some unconscious way Benny may have taken a little revenge on the rigid regulations of the new government . . .* Roly Moré, telephone interview, February 2007.

p. 148: *Celeste Mendoza also sang at this show . . .* Naser, 82.

p. 148: *Now bearing a rather outmoded name, the Conjunto Casino also played at the benefit.* Naser, 83.

p. 148: *. . . Dr. Ruiz telling Benny that he needed to stop playing late-night shows and get to bed much earlier.* Hilda Moré, interview.

p. 149: *. . . they played with the pile of yucca roots he had sweated to dig up . . .* Fuentes.

p. 149: *. . . half a bottle) per day . . . would have been more than enough to cause cirrhosis by his midthirties.* Dr. Howard J. Worman, e-mail, August 13, 2007.

p. 150: *. . . the Olympia in Paris.* Naser, 85.

p. 151: *Egües didn't understand until later what that meant.* Naser, 87.

p. 151: *Castellanos always considered Benny his best friend on earth, and was very moved by Benny's latest generosity.* Contreras, 159.

p. 152: *Dr. Ruiz asked him to sit, but Benny didn't listen and insisted on standing up to play.* Naser, 87–88.

p. 152: *It was the last time Cabrera saw him alive.* Contreras, 92.

p. 153: *. . . a dance out in Palmira . . .* To help reconstruct Benny's final days, I relied partially on the Naser book.

Chapter 15. Influence

p. 158: *Panamanian salsa star Rubén Blades . . .* Contreras, 218.

SOURCES

Primary Sources

Archival Material

Benny Moré municipal museum, Santa Isabel de las Lajas, Cuba
Díaz Ayala Cuban and Latin American Popular Music Collection, Florida
    International University, Miami
RCA Victor historical archives, Sony BMG headquarters, New York

Interviews and Correspondence with Author

MUSICIANS WHO PLAYED WITH MORÉ

Alfredo "Chocolate" Armenteros
Enrique Benítez, "El Conde Negro"
Generoso Jiménez
Bebo Valdés

OTHER MUSICIANS

Jimmy Bosch
Paquito D'Rivera
Miguel García
Frank Grillo Jr.
Arturo O'Farrill
Graciela Pérez
Arturo Sandoval
Mark Weinstein

MORÉ FAMILY

Roly Moré, grandson of Benny
Daughters Bárbara, Lázara, Hilda

MUSIC INDUSTRY AND OTHER PROFESSIONALS

Nicolás Argamasilla, researcher, San Luis Potosí, Mexico
Judy Cantor, journalist
Richard Davies, musician and author of *Trompeta*
Cristóbal Díaz Ayala
Raúl Fernández, Cuban music expert, University of California, Irvine
David García, author of *Arsenio Rodríguez and the Transnational Flows of Latin
    Popular Music*
Norman Isaacs, producer
Isabelle Leymarie, author of *Cuban Fire*
Ian Morrison, producer
Tatyana Praino, former manager for Mario Bauzá
John Storm Roberts, musicologist
Marcos Salazar, librarian and music collector, Mexico City
Sergio Santana, musicologist, Medellín, Colombia
Ned Sublette, author of *Cuba and Its Music*
Robert Farris Thompson, Professor of the History of Art, Yale University
Howard J. Worman, MD, Professor of Medicine and Pathology and Cell Biology,
    College of Physicians and Surgeons, Columbia University

Print Sources

Agrasánchez, Rogelio, Jr. *Cine Mexicano: Posters from the Golden Age, 1936–1956.*
    San Francisco: Chronicle, 2001.
Argamasilla, Nicolás. "La Gran Mentira." Ph.D. diss. manuscript, seen in 2006.
Argote-Freyre, Frank. *Fulgencio Batista.* Vol. 1, *From Revolutionary to Strongman.*
    New Brunswick, N.J.: Rutgers University Press, 2006.
Bardach, Ann Louise. *Cuba Confidential: Love and Vengeance in Miami and Havana.*
    New York: Vintage, 2003.
Candia, Alicia. "Memories of Benny." Undated clipping from *Latin Beat.* In Díaz
    Ayala Collection.
Cantor, Judy. "When Cuba Sang." *Miami New Times,* December 26, 1996.
Castro, Alicia, and Ingrid Kummels. *Queens of Havana: The Amazing Adventures
    of Anacaona, Cuba's Legendary All-Girl Dance Band.* Translated by Steven T.
    Murray. New York: Grove, 2008.
Cirules, Enrique. *The Mafia in Havana.* Translated by Douglas E. LaPrade.
    Melbourne, Australia: Ocean Press, 2004.
Contreras, Félix, ed. *Yo conocí a Benny Moré.* San Juan, P.R.: Plaza Mayor, 2003.
Davies, Rick. *Trompeta: Chappottín, Chocolate, and the Afro-Cuban Trumpet Style.*
    Lanham, Md.: Scarecrow Press, 2003.

Delgado, Celeste Fraser. "I Remember Benny." *Miami New Times*, November 20, 2003.

D'Rivera, Paquito. *My Sax Life: A Memoir*. Translated by Luis Tamargo. Evanston, Ill.: Northwestern University Press, 2005.

Epstein, Daniel Mark. *Nat King Cole*. New York: Farrar, Straus and Giroux, 1999.

Faget, Senobio. "Benny Moré: la informalidad o el turno del ofendido." In Contreras, *Yo conocí a Benny Moré*, 125–38.

Fernández, Raúl. *From Afro-Cuban Rhythms to Latin Jazz*. Berkeley and Los Angeles: University of California Press, 2006.

Figueroa, Frank. Untitled article. Clipping from *Latin Beat*, 2004. In Díaz Ayala Collection.

Fortune, Robert. "Sin—With a Rumba Beat." *Stag*, November 1950. At http://cuban-exile.com/doc_201–225/doc0208.html.

Fuentes, José Lorenzo. "Benny Moré ¡que bárbaro es usté." *Revolución*, November 15, 1962.

Galaor, Don. "Lo llaman Bárbaro y no protesta." *Bohemia*, 1954.

Giro, Radamés. *Panorama de la música popular cubana*. Havana: Letras Cubanas, 1995.

Jiménez, Generoso. Interview by John Parker-Rees for film *Cuba: Return to Havana*, unpublished.

Kasper, Dennis L., et al. *Harrison's Principles of Internal Medicine*. 16th ed. 2 vols. New York: McGraw-Hill, 2005.

Lam, Rafael. "La boda mexicana de Benny." In Contreras, *Yo conocí a Benny Moré*, 33–36. First published in *Granma*, September 1999.

———. "Esther Karula Lafayette: yo bauticé a Benny." In Contreras, *Yo conocí a Benny Moré*, 29–31. First published in *Cuba Internacional*, January 1998.

Leymarie, Isabelle. *Cuban Fire: The Story of Salsa and Latin Jazz*. London: Continuum, 2004.

Lowinger, Rosa and Ofelia Fox. *Tropicana Nights: The Life and Times of the Legendary Cuban Nightclub*. New York: Harcourt, 2005.

Loyola Fernández, José. "El Rey Benny." In Contreras, *Yo conocí a Benny Moré*, 187–92. First published in *Bohemia*, August 24, 2001.

Loza, Steven. *Recordando a Tito Puente: el rey del timbal*. New York: Random House Español, 2000.

Mallin, Jay. "Shanghai Theater, World's Rawest Burlesque Show." *Cabaret*, September 1956. Viewed at http://cuban-exile.com/doc_176–200/doc0198.html, accessed in 2007.

Martin, Lydia. "Brass Reunion." *Miami Herald*, November 21, 2003.

Martínez Rodríguez, Raúl. *Benny Moré*. Havana: Letras Cubanas, 1993.

Martré, Gonzalo. *Rumberos de ayer: músicos cubanos en México (1930–1950)*. Veracruz, Mexico: Instituto Veracruzano de Cultura, 1997.

Morales, Ed. *The Latin Beat*. New York: Da Capo, 2003.

Muguercia, Alberto. "Miguel cuenta cómo Benny ingresó en el Conjunto Matamoros." In Contreras, *Yo conocí a Benny Moré*, 27–28. First published in *Signos*, 1975.

Naser, Amin E. *Benny Moré: perfil libre*. Havana: Unión de Escritores y Artistas de Cuba, 1985.

Pagano, César. "Benny Moré and the Cuban Bolero." *Latin Beat*, March 2002.

Pérez, Louis A., Jr. *On Becoming Cuban: Identity, Nationality, and Culture*. Chapel Hill: University of North Carolina Press, 1999.

Ragano, Frank, and Selwyn Raab. *Mob Lawyer*. New York: Scribners, 1994.

Roberts, John Storm. *The Latin Tinge: The Impact of Latin American Music on the United States*. 2nd ed. New York: Oxford University Press, 1999.

Robinson, Linda. "A New Round in an Old Fight with Cuba: Fresh Controversy over Seized U.S. Property." *U.S. News and World Report*, October 16, 1995, 63–64.

Robreño, Eduardo. "Mis recuerdos del Benny." In Contreras, *Yo conocí a Benny Moré*, 47–52. First published in *Bohemia*, August 1974.

Rodríguez, Norayda. "Mi vida junto al Benny." In Contreras, *Yo conocí a Benny Moré*, 37–45.

Rosillo, Eduardo. "Entrevista a Enrique Benítez El Conde Negro." *La Habana*, 1967.

Schwartz, Rosalie. *Pleasure Island: Tourism and Temptation in Cuba*. Lincoln: University of Nebraska Press, 1999.

Serrano, Luis Hernández. "Me dicen el Conde Negro." *Juventud Rebelde*, October 26, 2003.

Sublette, Ned. *Cuba and Its Music: From the First Drums to the Mambo*. Chicago: Chicago Review Press, 2004.

Summers, Anthony, and Robbyn Swan. *Sinatra: The Life*. New York: Knopf, 2005.

Thompson, Robert Farris. "A Tango with Robert Farris Thompson." Interview by Ned Sublette. *Afropop Worldwide*, PRI, 2005. At www.afropop.org/radio/radio_program/ID/618.

Vázquez, Omar. "El Bárbaro sigue en pie." *Granma*, August 24, 1989.

Documentary Films

Al Bárbaro del Ritmo. Directed by Sergio Giral. Miami, 2004.

Cuba—The Forgotten Island. Part 2, *Return to Havana*. Directed by John Parker-Rees. London: Ironhill Pictures, 2001.

Hoy Como Ayer. Directed by Ileana Rodríguez. Havana and Andorra: Malanga Films, 2004.

DISCOGRAPHY

Except where noted, recordings were originally released by RCA Victor. Each song listing gives title, songwriter, and, when known, orchestra or group, style, and any record release code.

In Mexico

The Mexican musicologist Marcos Salazar has found that the Dueto Antillano singing as Lalo y Homero (Homero being Benny's pseudonym to avoid rights issues for Columbia Records) recorded "El can can," "Mira que eres linda," "Siguiéndote," "Tengo para ti," and other songs released on LP. Salazar also believes that the Humberto Cané group consisted of Florecita and Manolo Berrío on trumpets, Ramón Dorca on piano, Chico Piquero and Modesto on percussion, and Cané on bass, with Juancito Núñez doing backup vocals. Singers who provided chorus for Benny in Mexico included Lalo Montané, Tony Camargo, Eduardo Lara, Panchito Morales, and Toño Montané. The information in this section comes largely from Salazar and from the Cristóbal Díaz Ayala Collection at Florida International University, Miami.

1945, with Conjunto Matamoros

Buenos hermanos	Miguel Matamoros, son
La cazuelita	Hermenegildo Cárdenas, son
Se va a morir	Miguel Matamoros, rumba
Ofrenda criolla	Guillermo Rodríguez and Fernando Fernández, guajira son
Seré dichoso	Ramón Dorca, bolero son
¿Qué será eso?	A. Delachaux and Siro Rodríguez, son
Penicilina	Abelardito Valdés, son
Me la llevo	Rafael Cueto, son
Las ruinas de mi bohío	Miguel Matamoros, son montuno
Mexicanita veracruzana	Rafael Enrizo, son

1946

La televisión	José Carbó-Menéndez, Mariano Mercerón

1947

Manzanillo	José Carbó-Menéndez, Mariano Mercerón, son montuno (likely April 18, 1947)
Mi negrita rumbera	H. Jiménez, Humberto Cané, guaracha
Me como gozo	Antonio López-Martín, Humberto Cané, guaracha
Seboruco	José Carbó-Menéndez, Humberto Cané, son montuno
Hasta cuando	Rafael Ortiz, Humberto Cané, son montuno
Merengue pa' ti	Silvestre Méndez, Humberto Cané, guaracha
Puntillita	Félix Cárdenas, Humberto Cané, guaracha

1947–49, exact date unknown

Pensamiento/Soy Lucumí/ El fiel enamorado	Various songwriters, Arturo Núñez, Columbia Records
La sitiera	Rafael López, Arturo Núñez, guajira, Columbia Records
Tengo para ti	Arturo Núñez, Arturo Núñez, Columbia Records
Yo sabía que un día	Antonio Sánchez, Arturo Núñez, Columbia Records
Mazacote	Félix Cárdenas, Humberto Cané, guaracha-mambo

1948

Viejo cañengo	Héctor González, Pérez Prado, guaracha-mambo
El suave	Hermán Pou, Pérez Prado, son montuno
Parece que va a llover	Antonio Matas, Mariano Mercerón, guaracha
Me voy pa'l pueblo	Mercedes Valdés, Mariano Mercerón, guaracha
Las Posadas	Songwriter unknown, Mariano Mercerón, canción (with Lalo Montané)
Dinero no más	Mariano Mercerón, Mariano Mercerón, son montuno

1948–49, exact date unknown

La maricutana	Radamés Reyes, Mariano Mercerón, merengue
Mangolele	Benny Moré, Pérez Prado, son montuno
Será la negra	Justi Barreto, Pérez Prado, guaracha
Callen ese cornetín	V. Romero, Mariano Mercerón, guaracha

1949

Anabacoa	Juanchin Ramírez, Pérez Prado, mambo
¿Qué te pasa, José?	Justi Barreto, Pérez Prado, mambo
Se acaba el mundo	Frank Pérez, Mariano Mercerón, son montuno
Ya son las doce	Juan Bruno Tarraza, Mariano Mercerón, mambo
Loca pasión	Eduardo Domínguez, Mariano Mercerón, bolero
El bobo de la yuca	Marcos Perdomo, Rafael de Paz, mambo
Rabo y oreja	Justi Barreto, Pérez Prado, son montuno
Yo no sé	Justi Barreto, Pérez Prado, guaracha
La culebra	Obdulio Morales, Rafael de Paz, afro
Tú, solo tú	Felipe Valdés-Leal, Pérez Prado, mambo

1950

Batiri	Benny Moré, Pérez Prado, mambo
Babarabatiri	Antas Daly, Pérez Prado, mambo-batiri
Mambo eté	Guillermo Salamanca, Pérez Prado, mambo
La múcura	Antonio Fuentes, Pérez Prado, guaracha
Tocineta	Silvestre Méndez, Pérez Prado, mambo
Dolor Carabalí	Benny Moré, Pérez Prado, afro-mambo (with Hermanas Gaona)
Ana María	Pérez Prado, Pérez Prado, mambo
Pachito e'ché	Alejandro Tovar, Pérez Prado, mambo
A romper el coco	Otilio Portal, Pérez Prado, guaracha
La cocaleca	Victor Cavalli, Pérez Prado, mambo
¿Qué te parece, cholito?	Ulpiano Herrera, Pérez Prado, mambo
Guajiro	Benny Moré, Pérez Prado, mambo-guajira (with Hermanas Gaona)
Locas por el mambo	Benny Moré, Pérez Prado, mambo

María Cristina	Pérez Prado, Pérez Prado, mambo
San Fernando	Lucho Bermúdez, Rafael de Paz, porro
¿Dónde estabas tú?	Eduardo Duarte, Rafael de Paz, son montuno
Mi chiquita	Andrés Díaz, Chucho Rodríguez, guaracha
Yo no fuí	Consuelo Velázquez, Rafael de Paz, guaracha
Mambeando	Silvestre Méndez, Rafael de Paz, mambo
Sopa de pichón	Frank Grillo, Rafael de Paz, son montuno
Mamboletas	Benny Moré, Pérez Prado, mambo

1951

El marranito	Aarón González, Rafael de Paz, porro
Ah, Bárbara	Miguel A. Valladares, Rafael de Paz, bolero-mambo
La tomica	Pérez Prado, Pérez Prado, mambo (with Hermanas Gaona)
¿Qué pasará?	Arsenio Rodríguez, Rafael de Paz, bolero-mambo
Esta noche, corazón	Chucho Rodríguez, Chucho Rodríguez, bolero (with Tony Camargo)
Sin razón ni justicia	Chucho Rodríguez, Chucho Rodríguez, bolero (with Tony Camargo)
Qué cinturita	Walfrido Guevara, Chucho Rodríguez, guaracha-mambo
Que se me caigan los dientes	Chema Dávila, Chucho Rodríguez, guaracha
Deja que suba la marea	Pérez Prado, Pérez Prado, guaracha (with Tony Camargo)
A media noche	Pablo Cairo, Lalo Montané, bolero
Desdichado	Benny Moré, Lalo Montané, bolero

Released in 1952 but recorded earlier in Mexico

Encantado de la vida	Justi Barreto, Dueto Fantasma, bolero
No es así	Justi Barreto, Humberto Cané, bolero-mambo, Columbia Records
Llegó la rumba	Aurelio Estrada, Humberto Cané, rumba-mambo, Columbia Records
Ya tú sabes como é	Manuel Álvarez and Fernando Álvarez, Humberto Cané, guaracha, Columbia Records

Rumberos de ayer	Benny Moré, Moré Conjunto/Dueto Fantasma, rumba
Mata siguaraya	Lino Frías, Rafael de Paz, afro
Yiri yiri bom	Silvestre Méndez, Rafael de Paz, guaracha
Ensalada de mambo	Benny Moré, Lalo Montané, mambo
Mucho corazón	Elena Emma, Moré Conjunto/Dueto Fantasma, bolero
Bonito y sabroso	Benny Moré, Rafael de Paz, mambo
Qué aguante	Benny Moré, Rafael de Paz, guaracha

Released in 1963 but recorded sometime in Mexico

Bárbaro del ritmo	Benny Moré, Rafael de Paz, son montuno

In Cuba

1952, with Mariano Mercerón

Qué bandolera	Ramón Cabrera, guaracha-mambo
Candelina alé	Quico Cruz, montuno
La chola	Justi Barreto, son montuno
Demasiado santa	Quico Cruz, bolero-mambo
Fiesta de tambores	Mariano Mercerón, rumba
Esto sí es coco	Enrique Benítez, son montuno
Salomón	María Calderón, guaracha-mambo
Déjala	Luis Romagoza, guaracha

1952, with Ernesto Duarte

El brujo de Trinidad	Benny Moré, afro-mambo
Adiós, Palma Soriano	Ramón Cabrera, son montuno
Las mujeres de mi tierra	Justi Barreto, mambo
Ma Clotilde	Ernesto Duarte, mazumba

1953, with Ernesto Duarte

Compay seboruco	Parmenio Salazar, son montuno
No deben de llorar	Enrique Benítez, guaracha-mambo

Amor sin fe	Benny Moré, bolero-mambo
Como fue	Ernesto Duarte, bolero
Cha cha chá	Ernesto Duarte, mambo-cha
Buena bonita y barata	Benny Moré, son montuno
Guantánamo	Ramón Cabrera, son montuno
Aunque jamás me mires	José Slater, bolero
No me vayas a engañar	Osvaldo Farrés, bolero
Bombón de pollo	Enrique Benítez, son montuno
Por ser como tú eres	José Slater, bolero
Provocadora	Ramón Cabrera, son montuno

Exact date unknown, with Ernesto Duarte

Miguel	Ernesto Duarte, son
Magdalena	Ary Macedo and Ayrton Amorín, son

Banda Gigante

November 11, 1953

Manzanillo	Ramón Cabrera, son montuno, 23-6201
Oye una canción para ti	Félix Cárdenas, bolero, 23-6201
Tú me sabes comprender	Ricardo Pérez, bolero, 23-6203
Devuélveme un coco	Benny Moré, guaracha, 23-6203

November 25, 1953

No quiero matarte	Ofelio and Walfrido Guevara, bolero, 23-6234
Con Silvana Mangano	Francisco Fellove, guaracha, 23-6234
Semilla de marañón	Jesús Guerra, son montuno, 23-6235
Qué pena me da	Juan Arrando, bolero, 23-6235
Dulce desengaño	Armando Beltrán, bolero, 23-6236
Tú verás Margot	Jesús Guerra, guaracha, 23-6236

April 6, 1954

Perdón	Pedro Flores, bolero, 23-6348
Obsesión	Pedro Flores, bolero, 23-6348

May 4, 1954

| Tú me gustas | Rey Díaz Calvert, bolero, 23-6349 |
| Guajiro de verdad | Manolo Alfonso, son guajiro, 23-6349 |

July 6, 1954

| Hebra de plata | José Claro Fumero, bolero, 23-6461 |
| Santiago de Cuba | Ramón Cabrera, son montuno, 23-6461 |

August 3, 1954

Que te hace pensar	Ricardo Pérez, bolero, 23-6473
Baila mi son	Evelio Landa, son montuno, 23-6473
Ahora soy tan feliz	Benny Moré, bolero, 23-6488
En el tiempo de la colonia	Mario Recio, afro, 23-6488

November 30, 1954

| La vida es un sueño | Arsenio Rodríguez, bolero, 23-6574 |
| Solamente una vez | Agustín Lara, bolero, 23-6574 |

January 4, 1955

| Batanga no. 2 | Justi Barreto, batanga, 23-6592 |
| Me miras tiernamente | Luis Yáñez y Gómez, bolero, 23-6592 |

January 18, 1955

| Buscando la melodía | Marcelino Guerra, guajira, 23-6624 |
| Apúrate mi china | Eduardo Cabrera, son montuno, 23-6624 |

February 15, 1955

| Mi saoco | Benny Moré, son montuno, 23-6644 (alternate title: Me voy pa' Morón) |
| Celosa | Juan Bruno Tarraza, cha-cha, 23-6644 |

July 5, 1955

| Busco tu olvido | Mercedes Fernández, bolero 23-6760 |
| Las mulatas del chachacha | Evelio Landa, cha-cha, 23-6760 |

July 12, 1955

Y hoy como ayer	Pedro Vega, bolero-beguine, 23-6778
Nena, me muero	Enrique Benítez, son, 23-6778

August 9, 1955

¡Oh, vida!	Luis Yáñez y Gómez, bolero, 23-6809
Ya llegó la hora	Parmenio Salazar, cha-cha, 23-6809

August 23, 1955

Alma libre	Juan Bruno Tarraza, canción, 23-6793 (with Alfredo Sadel and Aldemaro Romero orchestra)
Yo no te engañé	Alfredo Sadel, bolero, 23-6793-2 (with Alfredo Sadel and Aldemaro Romero orchestra)

November 14, 1955

¡Ay! Cómo me gusta	Chiquitín García, merengue 23-6939
Será al volver	José Claro Fumero, bolero, 23-6939

December 26, 1955

De la rumba al chachacha	Benny Moré, cha-cha, 23-6871
Como arrullo de palma	Ernesto Lecuona, criolla, 23-6871
Santa Isabel de las Lajas	Benny Moré, son montuno, 23-6872
Todo lo perdí	Benny Moré, bolero, 23-6872

August 7, 1956

Cienfuegos	Benny Moré, guajira, 23-7063
Mi corazon lloró	Frank Domínguez, bolero, 23-7063
Compay José	Parmenio Salazar, son montuno, 45-1068
Bacalao con papa	Tony Martínez, mambo, serial no. G2ZB-7427/ CU-960 (unreleased)

January 8, 1957

Vano capricho	Alberto Barreto, bolero, 23-7185
Manigua	Ramón Cabrera, son montuno, 23-7185

April 10, 1957

El Conde Negro	Enrique Benítez, guaracha, 45-1008
Por una madre	Gertrudis Cruz, bolero, 45-1008
Soy del monte	José Ramón Sánchez, son montuno, 78-1035
Perdí la fe	Benny Moré, bolero, 78-1035
Se te cayó el tabaco	Benny Moré, guaracha, 45-1009
Rezo en la noche	Francisco Escorcia, bolero, 45-1009
Caricias cubanas	Benny Moré, son montuno, 45-1027
Vagar entre sombras	José Quiñones, bolero, 45-1027 (with Hermanos Benítez)
Cómo está mi conuco	Luis Mariano García, son montuno, 45-1044
Mulata con cola	Pío Leiva, son, 45-1044
No te atrevas	Benny Moré, bolero, 45-1090 (with Hermanos Benítez)
Dolor y pena	Evelio Landa, plena, 45-1090 (with Hermanos Benítez)

August 1, 1957

Qué bueno baila usted	Benny Moré, son montuno, 23-7334
Elige tú, que canto yo	Joseito Fernández, guaracha, 23-7334
Dolor y perdón	Benny Moré, bolero, 23-7325
Francisco Guayabal	Pío Leiva, son montuno, 23-7325
Corazón rebelde	Alberto Barreto, bolero, 45-1068
Cuando quieras volver	Félix Cárdenas, bolero, 45-1068

August 28, 1957

El agarrao	Eduardo Verde Aldea, son montuno, 23-7335
No hay tierra como la mía	Pedro Castillo, son montuno, 23-7335
No puedo callar	Mercedes Fernández, bolero, 23-7376
Trátame como soy	Pedro Brunet, guaracha, 23-7376

October 10, 1957

Marianao	Ramón Cabrera, son montuno, 23-7389
¿Por qué pensar así?	José Slater, bolero, 23-7389
Fiebre de ti	Juan Arrondo, bolero, 23-7406

| Pongan atención | Horacio de la Lastra, guaguancó, 23-7406 |
| Y te encontré | J. Grande and José Claro Fumero, bolero |

April 29, 1958

Maracaibo oriental	José Castañeda, changüí, 45-1005
Preferí perderte	Ángel Lores Jiménez, bolero, 45-1005
Que me haces daño	José Quiñones, bolero, 23-7443, 45-1006
Camarera del amor	José Quiñones, bolero-mambo, 23-7443, 45-1006

October 13, 1958

| Mi amor fugaz | Benny Moré, bolero, 23-7483, 45-1002 |
| Soy campesino | Senén Suárez, son montuno, 23-7483, 45-1002 |

October 20, 1958

Sin una despedida	José Quiñones, bolero, 45-1096
El santo de tía Juliana	Pedro P. Pérez, merengue, 45-1096
A mi padre	Néstor Mili, bolero, 45-1107
Tumba tumbador	Roberto Nodarse, son maracaibo, 45-1107
Como puedes pensar	Francisco Escorcia, bolero, 45-1121
Así es la humanidad	Pedro Hernández, guaracha, 45-1121

May 20, 1960

No lo dejes para luego	Rolando Vergara, son montuno, 45-1141
Conocí la paz	Benny Moré, bolero, 45-1141
Te quedarás	Alberto Barreto, bolero, 45-1148
Me gusta más el son	Enrique Benítez, son montuno, 45-1148
El cañonero	Enrique Benítez, montuno cha-cha, 45-1158
Mi amor, mi fe, mi ilusión	José Claro Fumero, bolero, 45-1158

Released only on 78 or 45 by Victor Mexicana, exact dates unknown

Piquito de oro	Pérez Prado, 70-8517
Lola Batiri	Pérez Prado, 70-8517
Mambo macaco	Chucho Rodríguez, 70-8619

Mamey Colorado	Chucho Rodríguez, 70-8597
Corazón herido	Rafael de Paz, 70-8642
Qué rico el mambo	Pérez Prado, 70-8279
A Santa Clara Queija	Mariano Mercerón
Amor fingido	Benny Moré
Chupando caña	Pérez Prado
Janeando	Benny Moré orchestra
Mambo del amor	Benny Moré, Mariano Mercerón
Baracoa	Ramón Cabrera

Also recorded in Mexico, dates unknown

El can can	Columbia Records
Mira que eres linda	Julio Brito, Columbia Records
Siguiéndote	Humberto Suárez, Columbia Records
Que me pasa	Pérez Prado orchestra, Benny Moré vocals
Timbero de Belén	Pérez Prado orchestra, Benny Moré vocals
Dinero no más	Mariano Mercerón orchestra, Benny Moré and Lalo Montane vocals
Margarita	Rafael de Paz orchestra, Tony Camargo vocals, Benny Moré chorus

For more detailed information on LPs and rereleases of Benny Moré material, the Cristóbal Díaz Ayala Collection at Florida International University may be consulted. The Web site of the Museo Municipal de Santa Isabel de las Lajas contains lyrics to Benny's songs and information on Benny's life.

INDEX

John Radanovich has written for the *New Orleans Times-Picayune, DownBeat, Jazziz,* and *OffBeat.* He lives in West Palm Beach, Florida.

CPSIA information can be obtained at www.ICGtesting.com
Printed in the USA
LVOW06s0540160915

454327LV00002B/2/P

9 780813 061863